GCSE
ENGLISH

Michael Baber
MA (Cantab.) Cert.Ed.

Stanley Thornes (Publishers) Ltd

First published in 1987 by:
Stanley Thornes (Publishers) Ltd.
Old Station Drive
Leckhampton
CHELTENHAM GL53 0DN
England

British Library Cataloguing in Publication Data

Baber, Michael
  GCSE English.
  1. English language—Grammar—1950–
  I. Title
  428   PE1112

ISBN 0-85950-712-2

Typeset by Blackpool Typesetting Services Limited, Blackpool in $11\frac{1}{2}/12\frac{1}{2}$ Zapf
Printed and bound in Great Britain by R. J. Acford, Chichester

Contents

Preface

GCSE ENGLISH is designed for Students taking GCSE in one year, and in particular for students in the 'New Sixth' and in Sixth Form, Further Education and Tertiary Colleges. It aims to offer:

- material chosen with the needs and interests of older students firmly in mind.
- a strong focus on Reading and Responding, Types of Writing and Oral Communication, introducing each in a systematic way.
- an introduction to a wide variety of language, from literary classics to popular journalism, and from modern literature to everyday speech.
- a major emphasis on coursework and the assignments needed to compile a strong coursework folder.
- examples that show the English language to be alive and evolving.

I hope you will find the order and approach logical and convenient. However, they are not prescriptive. Please use the material in the way that best suits your particular needs, adding your own ideas, experience and examples along the way. Remember too that the passages and extracts can be approached in a variety of ways, and not just the ones I have suggested.

Sections especially relevant to assessable coursework begin on pp. 15, 19, 24, 26, 28, 32, 34, 103, 110, 122, 129, 136, 145, 149, 153, 159 and 164.

The following symbols are used to introduce assignments particularly suitable for coursework assessment:

 – suitable for inclusion in a coursework folder.

 – suitable for the assessment of oral communication.

My thanks are due to all the students and colleagues with whom and through whom I first developed the approaches used here. Special thanks go to Christine Megson who proofread my draft material and offered many valuable comments and ideas, as well as suggesting useful exercises and relevant material.

Michael Baber
1987

Acknowledgements

The author and publishers are grateful to the following for permission to reproduce previously published material.

Associated Book Publishers (UK) Ltd. for extracts from *The Caretaker* by Harold Pinter, Methuen, and *Transcending* by David Cregan, Methuen; Avon Overseas Ltd. for material from one of their leaflets; The Bodley Head for an extract from *Sumitra's Story* by Rukshana Smith; Jonathan Cape Ltd. for 'The Waste Land' by Alan Paton from *Debbie Go Home*, for extracts from *The Hawkline Monster* by Richard Brautigan, and with the Estate of Arthur Koestler for an extract from *Darkness at Noon*; Chatto and Windus Ltd. and the Estates of Wilfred Owen and Cecil Day Lewis for 'Exposure' by Wilfred Owen from *The Collected Poems of Wilfred Owen* edited by C. Day Lewis; Consumers' Association for material from *Which* magazine; Cornell University Press for an extract from *Art in Indonesia: Continuities and Change* by Claire Holt. Copyright © 1967 by Cornell University; Dateline International Dating Systems Ltd. for an extract from a *Dateline* questionnaire; David and Charles Publishers plc for an extract from *Getting Through* by Godfrey Howard; Andre Deutsch Ltd. for extracts from *Sour Sweet* by Timothy Mo and *84 Charing Cross Road* by Helene Hanff; EMAP National Publications Ltd. for articles 'Human League' and 'Writing for a Living' and photograph from *Just Seventeen*; Equal Opportunities Commission for an extract from *Do You Provide Equal Educational Opportunities?*; Faber and Faber Ltd. for an extract from 'The Rain Horse' from *Wodwo* by Ted Hughes; The Geographical Magazine for an extract from an article by Beni Juel-Jenson, *Explore 86*; Victor Gollancz Ltd. for an extract from *Teenage Romance* by Delta Ephron, 1986; Grafton Books for extracts from *The Female Eunuch* by Germaine Greer and Tests 1, 2, 3 and 4 from *Standard Literacy Tests* by Hunter Diack; Heart of England Newspapers Ltd. for material from the *Leamington Spa Courier*; A. M. Heath on behalf of the Estate of the late Sonia Brownwell Orwell for an extract from *A Hanging* by George Orwell, Secker and Warburg Ltd.; Heinemann Educational Books Ltd. for an extract from *A Walk in the Night* by Alex la Guma, African Writers Series; The Controller of Her Majesty's Stationery Office for extracts from 'Energy Saving in the Home', 'Residential Burglary', and 'General Household Survey, 1980, OPCS; David Higham Associates Ltd. on behalf of the authors for extracts from *Beautiful Losers* by Leonard Cohen, Panther Books, *Vet in Harness* by James Herriot, Michael Joseph, *Luther* by John Osbourne, and 'Do not go gentle into that good night' from *The Poems* by Dylan Thomas; Hodder and Stoughton Ltd. for extracts from *Reading and the Consumer* by Alma Williams, Hodder and Stoughton Educational, and *The Fringes of Power* by John Colville; IOP Publishing Ltd. for an extract from *Journal of Physics* D: *Applied Physics*, 1978; The Lake District Mountain Accidents Association for material from 'Fell Walkers Read This'; Link House Magazines Ltd. for an extract from *SuperBike*, November 1986; Longman Group UK Ltd. for an extract from *Teaching English as a Second Language* by J. A. Bright and G. P. McGregor; Macmillan Publishers Ltd. for extracts from *The Shadow of a Gunman* by Sean O'Casey and 'The New Teacher' by Ninnie Seereeram from *Backfire* eds. U. and G. Giuseppe; Midland Bank plc for extracts from their magazine, *Cheque In*; John Murray Ltd. for an extract from *Full Tilt* by Dervia Murphy; National Girobank for material on 'Alcohol' from their magazine *Over 16*; The National Magazine Company Ltd. for book reviews by Pamela Carmichael, *She* magazine; Northern Examining Association for specimen GCSE questions from *Syllabus C: English for Mature Students*; The Observer for 'The Case for Nuclear Power in Britain' by Sir Alan Cottrell, *The Observer*, 28.9.86; Open University Press for an extract from *Teaching Students to Learn* by Graham Gibbs, 1981; Oxford University Press for 'Vergissmeinnicht' from *The Complete Poems of Keith Douglas* edited by Desmond Graham. Copyright © Marie J. Douglas 1978; Penguin Books Ltd. for an extract from *The Psychology of Interpersonal Behaviour* by Michael Argyle (p.154), Pelican Books, Copyright © Michael Argyle, 1967, 1972, 1978, 1983; Laurence Pollinger Ltd. on behalf of the authors for extracts from *Mother Courage* by Bertolt Brecht translated by Eric Bentley, *The Forest People* by Colin Turnbull, Jonathan Cape Ltd., *The Power and the Glory* by Graham Greene, William Heinemann Ltd. and The Bodley Head Ltd., and the Estate of Mrs Frieda Lawrence Ravagli for extracts from *Sons and Lovers*, *The White Stocking*, *Tickets, Please* and 'Intimates' by D. H. Lawrence; Python Pictures Ltd. for an extract from *Monty Python's Previous Record*; Quartet Books Ltd. for an extract from *The Monocled Mutineer* by William Allison and John Fairley; Radio Times for an introduction to *The Story of English* by Robert McCrum and 'Letters of Complaint' by Bob Smyth; Resources for Learning Ltd. for 'The Debt Trap' taken from *Over 16*, National Girobank magazine; Martin Secker & Warburg Ltd. for extracts from *What's to Become of the Boy?* by Heinrich Boll translated by Leila Vennewitz, and *Love and Glory* by Melvyn Bragg, 1983; Anthony Sheil Associates Ltd. on behalf of the Estate of Jean Rhys for an extract from *Wide Sargasso Sea*; Sidgwick & Jackson Ltd. for an extract from *Is That It* by Bob Geldof; The Society of Authors on behalf of the Bernard Shaw Estate for an extract from *Pygmalion*; Southport Visiter for a book review of *A Move in the Game* by Kathleen Conlon; Souvenir Press Ltd. for an extract from *The Peter Principle* by L. J. Peter; Spare Rib for a review of *Aliens* by Susan Ardill, October 1986; Time Out Ltd. for the article 'Teeth 'n' Smiles' by Chris Peachment, *Time Out*, 13–19 August 1986; Times Newspapers Ltd. for an article 'Hand it to them' by Caroline Rouf, *The Times Educational Supplement*, 18.7.86; Ed Victor Ltd. on behalf of Douglas Adams for an extract from *Life, the Universe and Everything*, Pan Books; A. P. Watt Ltd. on behalf of the Literary Executors of the Estate of H. G. Wells for an extract from *The Short Stories of H. G. Wells*; George Weidenfeld & Nicholson Ltd. for extracts from *The Millstone* and *The Garrick Year* by Margaret Drabble; Yorkshire Post Newspapers Ltd. for an advertisement.

We are also grateful to the following for prints and/or permission to reproduce illustrations:

BBC Hulton Picture Library (pp. 7, 8); Consumers' Association (p. 184); Hedges and Butler Ltd. (p. 107); Greenpeace (p. 108); Hodder & Stoughton – from Alma Williams: *Reading and the Consumer*, Hodder & Stoughton/UK Reading Association (p. 85); ITCCA – International Tai Chi Chuan Association (p. 100); *Looks* magazine (p. 86); McCain Foods (GB) Ltd. (p. 84); Ministry of Defence – Crown Copyright, reproduced by permission of Ministry of Defence (Navy) (p. 106); Northumbria Police (p. 80); Penguin – reproduced by permission of Penguin Books Ltd. (p. 105); Ken Pyne/Private Eye (p. 29); Viv Quillan (p. 4); Thomson – © D. C. Thomson & Co Ltd. 1986 (p. 22).

Every attempt has been made to contact copyright holders, but we apologise if any have been overlooked.

1 The English Language

– WHAT'S YOURS CALLED?

How many English Languages are there?

Have you ever written down something that you've been saying for years and then found it marked wrong? If so, you're not on your own. The differences between talking and writing cause problems for a lot of people.

Some differences are fairly clear, as in this passage:

> As he entered the classroom, I observed that he was a young man. His well-coiffured hair hung down to his shoulders. His penetrating brown eyes focused on us; his voice was slightly metallic. But what fascinated us most about him was his manner of speech. It was to say the least unexpected!
>
> He paced from one end of the room to the other.
>
> 'Ah name Ramoudit Singh; ah was born on de 30th December, 1950; ah came out from San Fernando. As all yuh know, ah come to teach English language, but as all yuh will find out, ah believes in talking de language of de people. Dat way all yuh understan' mih, an' ah understan' all yuh. Right?'
>
> He paused and looked at us intently.
>
> 'Ah know all yuh ain't too happy wid mih cutting in at dis present time, especially as dis is mih fust job, and wid English exam coming up just now, but we go have to try to get along and see wha' we could do. Right?'
>
> He resumed his pacing. He held the attention of the entire class. Eyes followed him from one place to another and back as he retraced a steady path. Utter silence from us students prevailed for that entire period. What was happening was unbelievable, but it was true.
>
> 'Ah ain't no bright man,' the new teacher continued, 'an' ah doh like people who feel dey hah too much in dey head. An nex' thing, doh feel all yuh inferior to mih, even doh ah hah mih GCE O Level, and all yuh ain't. We equal. De only ting is dat all yuh sitting down dey, an' I stannin' up here.

1

Ah ain't really hah no more dan yuh, an' yuh ain't hah no more dan me. If yuh shy, ah doh believe we go get along, fuh in English we hah to convey ideas to each odder. An' we mus' convey dem in we mudder-tongue. Leave de fancy style fuh writin'.'

It was on his third day, however, that he surprised the class. He handed out Xerox copies of a passage for comprehension. In order to save time, oral questions and answers were to follow. The passage was one of the most beautifully-written bits of prose I had read for a long time.

'Is I self write dat wen ah was at school,' Mr Ramoudit Singh claimed, 'an' now ah go ask all yuh questions to see if all yuh understan' it.'

I found it difficult to associate the passage with Mr Ramoudit Singh, and with the questions he began to ask in the 'mudder-tongue'.

Concerned as we all were about the possible results of our coming examinations, I was forced to wonder which posed the greater problem – translating 'English-as-written' into the 'mudder-tongue' for purposes of speech, or translating the 'mudder-tongue' into 'English-as-written' for exams and for communicating with the rest of the English speaking world?

'The New Teacher', by Ninnie Seereeram, in Backfire ed. U. and G. Giuseppe

This may seem a rather extreme example – the problems a West Indian student had in moving between 'written English' and 'spoken English'. Indeed he sees such a difference between them that he talks of 'translating' one into the other.

All of us, though, tend to speak one way and write another. And it can cause problems – especially if you are one of those students whose way of writing is too much like their way of talking. You may be left wondering why you make so many mistakes when writing. To help you we'll now look at some of the differences between speaking and writing in more detail.

REGIONAL ACCENTS AND DIALECTS

a)
Wee, sleeket, cowrin, tim'rous beastie,
O, what a panic's in thy breastie!
Thou need na start awa sae hasty,
      Wi' bickerin brattle!
I wad be laith to rin an' chase thee,
      Wi' murderin' pattle!

from 'To a Mouse' by Robert Burns

b)   'An' what dost think, my darlin'? When I went to put my coat on at snap-time, what should go runnin' up my arm but a mouse.
    ' "Hey up, theer!" I shouts.

'An' I wor just in time ter get 'im by th' tail.'
And did you kill it?'
'I did, for they're a nuisance. The place is fair snied wi' 'em.'
'An' what do they live on?'
'The corn as the 'osses drops – and they'll get in your pocket an' eat your snap, if you'll let 'em – no matter where yo' hing your coat – the slivin', nibblin' little nuisances, for they are.'

from Sons and Lovers *by D. H. Lawrence*

c) During the Second World War many children were evacuated from London to the countryside, to be safe from German bombing. A teacher was asked whether it had affected the way the children spoke. His reply was, 'Not particularly. They went away saying "we was" and they came back saying "us be".'

d)

The Note Taker	[*overbearing but good-humoured*] Oh, shut up, shut up. Do I look like a policeman?
The Flower Girl	[*far from reassured*] Then what did you take down my words for? How do I know whether you took me down right? You just shew me what you've wrote about me. [*The note taker opens his book and holds it steadily under her nose, though the pressure of the mob trying to read it over his shoulders would upset a weaker man.*] What's that? That aint proper writing. I can't read that.
The Note Taker	I can. [*Reads, reproducing her pronunciation exactly*] 'Cheer ap, Keptin; n' baw ya flahr orf a pore gel.'

from Pygmalion *by G. B. Shaw*

These examples show some of the differences between written and spoken English. They are mainly the result of dialect. Dialect isn't just a question of pronunciation and accent – it is also a question of vocabulary (words peculiar to that area like 'brattle') and grammar (*we was* or *us be* instead of 'we were').

In general, dialect isn't used when writing (or rather one particular dialect, variously called standard English, BBC English, etc., is used). For one thing it probably wouldn't be easily understood outside the area where the dialect is used.

EXERCISE 1.1

1 *Find a large outline map of the British Isles. On it fill in as many television series and television personalities as you can think of, locating each by their regional accent and dialect. Where would you locate East-Enders, Coronation Street, Crossroads and Brookside, for instance?*

2 *Listen to, and where possible tape record, examples of speech from different parts of the country. Radio and television will give you quite a* number of examples. Your school or college may have some records or tapes of regional speech.

Then prepare a table giving, for each dialect, an example of:

(i) pronunciation (e.g. the strong pronunciation of ng, for instance in the word hanging in Liverpool);

(ii) grammar (e.g. I be instead of 'I am' in Somerset);

(iii) vocabulary (e.g. brass for 'money' in Yorkshire); and

(iv) an idiomatic phrase (e.g. He's got all his chairs at home meaning 'He is shrewd and knows what he is doing' in the North of England);

which differs from standard English, and thus from the English you would write.

from The Pick-Up Book by Viv Quillin

3   Then prepare an extended list of such examples from the speech of your own area. Interview and record examples from your fellow students, families and friends as a starting point.

4 *Briefly explain the differences between:*
(i)   *accent and dialect.*
(ii)   *dialect and standard English.*

To give you a little help with these questions, here are a few more examples containing dialect speech:

e)   There's wee-er laddies than me that goes round there and start tossing stones at the laddies round there. They usually get battered fae them if they get caught . . .

f)   I says, I can remember when I used to shove a bairn about in a pram for a tanner a week. Lots of money a tanner then a week. And I says, I've been pushed for money ever since, so they divn't come back. Put them out on the road. Wey lad, get away, go on. Aye, he says, for a tanner. By, you can do a lot with a tanner.

g)   and there was Harry, his car or something had went wrong and he was . . . says I, Harry, what are you doing here, says I, you could be shot, says I . . .

h)   **Judge:**   What are these oonty-toomps you keep mentioning?

          Witness: What be oonty-toomps? They be the toomps the oonts make.

          Judge: But what are oonts?

          Witness: Why, them as make the toomps.

(This is an extract from a court case in Worcester. In case you're still wondering, 'oonty-toomps' are molehills.)

N.B.   Some aspects of the above – the sentences started but not finished, the repetition ('says I . . . says I . .') and so on – are not really characteristics of dialect. They are, as we shall see, typical of people speaking rather than writing.

So far I have suggested that speaking in dialect (provided the person you are speaking to is from the same area and understands) is fine, but that when writing you should use standard English.

Dialect is only one part of the problem, though. Let us look at some other variations.

SLANG, CATCH PHRASES AND COLLOQUIAL EXPRESSIONS

One of the richest sources of vital new slang has been – and still is – the United States. The pioneers of the Wild West were the fur trappers in the Rockies, the riverboat men on the Mississippi, the Forty-niners in California, the railroad workers on the Union Pacific, the cowboys on the Chisholm Trail.

From the fur traders we get 'work like a beaver' and because they used buckskins as currency, a 'buck' for a dollar. On the Mississippi, slaves might be 'sold down the river' (where the plantation owners were said to be harsher). A riverboat gambler might 'call your bluff', 'throw in his hand' or 'pass the buck' – here the 'buck' was a buckhorn-handled knife, placed in front of the dealer and passed by a player who did not fancy being in the 'hot seat' (gangster slang for the electric chair).

Once the Gold Rush started in 1849, Easterners hurried out West – 'to stake a claim'. They were looking for a 'bonanza' (a Spanish word meaning 'fair weather'). In California, they would hope that things would 'pan out', so that they might 'hit pay dirt' and 'strike it rich'.

Some of the slang used by railroad workers – 'step on board' or 'take your berth' – was simply borrowed from existing nautical jargon. But much of it was brand new. On its journey, a train might be 'in the clear'. Going uphill, it would 'make the grade' (if it wasn't 'sidetracked'), and finally it would 'reach the end of the line' – assuming it didn't 'go off the rails'. The Iron Horse gave us that archetypal Americanism 'to railroad' (meaning to coerce).

Samuel Clemens, who took his pen name, Mark Twain, from the Mississippi leadman's cry, wrote that 'slang was the language of Nevada', mischievously adding, for the affront of respectable Americans, that 'it was hard to preach a sermon without it, and be understood'.

Equally dramatic, perhaps, has been the influence of what used to be called 'broken English'. It's well established that phrases like 'nitty-gritty' and 'jam session' come via pidgin English from the languages of west Africa. Perhaps less well known is how much trendy, casual talk comes from the jazz parlours and jive talk of New York's Harlem in the 1920s.

One of the high priests of jive talk is Cab Calloway, who actually composed a song entitled 'Mr Hepster's jive-talk dictionary'.

What's a hepcat? A hepcat is a guy
Who knows all the answers and I'm
telling you why . . .
He's a high-falutin' student
Of the Calloway vocab.

From 'hepcat', we get the word 'hip', meaning sophisticated – or 'cool' (another Black English expression). In 1938 Calloway published a list of hip words, which included many that were adopted by the swinging 60s: 'beat' (exhausted), 'chick' (girl), 'groovy' (fine), 'hype' (persuasive talk), 'jam' (improvised swing music), 'mellow' (all right), 'riff' (repetitive musical phrase), 'solid' (great), 'latch on' (get wise) and 'too much' (a term of highest praise).

As the series will show, there are countless examples of the way in which the language of the street slowly passes into the mainstream

from all over the world. The Australianism 'walkabout', made famous by the Queen, comes from the aborigines. The computer industry has created 'interface', 'software' and a staggering 700 new terms. Space exploration has given us 'countdown' and 'blast off'.

The Mother Tongue
Caxton fixed spelling according to how we talked in the 1480s, but the spoken language continued to change

An English-speaking World

Tubular and totally red—LA group the Surf
Punks, California is a hothouse of slanguage;
the adman's 'Coca-colonialism' and Silicon
Valley computerese are copied all over the globe

Pioneers!
O Pioneers!

The new world of
America opened up
the frontiers of
English. The 1849
Gold Rush, for
example, gave us
'stake a claim' and
'strike it rich'

from a Radio Times *introduction to* The Story of English *by Robert McCrum*

EXERCISE 1.2

*Make a list of current slang or catch phrases. Then translate each word or
phrase into more standard English.*

Colloquial expressions ▬▬▬▬▬▬▬▬▬▬▬▬▬▬▬▬▬▬▬▬▬▬▬

These are expressions people use when speaking, perhaps to liven up the conversation, but which are usually too vague, imprecise or exaggerated to be used in writing. In any case they have normally been used so often that they have lost their effect. Examples include: *loads*, *tons* and *millions* for 'a large quantity'; or *fantastic, dead great, really great* and *ace* for 'good'. What examples of colloquial expressions can you think of?

IDIOMS

When we talk we sometimes also use idioms. In case you're wondering what an idiom is, look at the statements below. They all contain idioms.

Put your cards on the table.

You've got out of bed the wrong side this morning.

Out of the frying pan into the fire.

You've hit the nail on the head.

I can kill two birds with one stone.

Do you know the ropes?

Leave no stone unturned.

Never in a month of Sundays.

It never rains but it pours.

She hasn't got a leg to stand on.

You've got too much on your plate.

He couldn't see the wood for the trees.

EXERCISE 1.3

1   *Can you say what an idiom is?*

2   *The list above gives twelve examples. Can you match that by giving twelve of your own?*

3   *Suggest why idioms are better used when speaking rather than writing.*

So, spoken English may contain dialect, slang, idiomatic and colloquial expressions, and catch phrases – all of which should normally be *avoided* in writing (unless you are actually quoting people talking).

WRITTEN AND SPOKEN ENGLISH – BASIC DIFFERENCES

But the differences between written and spoken English go deeper than this.

EXERCISE 1.4

Look at the two extracts that follow and ask yourself these questions:

1 *Does spoken English follow the orderly sentence pattern of written English?*
   N.B. *For more information about sentences, see page 212.*

2 *Is there any necessary connection between the way words are written down (spelt) and the way they are spoken (pronounced)?*

3 *When you are talking to someone you can check whether they understand you, and they can always interrupt you if they're not clear what you're saying. Can you assume this when you are writing, or do you need to be more precise?*

4 *When you are talking to someone you can make clear your meaning by the look on your face, by stressing particular words, by how loudly you speak and by your tone of voice. Are there written equivalents, or do you again need to be more precise and detailed when writing – for instance, indicating whether the words were spoken angrily, gently, sarcastically or sadly?*

5 *When you are writing, does it matter if you stop for a few minutes to try and work out the most precise way of expressing yourself? Does it matter if you stop while talking to someone, and, if so, what may you find yourself doing to fill out the time?*

6 *When speaking, do you separate out your individual words as distinctly as in a sentence like this – or do you tend to run the words together? If you are not careful, do you sometimes end up writing the words together because that is the way you speak them?*

7 *How can you STRESS particular words when you write? Do you stress words in a different way when you speak?*

a) From a tape recording of a conversation

Listen – these two girls that I know that fly have been flying exactly three years – and they've been all over – and they – Rome, Athens, Greece, Egypt – every place – on their passes you know – they take two three weeks off and it's just fabulous – and this one girl met this guy in – uh – in Egypt – and she just fell madly in love with him – well it was so funny and now she can't – she had to come home in two weeks – that's one thing because she can't you know be with him or anything – Egypt – I mean how far away can you get – kind of a bad problem – she's supposed to be going back in August – he's sent her tickets – a ticket – her and her sister –for them to go back.

b)   As the above might appear in ordinary written English

Two stewardesses that I know have been flying exactly three years. They've been to all sorts of places. They can occasionally take two or three weeks off. When they do, they go everywhere – Athens, Rome, Egypt – on their passes. It's a wonderful experience for them. One of the girls met a man in Egypt and fell in love with him. But the difficulty was that she had to come home in two weeks. Now she can't be with him, because Egypt is too far away. This is a real problem for her. She's supposed to go back in August. The man has even sent tickets for her and her sister so that they can go back.

from A Practical Guide to the Teaching of English *by W. M. Rivers and M. S. Temperley*

What differences can you see?

EXERCISE 1.5

Summary

1   Written and spoken English
Some of the differences you have noticed in this chapter will probably have been new to you. To check that you have understood them, list all the characteristics of written English in one column, giving an example of each point. Now do the same for spoken English. Do the differences seem clear?

2   *Here are a few questions to see how well you can see the differences between written English and spoken English:*
   (i)   Can you think of seven different ways of spelling the sound ee?
   (ii) Can you think of six different sounds the letter a *might have?*
   (iii) George Bernard Shaw used to get very angry about our strange spellings. To show the problems he once wrote the word fish *as* ghoti. *How do you think he managed it?*
   The answers are on page 12.

3   *Read the following passage, which describes a conversation between a farmer and a vet. List the different features which distinguish the farmer's spoken English from standard written English. For each feature give an example.*

   And sometimes it isn't easy to get a clear picture over the telephone . . .
      'This is Bob Fryer.'
      'Good morning, Herriot here.'
      'Now then, one of me sows is bad.'
      'Oh right, what's the trouble?'

A throaty chuckle. 'Ah, that's what ah want *you* to tell *me*!'

'Oh, I see.'

'Aye, ah wouldn't be ringin' you up if I knew what the trouble was, would I? Heh, heh, heh, heh!'

The fact that I had heard this joke about two thousand times interfered with my full participation in the merriment but I managed a cracked laugh in return.

'That's perfectly true, Mr Fryer. Well, why have you rung me?'

'Damn, I've told ye – to find out what the trouble is.'

'Yes, I understand that, but I'd like some details. What do you mean when you say she's bad?'

'Well, she's just a bit off it.'

'Quite, but could you tell me a little more?'

A pause. 'She's dowly, like.'

'Anything else?'

'No . . . no . . . she's a right poorly pig, though.'

I spent a few moments in thought. 'Is she doing anything funny?'

'Funny? Funny? Nay, there's nowt funny about t'job, I'll tell that! It's no laughin' matter.'

'Well . . . er . . . let me put it this way. Why are you calling me out?'

'I'm calling ye out because you're a vet. That's your job, isn't it?'

I tried again. 'It would help if I knew what to bring with me. What are her symptoms?'

'Symptoms? Well, she's just off colour, like.'

'Yes, but what is she doing?'

'She's doin' nowt. That's what bothers me.'

'Let's see.' I scratched my head. 'Is she very ill?'

'I reckon she's in bad fettle.'

'But would you say it was an urgent matter?'

Another long pause. 'Well, she's nobbut middlin'. She's not framin' at all.'

'Yes . . . yes . . . and how long has she been like this?'

'Oh, for a bit.'

'But how long exactly?'

'For a good bit.'

'But Mr Fryer, I want to know when she started these symptoms. How long has she been affected?'

'Oh . . . ever since we got 'er.'

'Ah, and when was that?'

'Well, she came wi' the others . . .'

from Vet in Harness *by James Herriott*

Answers to Exercise 1.5, Question 2

(i) The sound *ee* is spelt differently, for example, in each of these words: key, quayside, green, receive, please, grieve, machine.

(ii) The letter *a* is pronounced differently, for instance, in each of these words: after, cage, all, about, fat, village.

(iii) *gh* = *f*, as in rough; *o* = *i*, as in women; *ti* = *sh*, as in nation. Therefore *fish* = *ghoti*!

2 *Effective Talking*
– ORAL COMMUNICATION IN PRACTICE

You may be used to talking and discussing in front of an audience. If so you can move straight on to the section on 'Reading Aloud and Play Reading'.

If you are not so experienced in this kind of talking and discussion, there is a whole variety of exercises available to get you talking as part of a group, and thus build your confidence before giving a solo performance. Here are some of them. Don't do them all in one lesson. Keep several in reserve to help prepare you before you start some of the more ambitious exercises later in the chapter.

EXERCISE 2.1

The snowball story
The class splits into small groups. Within each group one person starts to tell a story. At a signal he or she stops and the next person must continue it. This goes on until every member of the group has made several contributions and the story is complete.

EXERCISE 2.2

Visual description
Two students are chosen. One is given a piece of paper with the name of an object on it, such as a nail file, a pair of scissors, an umbrella or a sausage. The student must stand facing away from the blackboard and describe this object. He or she may describe the size, shape, colour, texture or any other aspect except what it is used for. The other student should try to draw the object on the blackboard from the description given. The first student cannot turn round, and will be unable to see and correct any mistakes or misunderstandings, so must be very precise in what he or she says. The rest of the group or class should try to guess what the object is.

This exercise can be repeated with various pairs of students, and a note made of the time taken before someone in the class correctly identifies each object.

13

EXERCISE 2.3

Fact finding

Work in pairs. One student in each pair should give a one-minute talk on a topic the other student doesn't know about. This could be a talk on a hobby, a TV programme, a sports match, a place or any other topic not known to the other student. The second student's task is then to find out as much as possible about the topic by asking questions. However, the student who has given the talk can only answer with one sentence for each question asked.

Reverse the roles and check which student is able to find out more about the other's topic.

Role play

EXERCISE 2.4

Gentle persuasion

Working in pairs, take it in turns to take on the role of persuader and person being persuaded. You can use any verbal or nonverbal means except *physical violence to help persuade your partner.*

1   *Persuade a friend to lend you the thing he or she treasures most.*

2   *Persuade a teacher or lecturer to excuse you from a mock examination.*

3   *Persuade a complete stranger to donate £10 to the charity of your choice.*

4   *Persuade the bus conductor to let you travel to school or college when you have no money (or have lost your bus pass). The bus is already very full with fare-paying passengers.*

5
  } *Devise your own examples of* Gentle persuasion.
6

EXERCISE 2.5

Many plays, films and television series rely heavily on conflict to generate audience interest and involvement. The conflict may be between people, between ideas, between different generations, between the sexes, between conflicting ideas within a character's mind, between people and the environment, or between different races and cultures. From Macbeth *to*

Dallas, *from* Romeo and Juliet *to* EastEnders, *conflict remains a key ingredient.*

1   *List as many examples of conflict as you can think of, from literature, film and television. In each case briefly suggest the main cause or source of conflict.*

2   *Choose one example which particularly interests you. Think it through in some detail. Then devise and note down a dramatic situation based on a similar conflict.*

3   *In small groups, work through each of the dramatic situations devised, taking an appropriate role in each case. Then decide which dramatic situation was most effective and why. Which seemed most realistic and which most powerful?*

 4   *Write* either *a* short story *or a* one-act play *based on one of the dramatic situations you have just explored.*

READING ALOUD AND PLAY READING

Reading aloud is something we don't do very often in everyday life, although we may read out a particularly interesting newspaper article or extract from a book to our friends if we think it's sufficiently unusual. Done well it can be very effective, bringing out the full impact the spoken word can have. However, reading aloud extracts and parts you haven't come across before will rarely produce the best results. This is one area where practice is particularly important. Read the advice that follows:

● Spend time *listening* to the way people talk – at home, in bus queues, at the supermarket, in pubs and in other places where people wait, shop or meet. Listen especially to the way people's voices change depending on the way they are feeling (shy, angry, surprised or happy, for instance) or the people they are talking to (children, friends or strangers, for example).

● Record your own voice on tape or cassette and experiment with the the effects your voice can produce. Remember that it has enormous potential. Practise changing the volume, the tone and the speed, and listen carefully to how these changes have an effect on what you are saying. Take a short speech from a play and experiment by placing the stress on different words or choosing a different place to pause. Again, listen carefully to the effect.

EXERCISE 2.6

Say the following in as many different ways as possible in order to give as many different meanings as possible. Don't change any of the words – just the emphasis and expression you give them.

(i) *Good morning.*

(ii) *Hello – Goodbye.*

(iii) *Come in. Sit down.*

(iv) *What's your name?*

(v) *Please do.*

(vi) *You will.*

(vii) *I do not know.*

(viii) *I like that.*

EXERCISE 2.7

Practise reading the following extract. Again, experiment with different approaches – including the use of pauses other than the one in the stage directions. Also, imagine you are speaking to the following different audiences:

(i) *a silent congregation in a cathedral.*

(ii) *a crowd in a busy market place.*

(iii) *the inmates of a lunatic asylum.*

Tetzel: Are you wondering who I am, or what I am? Is there anyone here among you, any small child, any cripple, or any sick idiot who hasn't heard of me, and doesn't know why I am here? No? No? Well speak up then if there is? What, no one? Do you all know me then? Do you all know who I am? If it's true it's very good, and just as it should be. However, however – just in case – just in case, mind, there is one blind, maimed midget among you today who can't hear, I will open his ears and wash them out with sacred soap for him! And, as for the rest of you, I know I can rely on you all to listen patiently while I instruct him. Is that right? I'm asking you, is that right, can I go on? I say 'can I go on'? [*Pause*]

Thank you. And what is there to tell this blind, maimed midget who's down there somewhere among you? No, don't look round for him, you'll only scare him and then he'll lose his one great chance, and it's not likely to come again, or if it does come, maybe it'll be too late. Well, what's the good news on this bright day? What's the information you want? It's this! Who is this friar with his red cross? Who sent him, and what's he here for? Don't try to work it out for yourself because I'm going to tell you now, this very minute.

from Luther *by John Osborne*

- At the risk of stating the obvious, make sure you know and under-stand your chosen extract. If there are long and complicated words or sentences try to work out their meaning. Don't be afraid to ask for help.

- If you are reading a part from a play establish the context – who you are, what your role is, your age, character and personality, who you are talking to, where, when and why. This will help you read 'in character'.

- Use the techniques you have experimented with earlier to bring your extract to life, but use them sparingly. Don't overuse the significant stress on words, the sudden raised or hushed voice, the change of tone to signal a change of mood or feeling, or the dramatic pause. Too little change will bore your audience – too much will confuse them.

EXERCISE 2.8

Use the extracts that follow for further practice and then present them in class, comparing the different approach each student employs. In the first extract take one verse each:

Our brains ache, in the merciless iced east winds that knive us . . .
Wearied we keep awake because the night is silent . . .
Low, drooping flares confuse our memory of the salient . . .
Worried by silence, sentries whisper, curious, nervous,
    But nothing happens.

Watching, we hear the mad gusts tugging on the wire,
Like twitching agonies of men among its brambles.
Northward, incessantly, the flickering gunnery rumbles,
Far off, like a dull rumour of some other war.
    What are we doing here?

The poignant misery of dawn begins to grow . . .
We only know war lasts, rain soaks, and clouds sag stormy.
Dawn massing in the east her melancholy army
Attacks once more in ranks on shivering ranks of gray,
    But nothing happens.

Sudden successive flights of bullets streak the silence.
Less deadly than the air that shudders black with snow,
With sidelong flowing flakes that flock, pause, and renew,
We watch them wandering up and down the wind's nonchalance,
    But nothing happens.

Pale flakes with fingering stealth come feeling for our faces –
We cringe in holes, back on forgotten dreams, and stare, snow-dazed,

Deep into grassier ditches. So we drowse, sun-dozed,
Littered with blossoms trickling where the blackbird fusses.
    Is it that we are dying?

Slowly our ghosts drag home: glimpsing the sunk fires, glozed
With crusted dark-red jewels; crickets jingle there;
For hours the innocent mice rejoice: the house is theirs;
Shutters and doors, all closed: on us the doors are closed, –
    We turn back to our dying.

Since we believe not otherwise can kind fires burn;
Nor ever suns smile true on child, or field, or fruit.
For God's invincible spring our love is made afraid;
Therefore, not loath, we lie out here; therefore were born,
    For love of God seems dying.

To-night, His frost will fasten on this mud and us,
Shrivelling many hands, puckering foreheads crisp.
The burying-party, picks and shovels in their shaking grasp,
Pause over half-known faces. All their eyes are ice,
    But nothing happens.

                                    from Exposure *by Wilfred Owen*

Aston	You could be . . . caretaker here, if you liked.
Davies	What?
Aston	You could . . . look after the place, if you liked . . . you know, the stairs and the landing, the front steps, keep an eye on it. Polish the bells.
Davies	Bells?
Aston	I'll be fixing a few, down by the front door. Brass.
Davies	Caretaking, eh?
Aston	Yes.
Davies	Well, I . . . I never done caretaking before, you know . . . I mean to say . . . I never . . . what I mean to say is . . . I never been a caretaker before.
	[*Pause*]
Aston	How do you feel about being one, then?
Davies	Well, I reckon . . . Well, I'd have to know . . . you know . . .
Aston	What sort of . . .
Davies	Yes, what sort of . . . you know . . .
	[*Pause*]
Aston	Well, I mean . . .
Davies	I mean, I'd have to . . . I'd have to . . .
Aston	Well, I could tell you . . .
Davies	That's . . . that's it . . . you see . . . you get my meaning?
Aston	When the time comes . . .
Davies	I mean, that's what I'm getting at, you see . . .
Aston	More or less exactly what you . . .
Davies	You see, what I mean to say . . . what I'm getting at is . . . I mean, what sort of jobs . . .
	[*Pause*]

Aston   Well, there's things like the stairs . . . and the . . . the bells . . .

Davies   But it'd be a matter . . . wouldn't it . . . it'd be a matter of a broom . . . isn't it?

Aston   Yes, and of course, you'd need a few brushes.

from The Caretaker *by Harold Pinter*

EXERCISE 2.9

Find two *of the following and prepare them for reading aloud. Choose examples which you enjoy reading and which are likely to be effective when read aloud:*

(i) *a poem.*

(ii) *an extract from a play.*

(iii) *an extract from a novel or short story.*

(iv) *an extract from a speech.*

GIVING A TALK

Giving a talk is not the most common form of oral communication; it is not as common as just talking to your friends, for instance. However, if you ever become involved in management, trade union activity, teaching, politics, the organisation of a club or society, etc., you may find the ability to talk to a group or meeting useful. (It is also, incidentally, one of the easiest forms of oral communication to mark with some degree of accuracy – hence its inclusion on many courses.)

Giving a talk: some practical hints

Imagine that you have been asked to give a talk, lasting 3–5 minutes, on a topic that interests you:

Before the talk: preparation

A Choose something you are *genuinely* interested in, as this will help you to be more enthusiastic. (And don't say you have no interests – no one can be *that* boring!)

B Jot down, over a period of time, anything that comes to mind. It is better to start with too much than too little – and it gives you confidence to know you have plenty to talk about.

C Use different approaches to give yourself ideas on the topic, for instance:
   • Ask yourself questions about the topic, such as who? what? why? where? when? how? what if?
   • Think of your *senses*. For example, what would be seen? heard? smelt? touched? tasted?
   • Try a *word association* exercise. Give yourself 30 seconds to jot down the first words that come to mind when you look at the topic. This may produce some unexpected ideas or connections.

D Think of a good start and a good ending, to give your talk a positive approach. An interesting or amusing example or anecdote could be useful here; it's always helpful to get the audience on your side.

E Practise and rehearse your talk. If you are shy, talk to the mirror or your dog; if you have sympathetic friends or relatives, use them as an audience. In particular:
   (i) Check that the talk is the right length.
   (ii) Check that you have a positive start and finish.
   (iii) See what works and what doesn't.

F As you get to know the talk, reduce it to a series of main point headings – only as many as will fit on a postcard.

   (Practical point: If you are nervous when standing in front of your group a postcard will not shake as much as a sheet of paper!)

G Is there any way you can illustrate your talk – by giving a short demonstration, using slides or displaying examples of what you are talking about?

H Check that the language you use is understandable. Too many technical terms or too much jargon will soon bore your audience.

I   Time your talk by practising it beforehand. Don't rush and don't read long prepared notes. (Headings on a postcard will also remove this temptation.) Remember that a pause before a dramatic point or the punchline can be very effective.

J   Make sure you are relaxed. Use the following suggestions:
   (i)   More practice means more confidence.
   (ii) Take two or three big deep breaths.
   (iii) Relax your neck and shoulders.
   (iv) Take your time coming out and getting ready.
   (v)   Be sure to look at everyone first. Catch their eyes and talk to *them*, not to the desk or the ceiling.

K   Be aware of the context. For instance:
   ● Are you giving your talk to five people or to 50?
   ● Will you be speaking in a large room or a small one, and will it be empty or full?
   ● Who are your audience? Are they young or old, male or female, experts or non-specialists? Do they know you?
   ● Why are you giving a talk? Are you trying to persuade people about something, to entertain them, to give them information, etc.?
   ● Is your audience friendly, or perhaps not so friendly?
   The more aware you are of these factors the more you can aim to adjust your talk accordingly. This might affect how loudly you speak, whether you use simple or complicated language, whether you try to be serious or amusing, what kind of examples you use, etc.

   So, in the exercises that follow, remember to ask:
   ● *Who* am I talking to?
   ● *Where* am I giving the talk?
   ● *Why?*

   This will help you decide *what* to say and *how* to say it!

EXERCISE 2.10

Before giving an individual talk, and to check that you have followed the points so far, read the picture strip on page 22. Then, in small groups, discuss what makes some topics appear initially boring and what can be done to make them seem more interesting. For instance, if you were Nick and you had decided to give a talk at school or college about motorbikes what could you do to make it interesting to other people – even to someone like Cathy?

from Patches

EXERCISE 2.11

1 *This question was triggered off by the following essay question:*

What factors do you think ought to govern the amount of money people are paid for the work they do?

Choose one of the occupations from the list below. You now have 20 minutes to prepare a pay claim, stating why your particular choice deserves a pay rise more than any of the others. Then put your case to the rest of the class. They should then vote on how convincingly your case was argued (rather than on what their own feelings were previously).

Housewife	Miner
Nurse	Bank manager
Doctor	Dustman
Cleaner	Clerk
Secretary/typist	Managing director of ICI
Factory worker	Window cleaner
Masseuse	Salesman
Shop assistant	Newsagent
Hairdresser	Advertising artist
Social worker	Pop singer
Primary school teacher	Professional footballer
Film star	Car worker

 2 Prepare a three-minute talk on one of the following:

  (i) a demonstration of some skill or process.

  (ii) a hobby or interest.

  (iii) 'if I were . . .'

3 After requests from students your school or college has just set up its own internal radio station, run by the students, and operating for an experimental period of one term from 12 to 2 each day. You have been given the job of preparing a two-minute news broadcast to be given at 1 o'clock each day.

Prepare the script for such a broadcast for each of three successive days, using the morning newspapers to prepare a brief summary of the major items. As the programming schedule is very tight you must ensure that each news broadcast does last for just two minutes. (This will be timed.)

 4 Choose one area or aspect of the school or college you consider to be in need of change and improvement. It will be your job to persuade a meeting of the school council or student union (simulated by the class itself, or several classes combined) that change and improvement are needed, by means of a short speech lasting 3–5 minutes. (Different members of the class should take it in turns to chair the meeting, and to act as secretary and produce minutes of the meeting. These could also be taped or videoed, should facilities be available.)

5 *Prepare a talk, 'An introduction to . . .' (the course you are following at the moment). The talk should be of roughly five minutes' length and suitable for inclusion in a radio programme for schools and colleges entitled* Courses at 16 + : The Alternatives. *Each talk will be taped – and the best talks will be played to new and prospective students next year.*

Write a script for the talk (with directions, as necessary, on how it should be given). Before the script, write an introduction that indicates how your talk has taken into account:

(i) the intended audience.

(ii) the medium used (radio or cassette).

(iii) the suitability of the topic in terms of (i) and (ii) above.

TAKING PART IN A DEBATE

Taking part in a debate is a rather formal way of discussing a topic. The formality does have some advantages though. It allows an argument to be developed – and challenged – in detail. It develops the ability to speak to an audience. It can also encourage more careful listening to others.

A typical debate will have:

- a motion or proposal for debate, such as
  Cigarette smoking should be made illegal and a ban placed on the production and sale of cigarettes.

- someone in the chair to keep order in the debate and make sure everyone gets a fair hearing.

- a main speaker in favour of the motion and a main speaker against, to introduce the major arguments.

- a supporting speaker on each side, to introduce additional arguments and challenge those made by the other side.

- the opportunity for members of the audience to give their points of view, provide further information or ask relevant questions after the speakers have put their case.

- a final summary by the main speakers on each side.

- a vote on the motion. Ideally you should vote for whoever has put the more convincing case in the debate, rather than simply voting for what you happened to believe already before the debate.

Before speaking in a debate reread the advice on giving a talk (pages 19–21). Decide which advice will be most important. Because you will be arguing a case rather than simply giving a talk you will need to give much more thought to persuading people to support your point of view.

Consider these questions for instance:

● Have you researched the topic carefully and found the strongest arguments and examples?

● What do you know about your audience – their background, experience and points of view? Will you be challenging or building on what they believe?

● Can you make your case relevant to the interests of each of the people listening, by showing how they would benefit or be affected by the topic debated?

● Can you bring your case to life by providing interesting, amusing, dramatic or thought-provoking illustrations?

● Can you anticipate the arguments your opponents will raise and are you able to provide a convincing answer to these arguments?

● Is your line of argument clear and jargon-free? (To make sure your message is clear, it may not harm to repeat important points.)

EXERCISE 2.12

Hold formal debates on three *of the following motions. Alternatively, you may prefer to suggest your own topics for debate based on particularly topical local or national issues.*

  (i) *BBC Radio and Television should be financed by advertising.*

  (ii) *Honesty is not always the best policy.*

  (iii) *The school leaving age should be lowered to 14.*

  (iv) *Britain should commit itself to unilateral nuclear disarmament. (You may need to find out what 'unilateral' means first!)*

  (v) *In English law a person accused of a crime is assumed to be innocent until proven guilty beyond all reasonable doubt. This assumption should continue even if it sometimes means guilty people go free.*

  (vi) *We should all give 5% of our weekly income to help those in Third World countries.*

  (vii) *The death penalty should be reintroduced for convicted murderers.*

INTERVIEWS – BEING INTERVIEWED

Before you are offered a job, or a place at a college, polytechnic or university, you will usually have to attend an interview. To help you perform as well as possible, form small groups and discuss the following questions. Appoint one person in each group to act as secretary and note down the group's recommendations. To help focus discussion, each group should first choose one type of full-time job likely to be open to applicants of your age range.

Getting the interview

- How can you make sure your application is neat, accurate and answers all the questions?

- How can you make sure the people you name as referees will say complimentary things about you?

Before the interview

- What might you need to take with you to the interview?

- How should you dress for the interview?

- What sort of questions might you be asked?

- What sort of person is the interviewer likely to be looking for?

During the interview

- How should you sit, speak and behave?

- How can you show that you really want the job?

- How can you show that you have the qualities needed to do the job well?

EXERCISE 2.13

1 *From what you have discussed so far try to work out 20 possible questions you might be asked at an interview to gain a place in Further or Higher Education. Remember that the emphasis in this kind of interview will be rather different from the emphasis in a job interview – it will be on your educational ability in particular.*

2 *Reply to this advertisement:*

POST CLASSIFIED
FREE SERVICE
To Unemployed Youngsters

From August 6th a special classification entitled 'Jobs Wanted – School Leavers' will be appearing daily in the *Evening Post*.

If you are under 18 and still seeking a job you are invited to submit your advertisement, and it will be published free of charge.

Tell prospective employers about yourself, about your education and about the kind of job you are looking for. Keep your advertisement to within 50 words and include your full name and address, and also your telephone number if you have one.

Send it, marking the envelope 'School Leavers Column' to:

Ann Menzies Neal,
Classified Sales Manager,
Yorkshire Post Newspapers Ltd.,
Wellington Street,
Leeds
LS1 4QZ.

P.S. If you get a job from your advertisement, Ann will be delighted to hear the good news.

3 *First, check that you know what the following are:*

a *a Personnel Manager.*

b *mobility.*

c *references.*

d *a job description.*

e *a testimonial.*

f *a short list.*

Then:

(i) *Collect as much material as you can on a type of job you are interested in (for instance, using material from the Careers section of your school, college or library, or talking to people who know about that sort of job).*

(ii) *From this material prepare a job description of the kind a Personnel Manager might draw up when trying to decide what sort of person to appoint, and of the kind that could be sent to applicants to explain what the job would involve.*

(iii) *From this material also prepare a job advertisement, of the kind that might appear in the 'Situations Vacant' section of a newspaper.*

(iv) *Prepare an application form, suitable for this sort of job, designed to give the kind of information needed to check whether applicants measure up to the job description.*

(v) *Then, fill in the application form to the best of your ability, including giving referees.*

(vi) *Staple together the job description, job advertisement and completed application forms, and circulate them round the class for discussion, suggested improvements, evaluation, etc.*

(vii) *Those students who are agreed to have completed their application forms effectively will be interviewed for the posts in question.*

INTERVIEWS – SURVEYS AND QUESTIONNAIRES

These days surveys are big business. Companies carry out surveys to check whether new products will sell. Newspapers carry out surveys to check what people think about social and political issues – and, of course, who will win the next General Election. The demand for surveys is such that some organisations have been set up just to carry out surveys (Gallup, Marplan, MORI, etc.), whilst major companies have their own survey departments.

Here is a quick guide to surveys and questionnaires:

A   What do you want to know – and who will have that information?

B   Ask only the people who will have that information. (This may mean only certain age groups, occupations, or people living in certain areas etc. Check this carefully.)

C   Asking everyone who has the information usually takes too much time – so ask a *representative sample* (e.g. 1 in 20, 1 in a 100, 1 in a 1000 of that kind of person).

"SAME HERE— I CAN'T FIND AN ORDINARY MAN IN THE STREET ANYWHERE!"

D   People don't usually mind answering a few questions – but they are more likely to answer if they are asked politely, told why you are asking the questions, and assured that their replies will be treated confidentially.

E   Even so they may not have all day to stand and answer questions, so try to keep the number of questions reasonably small (no more than ten, for instance).

F   Choose your questions carefully. Keep them:

   • short,

   • easy to understand, and

   • easy to give an accurate answer to.

   Avoid any question that could be ambiguous, misleading, difficult to remember, or to remember the answer to, embarrassing, vague, over-technical, etc.

G As you will need to record the answers as they are given (for non-postal surveys, anyway), prepare:

- questions it is easy to record answers to. The answers to *multiple choice* questions are easy to tick off, and relatively easy to analyse afterwards. For example:

    Do you think xyz is:
not important	𝓙𝓗𝓣 ‖	(7)
fairly important	𝓙𝓗𝓣 ‖‖‖	(9)
important	𝓙𝓗𝓣 𝓙𝓗𝓣 ‖‖‖	(13)
very important	𝓙𝓗𝓣 ‖	(6)

    Open questions mean you have to write down everything the person says, which gets tiring – and the answers are more difficult to analyse quickly.

- question forms that are easy to use, and have, for instance, plenty of space to tick off answers.

H When you have all your answers, tot them up, and then present them in a form that is easy to follow. If there are a lot of figures involved, it can help to present them in the form of tables, graphs, charts, pictograms, etc. Generalisation can help too. For instance, 'The vast majority believed . . ., whilst only a few . . .'

I Draw appropriate conclusions from your results. For instance, you could say, 'The fact that so many people declared . . . would suggest . . .'

J Remember that a well-conducted survey will usually give a pretty accurate picture, but it cannot guarantee 100% accuracy. There are different reasons for this:

- People may make honest mistakes. A BBC survey found that 5% of housewives interviewed were mistaken about which TV channel they had been watching a couple of minutes earlier – probably because were thinking in terms of *programmes*, not TV channels.

- People may forget, or misunderstand.

- They may be afraid to give an honest answer, or embarrassed to.

- They may even just change their minds.

- The representative sample may not have been as 'representative' as it was supposed to be.

This is why it is so important to prepare your survey carefully in the first place, and then, when considering the results, to concentrate on the overall picture (which should be fairly accurate) rather than on exact percentages (which probably will not be so accurate).

EXERCISE 2.14

1   If you were preparing a survey on the following, what kind of people would you ask, and what would be a reasonable representative sample?

   (i) local sports facilities (from a player's point of view)

   (ii) local sports facilities (from a spectactor's point of view)

   (iii) the musical tastes of young people in your area

   (iv) purchase of LPs by young people in your area

   (v) how important local employers think it is for applicants to be well educated

   (vi) what local employers think 'well educated' means

2   Think of five things you would like to know, which a survey could help you find out.

3   Even if we don't really believe in astrology, most of us have probably read our own horoscopes at one time or another. Here is a short project to test the value of star signs.

   There are twelve star signs – Aquarius, Pisces, Aries, Taurus, Gemini, Cancer, Leo, Virgo, Libra, Scorpio, Sagittarius and Capricorn.

   Choose one star sign each, making sure that, where possible, each sign is represented within the class. Research what are supposed to be the characteristics of people born under your chosen star sign, using libraries or any other sources of information you have access to. Try to find out both physical and personal characteristics.

   When you have identified the major features, prepare twelve questions designed to identify whether someone has the relevant personal characteristics. (You will probably be able to check the physical characteristics by observation.) Now interview at least five people born under the chosen star sign. These could be staff, students, family or friends.

   Check how many times there is a match between the characteristics you have researched and the characteristics of the people you have interviewed. Use this information to prepare an illustrated information sheet which can be mounted as part of a wall display, and then discuss your findings with the rest of the group.

   If you find this topic particularly interesting you can take it a stage further by doing a similar exercise examining weekly horoscopes in a range of magazines. Investigate how far the horoscopes for any one star sign agree with each other and how far they correspond with what actually happens to people during the period predicted.

4 *Choose* one *topic you would like to know more about. Then prepare, carry out, and present the results of, a suitable survey.*

Keep a list of any problems that you found in preparing, carrying out, or presenting the results of this survey, together with details of how you tried to deal with these problems.

IN-DEPTH INTERVIEWS

Television and radio programmes, as well as newspaper and magazine articles, often carry detailed interviews with well-known people. These can range from interviews with leading politicians on national news bulletins to the more varied questions asked of 'personalities' on chat shows and for magazine articles. Here the aim is not to find out the general trends a survey would reveal, but to find out more about a particular person. A similar approach is used by journalists when they interview people about a news event such as a crime or an accident. They are looking for comments they can quote, and which they can attribute to named individuals.

For in-depth interviews the preparation will be similar to that for surveys and questionnaires. You will still need to decide what you want to know and who will have that information. However, you will also need to:

- find out more about the person you will be interviewing *beforehand.* This is partly to give you more ideas for questions and partly to help you know which answers to follow up.

- think of a much wider range of questions and possible follow-up questions to the answers you are given.

- be very careful how you word your questions, so as to encourage your interviewee to talk naturally and openly. If you have any controversial questions in mind, it makes sense to start with factual and less controversial areas and move on to the questions likely to produce strong reactions later. (If one person refuses to answer questions on a survey the survey can still go on; if the person being interviewed in depth refuses to answer that's the end of your interview!)

    N.B. Whether you are carrying out an in-depth interview or a more general survey, it is always wise to 'clear' questions with your teacher or lecturer first.

EXERCISE 2.15

1 *Find someone in your school, college, family or area who has either had a particularly interesting life or recently been involved in a newsworthy activity. Arrange to interview him or her with a view to producing a magazine-type article based on the interview.*

EXERCISE 2.16

Assume that you are working for an introduction agency. This introduces single people who wish to develop long-term relationships, but find their current social and study or employment circles have not yet produced the 'right' partner. It is part of your job to:

- *carry out an in-depth interview of each client, discussing each person's background, interests, tastes, personality and ambitions.*

- *discover what kind of person each client is interested in being introduced to.*

Prepare a suitable in-depth interview and then find someone outside your group or class who is willing to be interviewed. Record and write up the results of the interview, but do not give the name of the person you have interviewed.

To help you with this interview, here is an extract from a survey by Dateline. It is intended to be completed on a postal basis, so it may need altering to meet the needs of a personal interview.

Your Personality

This section looks at the role you play in your relationships, your emotional reactions to other people and how you feel you get on best with them.

98 I'm good at drawing people out when talking. ☐
99 I find it easy to say 'no' when necessary. ☐
100 I lose confidence when I am criticised. ☐
101 I will complain when unfairly treated. ☐
102 I feel rude if I leave boring company. ☐
103 I am concerned about how others see me. ☐
104 I usually end up getting my own way. ☐
105 I soon give up trying to keep a conversation going. ☐
106 I am usually the one who talks the most. ☐
107 I am easily persuaded ☐

108 I find it easy to express my views. ☐
109 I don't care too much what other people think of me. ☐
110 I find it easy to express my emotions. ☐
111 I prefer someone else to make the decisions. ☐
112 I usually fit my views in with those of others. ☐
113 I don't like to make a scene by complaining. ☐
114 I prefer listening to talking. ☐
115 I don't hesitate to leave boring situations. ☐
116 Personal criticism does not hurt me. ☐
117 I like to keep my emotions under control. ☐

EXERCISE 2.17

 Glaxo Tac, an intelligent and English-speaking alien, has come from another galaxy and has chosen to interview members of this group to find out about life on earth. Spend five minutes noting down the kind of questions the alien might ask. Then work in pairs, one taking on the role of Glaxo Tac and the other the role of interviewee.

GROUP DISCUSSION

Earlier we looked at one type of oral communication – giving a talk. More common, however, in everyday life, are occasions when we talk to another person, or to others in small groups (e.g. friends, colleagues, shop assistants, relatives, etc.), and when they reply, so that there is *dialogue*. A similar, if perhaps more formal, type of communication occurs in meetings (such as committee meetings).

Different people communicate in different ways in groups. Shortly we shall look at a range of suggestions, based on observations of people actually communicating in groups.

Perhaps the most useful lesson *you*, as a student, can learn from these suggestions is *how many different ways* it is possible to communicate in. When you do the exercises that follow try dividing the class in half. One half will act as the group that carries out the exercise. The other half will observe the technique they use. (It is easier for each observer to watch and make notes on a different student, and then report back after the discussion.)

One thing many students find at first is that, although they feel they are using a variety of techniques, most of what the observers find they are doing is proposing, supporting, defending or attacking. Some techniques such as 'open behaviour' (for example, admitting mistakes), or bringing other people into the discussion and asking their opinions, are very rarely used. It is also noticeable that some students may try to get involved in the discussion, but each time they start to speak, a more vocal student will start to speak as well, not giving them a chance. Again, some students will try to dominate the discussion, and perhaps cause resentment among the others. As the exercises continue, and as the students find out more about the ways in which groups operate, however, some students may try new techniques. Often they will find that this wider range helps them to be more successful, and helps the group work more smoothly or efficiently. Try doing this yourself.

Group discussion: group behaviour ━━━━━━━━━━━━━━━━━━

To help you use a variety of techniques when discussing, and to describe what other people do in discussions, here are some suggested definitions. You might not agree with every definition, or you might feel some techniques have been missed out. If so, amend the list for your own use. This is just to start you thinking.

Proposing   Putting forward a new idea, suggestion or proposal – e.g.
'Why don't we . . .?'

Building   Taking a proposal suggested by someone else, and developing it, or adding to it – e.g.
'Yes, and then we could . . .'

Supporting   Agreeing with someone else's idea – and explaining *why* you agree – e.g.
'That seems sensible. It would solve the problem of . . .'

Disagreeing   Disagreeing with someone else's idea – but explaining *why* you disagree – e.g.
'I'm not sure. Aren't you forgetting about . . .?'

Defending   Agreeing with someone, but giving no good reason – e.g.
'I agree!'

Attacking   Disagreeing with someone, but giving no good reason – e.g.
'Well, I don't (agree) . . .'

EXERCISE 2.18

Here's an opportunity to try out the techniques mentioned. It will probably work best if half of you act as the committee, and the other half as observers, making notes on the techniques used, and then reporting back on what you saw and heard.

Survivors

It is the year after World War Three and most of the world's population is dead. The survivors live in nuclear shelters underground, where they must remain until it is safe to return to the surface. You are members of a committee set up to decide how the survivors should be trained or retrained to be of maximum usefulness:

(i) during the long period underground.

(ii) when they return to the surface.

As a committee you must decide on, and make a list of, the order of importance of the following occupations as far as training priorities are concerned:

Nurse	*Farmer*
Telecommunications engineer	*Soldier*
Dentist	*Carpenter*
Musician	*Blacksmith*
Teacher	*Waste disposal expert*
Tailor	*Fisherman*
Actor	*Doctor*
Miner	

Here are some further suggested definitions of what people do in discussion. Bear these in mind when taking part in, or observing, future exercises.

Blocking
Trying to block a suggestion, but giving no good reason, and suggesting no alternative – e.g.
'It won't work.'
'We can't do that.'*

Open
Being willing to admit a mistake or lack of ability in some areas – e.g.
'Yes, perhaps I was wrong to . . .'
'Yes, looking back I didn't handle that too well, did I?'†

Testing understanding
Checking an earlier point has been understood – e.g.
'Are we all clear about what Janet was saying? If we . . . then we must also . . .'

Summarising
Restating briefly what has been said so far, such as the main points of the discussion, or a part of the discussion – e.g.
'So we're all agreed then. We've decided to . . . and . . .'

*Bald statements like the above are blocking statements, but if the speaker had said, 'It won't work. If we . . . then . . . and in any case . . .' he or she would have been giving reasons and thus disagreeing rather than just blocking. Also, defending and attacking behaviour are used towards another *person*; blocking is against an *idea* or *suggestion*.

†As people are often unwilling to admit their own mistakes or failings, this technique is sometimes not used. However, it can be very useful. If you are under attack, stubborn resistance to criticism may lead to more criticism – while simply admitting a mistake (perhaps with an 'extenuating' circumstance) can cut the ground away beneath your critic's feet. If someone continues to criticise you even after you have admitted a mistake, you will normally pick up sympathy from others who will then feel your opponent is taking things too far.

Seeking information	Finding out information (facts, figures, opinions etc.) – e.g. 'So how much will this cost altogether?' 'What do you two think?'
Giving information	Offering information (facts, figures, opinions etc.) – e.g. 'John couldn't make it today. But he asked me to tell you . . .'

Paradoxically, open behaviour is often used by confident and successful people. They are sufficiently confident of their general ability to be willing to admit to a few mistakes, and astute enough to realise its effectiveness in meeting justified criticism. People who insist that they are always right aren't always too popular. Making the odd mistake, and admitting it, simply shows you are human too.

EXERCISE 2.19

Your school or college has been asked to send a small team of staff and students to a local 11–16 secondary school to talk about courses available for 16+ students.

In small groups (three or four people each) work out a short (ten-minute) illustrated talk on:

> *Life as a sixth-former/further education student/sixth-form college student*

which you feel would appeal to the students at the school (without sacrificing accuracy).

Now adapt the talk for a parents' evening at the school.

What, if anything, would you add, leave out, change or amend – and why?

Group discussion: problems of observing

If you were observing, did you find it difficult to listen to the discussion, *and* watch it, *and* think what different techniques were being used, *and* make notes on them? If so, don't worry – people usually find it difficult the first few times.

To make it easier:

(i) Just watch *one* person and note what he or she does.

(ii) Once you've watched a few discussions, you'll be clearer in your mind what techniques are being used.

(iii) Prepare a checklist *before* the discussion, and just write a stroke each time a particular technique is used. These can be added up once the discussion is over. For example:

Observation on Student A during a discussion
Proposing ⤶Ⅼ Ⅱ 7 times   *Supporting* ⤶Ⅼ ⤶Ⅼ 10 times
Building   Ⅱ   2 times   *Disagreeing* Ⅲ   3 times
etc.

(iv) If possible, tape (or even videotape) the discussion. That way you can play it back as often as you need to for discussion of the techniques used.

(v) As there are so many techniques, and perhaps some behaviour that wasn't covered in my earlier suggestions (not just *what* people said, but also *why*; were they trying to help the group reach a decision? were they trying to give a good impression of themselves? etc.) have a look at this slightly different way of analysing group behaviour. It is particularly useful because it groups the behaviour under three main headings, which makes it easier to handle:

Task-centred	Proposing Information-seeking Information-giving Clarifying/testing understanding Evaluating/summarising Dissenting
Relationship-centred	Active listening (seeming interested in what other people say) Refereeing (if disputes arise) Bringing in (the quieter members of the group) Reducing tension Compromising Seeking feelings
Self-centred	Blocking Defending/attacking Shutting out (not letting other people get a word in) Dominating Avoiding Seeking recognition Nit-picking

Where the members of the group are most concerned to achieve an objective (such as reaching the best decision in a limited time) they will probably use 'task-centred' techniques.

If the group meets regularly, and its members are friends, rather than offend other members of the group they will probably tend to use 'relationship-centred' techniques – even if this means postponing or avoiding a controversial decision.

Where the members of the group are most concerned about themselves and their own 'images', the objective and the other members of the group may tend to be used simply as means to that end.

Now try the following. If possible half of you should act as the jury, and half as observers, changing places after each case.

EXERCISE 2.20

Discussion: murder most foul?

Below are details of some murder cases. In each case your group should try to operate as a jury, that is, discuss the case, and try to reach a unanimous decision on whether the accused was guilty of murder. (Some of the cases may seem rather old, but they are not out of date, and occur in many modern law books because they raise interesting questions about murder.)

To help you decide here are some basic principles of law. Normally, to be guilty of a crime the accused must have:

- *performed a guilty action (that is, a criminal act)*

- *with a guilty intent (that is, it was not an accident, or even negligent, but done deliberately).*

The guilty intent need not be to do exactly what actually happens, but must be something very similar. For instance, if you hit someone hard on the head repeatedly with a sledgehammer, with intent to commit grievous bodily harm, and they die, that is a result you might reasonably have expected and you would be guilty of murder. However, if you push someone aside, feeling annoyed with them, and they die of a heart attack, that would be such an unexpected consequence that you would not be guilty of murder because you would have had no intent to commit murder or grievous bodily harm.

(i)   **R. *v.* Jordan (1956)**
Court of Criminal Appeal
The appellant stabbed the deceased in the abdomen. The deceased was taken promptly to hospital and the wound was stitched. A few days later he died. Jordan was convicted of murder at Leeds Assizes and on appeal

sought to adduce further medical evidence. This evidence disclosed that the wound, which had penetrated the intestine in two places, was mainly healed at the time of death. At the hospital Terramycin was administered to prevent infection. The deceased was found to be intolerant to this antibiotic. A doctor who was unaware of this ordered its continuance. Two fresh witnesses also testified that abnormal quantities of liquid had been given intravenously. This caused the lungs to become waterlogged and pulmonary oedema was discovered.

(ii)

R. *v.* Rose (1884)

The accused was a weakly young man of 22; his father was a powerful man. Recently the father had been drinking excessively and whilst intoxicated he was of the opinion that his wife had been unfaithful to him. He had threatened her life and she was so frightened that she had frequently hidden everything in the house that could be used as a weapon. On the night in question the family had retired to separate bedrooms when the father had started abusing and arguing with his wife, threatening to murder her. He said he was going to get a knife which they knew was in his room. He rushed from his room, seized his wife, and forced her up against the balusters in such a way as to give the impression that he was cutting her throat. The daughter and the mother shouted 'murder', whereupon the accused ran from his room. He is said to have fired a gun to frighten his father – no trace of this shot was found, and then he fired again, hitting his father in the eye and killing him. On arrest he said, 'Father was murdering mother. I shot on one side to frighten him: he would not leave her, so I shot him.' He was charged with murder.

(iii)

Director of Public Prosecutions *v.* Smith (1961)

Smith was driving a car containing some stolen property when a policeman told him to draw into the kerb. Instead he accelerated and the constable clung on to the side of the car. The car followed an erratic course and the policeman fell off in front of another car and was killed. Smith drove on for 200 yards, dumped the stolen property, and then returned. Smith was charged with capital murder.

(iv)

R. *v.* Blaue (1975)

The accused stabbed a girl. She was taken to hospital, where according to doctors a blood transfusion would probably have saved her life. However, she was a Jehovah's Witness, refused a blood transfusion, and died.

Group discussion: quantity versus quality

So far we've been looking more at quantity than quality – for instance, at *how many* techniques a person used, and *how often*. This is useful if we are trying to encourage people to use new discussion techniques. It is also easy to keep a record of.

However, the person who uses the greatest variety of techniques isn't necessarily the most effective member of the group – just as the person who talks most isn't necessarily the most effective. It's not *how much* you say, so much as *what* you say and *how* you say it.

Knowing effective discussion techniques is useful – but knowing *when* to use them is also important.

How can you check who is being most effective in a discussion? Here are a few suggestions.

A   Don't just count the number of proposals a person makes. Check how many of them are actually followed up by the rest of the group.

B   How easy does each person find it to get a hearing? Do others automatically stop to listen – or does he or she have difficulty getting a word in? Do others show approval of what he or she is saying (by nodding, making sounds of agreement, listening more intently, etc.), or do they show a lack of interest (whispering to friends, looking bored, etc.) or a lack of agreement (butting in to object, shaking their heads, frowning, etc.)?

C   Do others take the person's word, or do they question or doubt what he or she says?

D   What part does the person play in

 • keeping the group together?

 • keeping to the task in hand (being a good listener, asking other people's opinions, avoiding disputes, and generally keeping the discussion moving if it looks like getting sidetracked)?

In the exercise that follows look for the *quality* of contributions in particular.

EXERCISE 2.21

A former student has left £50,000 to your school or college on condition that the decision as to how the money is spent is made by the students themselves. After a series of meetings a list of possible choices has been drawn up. Unfortunately, the total cost of these would be £200,000. It is the task of your group to agree a final list within the original budget.

First read the list carefully and make a note of your individual choices. Then discuss these choices and try to reach agreement as a group.

 (i) *New sports equipment to the value of*   *£5,000*

 (ii) *50 travel scholarships of £100 for students to go on foreign exchange schemes.*   *£5,000*

 (iii) *A large screen video projector and a new film projector, to show TV programmes, videos and films to large audiences*   *£5,000*

(iv) A school or college minibus	£15,000
(v) 20 guitars and a guitar tutor	£15,000
(vi) Driving lessons for 150 students aged 16 or over	£15,000
(vii) Fitting out a new student common room	£15,000
(viii) 1,500 new books for the school or college library	£15,000
(ix) A TV studio for students to learn how to make their own video films	£20,000
(x) Purchase of land close to the school or college to provide more convenient games facilities	£20,000
(xi) Establishment of a campus radio system to be run by and for students	£20,000
(xii) A computer room with a network of 20 microcomputers	£20,000
(xiii) A burger master franchise to enable the canteen to operate a fast food service like MacDonalds	£30,000
	£200,000

EXERCISE 2.22

Some final discussion exercises

Read these passages on perception and then do the exercise which follows.

Research suggests our perception of the world around us and the people in it varies for all sorts of reasons, as in the following examples:

(i)   Some years ago there was a story in the papers to the effect that riots had broken out in an undeveloped country because of rumours that human flesh was being sold in a store. The rumour was traced to food cans with a grinning boy on the label.

from The Visual Image *by E. H. Gombrich*

(ii)   If you observe the behaviour of a neurotic person, you can see him doing many things that he appears to be doing consciously and purposefully. Yet if you ask him about them, you will discover that he is either unconscious of them or he has something quite different in mind. He hears and does not hear; he sees, yet he is blind; he knows and is ignorant.

from Man and his Symbols *by Carl G. Jung*

(iii) A psychological test was carried out in the United States a number of years ago. A cross-section of people were shown a picture of a crowded subway (tube train) compartment. The compartment was full of people. One of them, a white man, was brandishing an open razor at a black man who stood nearby. The people were later asked to describe what they remembered about the picture. Those people who were racially prejudiced tended to 'remember' the black man, not the white man, holding an open razor.

(iv) **Wife**   Do you want to come with me to see the new film at the ABC?
Husband   No, I want to watch the snooker final.
Wife   You never want to do anything with me these days.
Husband   You know that isn't true.
Wife   [*Becoming upset*] I'm beginning to wonder if you love me any more.

Now look at the following example and discuss the question it raises:

A racially mixed British band is playing reggae-derived music in a club, before a very varied audience.

What differences are there likely to be between what each of the following might see and hear?

You
An old age pensioner
A four-year-old child
A National Front supporter
A classical musician
A Japanese tourist
The ex-girlfriend of the lead singer
The bass player's mother

A barmaid
The club owner
A writer for a pop music magazine
A Jamaican Rastafarian
Someone who has just escaped from a local mental hospital
A TV camera and a tape recorder

EXERCISE 2.23

Following a review of educational buildings in the area, the Local Authority has decided to offer a vacant primary school for use by your school or college. The primary school, which is just five minutes' walk away, will be converted into a school/college annexe. There are two aims: to provide additional facilities for current students, and to provide wider educational opportunities for the community generally.

Examine the plans on page 44, decide how you would use both the annexe as a whole and each part of it, and then make a note of your recommendations.

Now discuss this with the rest of your group and see if you can agree on how best to use the annexe.

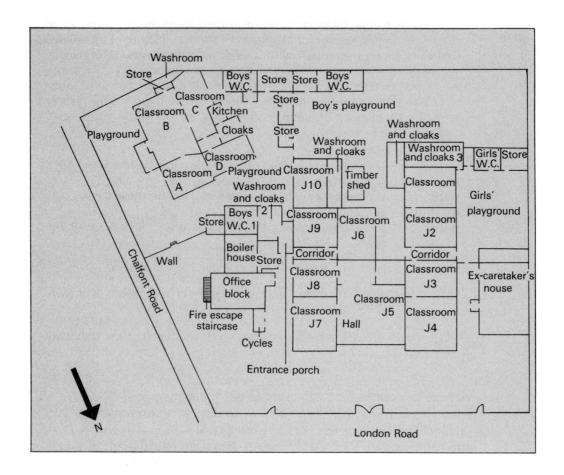

EXERCISE 2.24

Your task as a group is to decide how you could establish yourselves as a profitable Young Enterprise company. In particular you should aim to achieve the following:

(i) *Identify at least twelve types of business activity you could realistically consider starting.*

(ii) *Agree a short list of the three ideas you would like to investigate in more detail. For each of these ideas you should decide on a possible company name, what demand there would be for your product or service, what competition you would face, how much time, money, space and materials you would need, how you would raise money to start up in business, how you would market your product or service, and what contribution each of you could make.*

(iii) *Decide which idea seems most likely to succeed.*

To help your discussion here is an article outlining the way the Young Enterprise Scheme works:

The Young Enterprise Scheme gives young people between the ages of 15 and 19 the chance to find out how business works in the most practical of ways, by running a company of their own.

Every year over 700 Young Enterprise companies set themselves up, with company members going through all the activities of bringing the company into being, giving it a name, appointing people to key positions, deciding what activities to undertake, carrying through the work, organising sales and accounts, then ending it all and distributing the profits.

Midland Bank has been closely involved with, and has supported, Young Enterprise for a number of years. The Bank arranged for the re-design of the Company Kit and currently provides these directly to Young Enterprise. The kit is given to each new company and contains all that is required to incorporate, operate and liquidate a Young Enterprise company.

Midland also organise the annual Company Competition, the finals of which take place at the National Achievers' Conference in July each year. In addition, many Midland staff act as advisers to companies and are members of the Young Enterprise Area Boards.

Companies usually start up in September and wind themselves up around mid-May. Adult advisers help with the setting up of each company and help and advise throughout the year. A fairly typical Young Enterprise project brought together members of Dr. Challoner's Grammar Schools for Boys and Girls and Chesham High School in Buckinghamshire. Most of the twenty students taking part were in the VIth form, aged 16–17.

Roger Gibbins, manager of the Midland Bank at Chalfont St. Peter, was one of the advisers to the group, "My job was to give them financial advice," he says.

He explained to them how to form the company, raise money by selling shares, and draw up accounts so they could keep track of the cash flow and make sure that the cash coming in was enough to cover the payments that they had to make.

"They did very well," he says. "They made the biggest profit of the Young Enterprise projects in the Chiltern area, £500 from a turnover of £2,500."

He even seems quite pleased that the group managed to have a strike. "The work force felt they didn't know what the management were up to. They wanted more information. It was so true to life. We all learned something."

Michael Creasey, one of the group, found himself elected into the position of Research and Development Manager. This meant looking for products that they might make. Others took on the jobs of organising production, arranging for sales and so on. They started by making jewellery, which gave them a name for the company, Aphrodite, the Greek goddess of love and beauty. They went on to make up baskets of fruit which they sold to local firms to give to staff at Christmas, they ran a disco to raise money, and they opened up a tuck shop at school.

"We learned a lot on the finance side," says Michael, "particularly on the cash flow problems where you're trying to buy materials when you don't have any money in the bank." They solved that problem on the fruit baskets by cleverly getting a 50 per cent deposit on every order.

Most of the production was done at their two-hour meeting every Wednesday evening, although people had to put in more time getting materials, delivering the fruit baskets and running the shop. They learned something when someone bought huge bars of chocolate that looked like a bargain but cost too much for people to afford.

Carolyn Ayton was elected Managing Director at that first meeting. "I wanted to get involved," she says, "but I hadn't expected that and it came as a bit of a shock.

I was thrown in at the deep end and I didn't know what I was doing for the first couple of weeks. But the advisers were there to help me, although as time went on they did less and less and I did more and more."

She ended up doing about six hours' work a week, preparing beforehand for meetings, liaising with the accountant because the takings from the shop had to be added up each night, and so on.

"It was quite hard work," she says. "What I learned was you have to find the right degree of getting on with people and getting them to work properly."

All involved were pleased with the final results. "The company taught us a lot in a short space of time," says Michael Creasey. "We had fun and we made a bit of money."

The Young Enterprise Scheme itself has been going for 22 years so it has a fair bit of experience. It is organised through areas which arrange for the volunteer adult advisers.

At the beginning of the year each company raises money by selling shares to the people taking part and their friends. These cost 25p each and are limited to a maximum of five a person. At the end of the year, so long as the company has been successful, the money from the shares is given back plus a proportion of the profits.

At the end of the year each company draws up a proper report on its activities and its final accounts. These accounts show the income it made from sales and the outgoings on materials, wages, and so on. In the final balance sheet the cash the company ends up with is set against the liabilities to the original shareholders, the contributions to the Young Enterprise Scheme and assessments for corporation and value added tax.

It's paying tax that brings home to everyone that these companies actually are the real thing. To find out more, send a stamped addressed envelope to Young Enterprise, Robert Hyde House, 48 Bryanston Square, London W1H 7LN. Telephone 01-723 4070.

from Cheque In, *published by the Midland Bank*

EXERCISE 2.25

Written exercise on group discussion

To see what you have learnt from all this experience of group discussion, write a paragraph on each of the following, and use the paragraphs as a basis for an overall discussion on group work afterwards:

(i) *the advantages of working as part of a group.*

(ii) *problems that may arise.*

(iii) *ways of overcoming them and improving group discussion.*

(iv) *how I behave as a part of a discussion group.*

(v) *any changes I have noticed in myself or other people while doing work on group communications.*

(vi) *opportunities for group discussion outside of school and college.*

(vii) *possible uses of group discussion techniques in school and college – for instance, to help learning.*

3 *Before you Start your Coursework Folder*

– WHAT WILL YOUR WRITING TELL PEOPLE?

The way you dress, the way you speak, the way you behave – all these things suggest what kind of person you are. So too does your handwriting. Indeed some people believe they can work out your personality and even events in your past life just by studying how you write. See the extract that follows.

Reading beyond the lines

Interviewer Russell Harty, who has the reputation for asking odd questions, had the tables turned on him recently.

The beautiful lady called Justine asked him: 'Have you ever done anything to your left leg?'

'Yes, I have as a matter of fact,' he replied, sounding shaken if not completely off-balance. 'It's shorter than the right one.'

Justine hadn't seen Russell stand, let alone walk. The secret was in his handwriting. Australian-born Justine is a graphologist, the niece of A. Henry Silver, one of the pioneers of the science, and she made the intriguing revelation on a mid-week radio chat show that Russell Harty chairs.

And I know how she did it because a couple of years ago she surprised me in a similar manner. I had damaged a knee ligament and it actually showed in my signature at the time. There was a slight twist in the way I wrote the capital 'E' of my first name. As the knee improved my signature straightened out.

'Russell's give-away was the break in the 'Y' loop at the end of his name,' Justine told me. 'My uncle first demonstrated this technique from a signature of a divorced friend of mine. She included her previous married name in the middle and there was a break near the top of the first letter. 'Were you injured on the chin during your previous marriage?' he asked her. She had been. A honeymoon ski-ing accident left her with a virtually invisible scar under the point of her chin.'

It's amazing how revealing graphology can be. Particularly in the case of one you'd imagined to be so totally hale . . . and Harty.

from an article in TV Times *by Ed Stewart*

This is arguable. What is less arguable is that clear, readable handwriting is an asset – whether you are taking an examination, applying for a job, or just leaving a note for the milkman. There is, in fact, some evidence which suggests that teachers and examiners tend to give higher marks for 'good' handwriting. And when employers are considering hundreds of application forms for a few jobs, can you blame them if they tend to concentrate on the application forms that are clearly written?

EXERCISE 3.1

1 *Discuss:*

  (i) what 'good' handwriting is.

  (ii) how your own handwriting rates. (Look back at recent exercises and essays for examples.)

  (iii) whether you were surprised to discover how important handwriting could be.

2 *This article was written for teachers. Are there any ideas which you as a student could use to help you improve your handwriting?*

Hand it to them

Caroline Rouf

The development of handwriting is not the learning-to-ride-a-bike type of skill it is often assumed to be, especially by secondary school teachers. Most people do not develop their mature hand until they are adult. This is not simply a question of whether or not a cursive script was taught at an early age – we can all remember experiments with handwriting: the flourishes and affectations of an adolescent hand, reflected in a similar way by dress, hairstyle, make-up and mannerisms.

For many secondary pupils, time needs to be given to handwriting. Do they know why 'joined-up writing' is thought to be desirable, and which particular features of their writing make it difficult to read? Handwriting needs to be discussed periodically right through adolescence, and the different handwriting registers one is required to develop in life rehearsed.

Most people practise at least four different kinds of writing – a formal 'best' (letters of application), a fast but clear (exams, letters to friends), capitals or other non-cursive script (parcels, diagrams, notices, forms) and a private hand or scribble (fast, using abbreviations and other personal shorthands).

All too often, a teenager's immature hand is allowed to deteriorate rapidly by being forced to write too fast before a really free and legible style has had a chance to develop. In such cases, it then becomes increasingly difficult to produce a formal best handwriting when the need arises.

For children who panic easily, either because 'you're going too fast, Miss, I can't get it all down', or under exam pressure, it can be very reassuring to use a stopwatch and time them over half-a-page or so, once at their panic-stricken fastest, and once at their fast but clear speed.

This reveals to them that the difference in time is usually of the order of half-a-minute or so over a three-minute stretch of fast writing, and that illegibility has more to do with their state of mind than reality.

Several other approaches are also needed. When teachers dictate too fast or rub off the blackboard too soon, pupils pay the price in exercise books which are useless tools for revision or further study.

The whole question of handwriting as a skill, of pupils' notebooks as tools for learning, and the merits and demerits of dictation and copying needs to be discussed as a matter of policy among the teachers.

One can also encourage pupils to take an intelligent interest in the development of their own hand, and to develop enough objectivity to realise that a small reduction in speed usually results in a much-improved end-product. Confidence is crucial, for not only is it the best guard against panic, but a confident request to the teacher to slow down is more likely to be effective.

There are also those young writers with reasonably well-formed letters and fluent hands whose final script is so messy and full of crossings out that it is indecipherable on that account – nothing to do, this time, with having been rushed or confused by anyone but themselves.

Here again, everything seems to turn on the confidence with which they approach their subject matter, and their command of it. Has sufficient time been given for drafting, for revision, for discussing the work in hand with others in the class and the teacher?

And finally, is it sufficiently appreciated how close the connection is between a free, comfortable and legible hand and the ease and clarity with which one puts thoughts on paper? It's no wonder word processors are selling so well. But until they compete in price and bulk with a ballpoint and a pad of paper, I'll go on teaching handwriting.

from The Times Educational Supplement

In the same sort of way it matters how accurate your punctuation, grammar and spelling are. Some people, fairly or not, take these to be indicators of intelligence and education, and will judge you accordingly. Often (as in examinations, job application forms or letters) you are not there yourself – so all the other person has to go on is your writing. Will it stand the test? Is it clear and accurate?

PUNCTUATION AND GRAMMAR: DO THEY REALLY MATTER?

- Look at this sentence. What does it mean?

  My mother said the girl is wasting her time.

  Does it mean:

  'My mother,' said the girl, 'is wasting her time.'

  Or does it mean:

  My mother said, 'The girl is wasting her time.'

  The words used are exactly the same in both sentences, but the meaning is quite different. What made the difference was the punctuation. So punctuation matters because it can affect meaning.

- Look at these sentences. Does each have one clear meaning or is there some possible confusion or ambiguity?

  Nobody knew nothing about the kidnapping.
  Walking down the street, the sun was shining.
  He likes dancing a lot – more than me.

  Correct grammar is important because it can help avoid these kinds of misunderstanding.

- To gain a grade C pass in GCSE English you will need to achieve a good standard in your work. According to The National Criteria for GCSE English this will include competence in 'writing in paragraphs, using sentences of varied kinds and exercising care over punctuation and spelling'.

- 'If a job's worth doing it's worth doing well.'

  What do you think?

EXERCISE 3.2

Now look back at the article on the Young Enterprise Scheme on pages 45–7. Examine the punctuation and grammar in the article, and then use it to draw up your own guidelines on:

(i) sentences.	*(iv) quotation marks.*
(ii) full stops.	*(v) subject–verb agreement.*
(iii) commas.	*(vi) the correct use of tenses.*

As a class compare your findings and use them to produce your own class guide to punctuation and grammar.

N.B. There is a reference section on punctuation and grammar at the back of the book. If you find you are making mistakes with a particular area of punctuation or grammar, use the exercises and examples in the relevant section to help you improve your work.

You may also need to refer to specialist books on punctuation and grammar – such as Angela Burt's *A Guide to Better Punctuation* and *A Guide to Better Grammar.*

SPELLING: HOW IMPORTANT IS IT?

EXERCISE 3.3

Read the following sentences. What mistakes have been made?

(i) *It would be a good idea if more of our policemen were trained in the marital arts.*

(ii) *Two big men, dressed smartly in three-piece suites . . .*

(iii) *We request your presents at the meeting.*

(iv) *His clothes are all at the pornshop.*

The spelling mistakes you make as a student, like the ones above, sometimes amuse your English teacher. More often, however, they will irritate or annoy (especially if they are common words, or mistakes he or she's pointed out to you before) . . .

. . . and they'll annoy examiners, employers, etc.

The difficulty of teaching spelling, though, is that different students make different mistakes. So instead of a reference section on spelling, here are some guidelines for helping yourself.

Get a little note pad. Head each page with a different letter of the alphabet. Each time you make a mistake (and not just in work for English) find out the correct spelling (you do have a dictionary, don't you?) and write it up in your notebook. Test yourself regularly and try to use the corrected words in your writing. That way you can learn the spellings *you* need.

N.B. If you find that you keep having problems with a particular kind of word you may need to refer to a specialist book on spelling – such as Angela Burt's *A Guide to Better Spelling* (Published by Stanley Thornes (Publishers) Ltd.).

It will also help to look for *patterns* of spelling. As we saw in Chapter 1, there is no necessary connection between the way a word is pronounced and the way it is spelt. However, there are *some* connections, otherwise spelling would be even more difficult. As an example look for connections between spelling and pronunciation in the following groups:

A		B	C			
hop	hope	gnat	hat	heart	hate	
not	note	reign	cat	cart	cater	
rob	robe	resign	mat	martin	mate	
hat	hate	phlegm	back	bark	bake	
fat	fate	sign	lack	lark	lake	lace
mat	mate	feign	mac	mark	make	mace
man	mane		pack	park		pace
Sam	same		stack	stalk	stake	
plan	plane		tack	talk	take	
Tim	time		wack	.walk	wake	
bit	bite					
kit	kite					

These patterns mean that a number of spelling rules can be suggested – making it easier for you to improve your spelling in a systematic way.

EXERCISE 3.4

Each week take a different question from the list below. Find out the answer and check that you understand and can use the spelling rule involved. Then give as many examples as you can of words which follow the rule.

1 *When does 'i' come before 'e'?*

2 *How do you decide between 'c' and 's' in words like 'practice' and 'practise', or 'advice' and 'advise'?*

3 *What rules are there for deciding how to spell the plurals of words?*

4 *Are there any rules about words ending in 'l' or 'll'?*

5 *When do you double the letter at the end of a word when adding '-ing' or '-ed'?*

6 *In what ways can the sounds of vowels ('a', 'e', 'i', 'o' and 'u') give a guide to the spelling of words?*

7 *When should you use and when should you lose the letter 'e'?*

8 *When does 'cc' act like 'x'?*

9 *Do you add any extra letters to a word when adding the prefix 'dis-' or 'mis-'.*

10 *What are the most common 'silent' letters (that is, letters which are written but not pronounced – as with the 'k' in knot)?*

VOCABULARY: HOW MANY WORDS DO YOU KNOW?

EXERCISE 3. 5

You need a sheet of paper or a pencil.

Beginning at word Number 1, read through the words of the first test on page 55 in the order numbered. As you come to a word you do not know, write the number of the word on your sheet of paper. Carry on in this way until you have ten numbers on your sheet. At that point stop, whether or not you know the next word. That is to say, you read through the test until you have met ten words that you do not know the meaning of. Now you must show that you really do know the words you claimed to know. It is enough if you show that you can give a correct meaning to the last five words you claimed to know – that is, the last five words whose numbers you did not write down. You can do this in each case by making a small sketch to illustrate the meaning, or by writing about the meaning, or by showing in a sentence how the word is used.

Repeat this process for Tests 2, 3 and 4.

Test 1

Level 1

1 extravagant
2 industry
3 litter
4 menagerie
5 pavilion
6 repetition
7 shudder
8 torch
9 vacant
10 whimper

Level 2

11 classic
12 discordant
13 fanfare
14 keel

15 incubate
16 locate
17 outwit
18 privilege
19 rectangle
20 sequel

Level 3

21 dialect
22 hostage
23 ingratiate
24 ingenuous
25 magnate
26 neutral
27 passive
28 pinion
29 supersede
30 velocity

Level 4

31 bifurcate
32 gaffe
33 incidence
34 junker
35 liturgy
36 marsupial
37 obsequious
38 pristine
39 rapprochement
40 sibilant

Level 5

41 anodyne
42 barton
43 cinquecento
44 galliard

45 glacis
46 isocheim
47 lallation
48 maenad
49 patristic
50 scutage

Level 6

51 agio
52 bolometer
53 chance-medley
54 epact
55 glyptics
56 jerque
57 labret
58 marquois
59 pappus
60 usufruct

Test 2

Level 1

1 barge
2 cable
3 continent
4 exactly
5 habit
6 landlord
7 mascot
8 orchestra
9 passport
10 resolve

Level 2

11 astronomer
12 banish
13 camouflage
14 excess

15 fallow
16 obliterate
17 optimism
18 twinge
19 tyranny
20 unassuming

Level 3

21 abscond
22 barrage
23 calibre
24 elliptical
25 financial
26 negligent
27 nocturnal
28 ritual
29 stoic
30 typical

Level 4

31 analgesic
32 anachronism
33 bathos
34 cacophony
35 diatom
36 empirical
37 Nemesis
38 rondo
39 ubiquity
40 vignette

Level 5

41 azoic
42 behemoth
43 calx
44 foudroyant

45 rondeau
46 sansculotte
47 sillabub
48 tympanum
49 uhlan
50 xenophobia

Level 6

51 anacoluthon
52 banket
53 cadastre
54 dalton
55 fumatory
56 netsuke
57 pandect
58 runagate
59 systaltic
60 thurifer

Test 3

Level 1

1 badger
2 capture
3 fresh
4 hiss
5 ironmonger
6 ladle
7 mermaid
8 parade
9 rear
10 swindle

Level 2

11 brewer
12 charity
13 generosity
14 idol
15 lathe
16 orderly
17 orient
18 quest
19 rowlock
20 summit

Level 3

21 breaker
22 cumbersome
23 detention
24 fumigate
25 humane
26 juggernaut
27 kayak
28 lineal
29 objective
30 sorcery

Level 4

31 chicanery
32 gravamen
33 holocaust
34 lethargic
35 monograph
36 pinnace
37 ramify
38 scrutineer
39 tangential
40 unction

Level 5

41 ablaut
42 belvedere
43 dimity
44 gelation

45 homoeopathy
46 morpheme
47 pis aller
48 psephology
49 regulus
50 sawder

Level 6

51 chibouk
52 disembogue
53 gemmule
54 idolum

55 lasque
56 oreide
57 quintan
58 rampion
59 scammony
60 sullage

Test 4

Level 1

1 amazed
2 belfry
3 cautious
4 distant
5 explain
6 guide
7 modern
8 season
9 soot
10 tame

Level 2

11 accute
12 callous
13 diplomatic
14 entrant

15 feint
16 gender
17 hawk-eyed
18 minimum
19 professional
20 quartet

Level 3

21 alleviate
22 category
23 dissuade
24 ego
25 indecision
26 levy
27 millennium
28 pedantic
29 tariff
30 vestige

Level 4

31 contingency
32 emolument
33 felicitous
34 malaise
35 meticulous
36 proctor
37 revert
38 trauma
39 vicissitude
40 volition

Level 5

41 apothegm
42 cathode
43 courgette
44 draconian

45 exegesis
46 glissando
47 pomander
48 scrip
49 tong
50 vesicular

Level 6

51 brandreth
52 corposant
53 euphorbia
54 glendoveer
55 mandamus
56 myoclonic
57 reseda
58 saxatile
59 smallage
60 trave

from Standard Literacy Tests *by Hunter Diack*

So – how many words *do* you know?

The mark in each test is the number of words known in that test up to the tenth unknown word. The total vocabulary is the average score in three tests multiplied by 600, e.g. average score 25 = total vocabulary 25 × 600 = 15,000 words. You may find this hard to believe but extensive tests have shown this to be a very accurate estimate of how many words a person knows. So, multiply your average score (that is, your total over 4 tests ÷ 4) by 600, to find out how many words you know. This exercise will probably show you both how much you know already, and also how much more you could learn!

Increasing your vocabulary

The best way to increase your vocabulary is by wide reading. That way you will not only meet new words, but also see how words can have different meanings depending on the context. Just think how many meanings a simple word like *run* can have, for instance. The more new words you come across, the more often you come across them, and the more ways you find to use them yourself, the more your *active* vocabulary will grow. That means you won't just be able to recognise new words – you will soon feel confident using them yourself.

The next section deals with prefixes. They are included as useful vocabulary builders, since knowing prefixes can make it easier to remember words you come across and to work out what they mean.

EXERCISE 3.6

Prefixes: some common examples

Copy the following and fill in the blank spaces. Where the blank space is for examples, try to give at least three.

Prefix	Meaning	Examples
semi-	half	semicircle semiconscious semidetached
	one/single	monocle monogamy monopoly
	three	triangle tripod trilogy
post-	after	
mal-	badly	
tele-	from afar	
		misbehave mistreat misunderstand
		non-alcoholic nonsense nonentity
		quadrangle quadruple quadruped
		prearranged preconceived premature

Now, having done this, start to draw up your own list, taking one prefix a day, and finding as many examples as possible. In a few weeks your vocabulary will increase considerably.

Another way of increasing your vocabulary is by becoming a linguistic detective. Search out words that look or sound a little out of the ordinary and find out where they come from. A good dictionary will be a great help here.

EXERCISE 3.7

The English language is in a state of gradual evolution, as it has been for hundreds of years. Words are borrowed from other languages or invented as the need arises to describe new ideas or objects. You can get some idea of this process by examining the words on the left below. Each has been borrowed from another language. Can you match up each borrowed word with its origin from the list on the right?

Shampoo　　　*The Australian word for a large marsupial creature.*

Robot　　　*An Urdu word originally meaning to press, later used to describe a process including massaging the head.*

Kangaroo　　　*From the Mexican word* tomatl, *meaning a red pulpy edible fruit.*

School　　　*The Italian word for a small dagger.*

Thug　　　*A word from Czechoslovakia, originally meaning forced labour, and now referring to a machine-like creature which can carry out such labour.*

Stiletto　　　*From the Greek word* demokratia, *meaning government by the people.*

Taboo　　　*From the Latin word* schola.

Mattress　　　*From a Hindi word describing a member of a sect of religious assassins in India.*

Assassin　　　*From the Tonganese word* tabu, *meaning to set apart someone or something as either cursed or sacred.*

Yacht　　　*A word brought back by the Crusaders, from the Arab word for the killers who set out to murder the Christian leaders after taking hashish.*

Banana　　　*A native African word from the Congo which is used to name a common fruit.*

Alligator　　　*From the Spanish word* el lagarto, *meaning lizard.*

Tomato　　　*From the Arab word* almatrah, *meaning a cushion.*

Democracy　　　*A light sailing ship, built to be raced, from the Dutch word* jaght(e).

WHO ARE YOU WRITING TO?

The way we write depends on three things in particular:

● who we are writing to,

● why we are writing, and

● how people normally write in this situation
(probably how they have been taught to write in this situation).

These three factors will affect *how much* we write, *how we set it out*, *what words we use*, *what tone and register* (for example, formal or informal), and perhaps even *how neatly* we write and what kind of pen or pencil we use.

EXERCISE 3.8

Read the following questions and ask yourself how different answers would affect the points mentioned above.

1 *How old is your reader – in relation to you?*

2 *What sex is your reader?*

3 *Is there just one reader – or many?*

4 *How well do you know the reader(s)?*
   (for example, boyfriend or girlfriend/close friend/friend/family/relative/colleague/acquaintance/friend of friend/stranger).

5 *What status is your reader – in relation to you?*

6 *What nationality is your reader?*

7 *How much do you know about your reader?*

8 *How much does your reader know about you?*

All these should affect the form and language you use.

EXERCISE 3.9

You are not able to see the following people in time so have to leave a note or message. Apply what you have learnt from discussing Exercise 3.8:

(i) *Your mother: tell her you have gone out with friends and will be back late. (She's the worrying kind, incidentally.)*

(ii) *Your form teacher or personal tutor: explain you are going into hospital for a few days so will be away from school or college.*

(iii) *The new milkman: he left too much milk yesterday, so you will need less today and the normal amount from tomorrow onwards.*

N.B. There is more work on this in Chapter 4, 'Reading and Responding'.

WHY ARE YOU WRITING ANYWAY?

This question can mean two things. If it is asking what you are trying to communicate, the answer will probably lie in one of the following suggestions.

- to inform – for example,
    I shall be home early tonight.

- to persuade – for example,
    Do try to be home early tonight.

- to maintain relations – for example,
    I hope you've been keeping well since I last saw you.

Would the words you would choose vary, depending on your purpose? Give some examples of this.

If it is asking why you are using writing rather than any other medium of communication (e.g. talking) then the answer will normally be something along these lines:

- *writing is permanent* (so that you can check it later – for example, a contract or notes for revision).

- *writing is cheap and space-saving* (for example, you can store lecture notes on tape but it is a more expensive and bulky method than writing them on a sheet of paper).

- *writing enables you to communicate without being there in person* (from a note left for the milkman to a book written by someone who could never communicate personally with all his or her readers otherwise).

- Writing, when published, can reach an audience of thousands or even millions of people.

EXERCISE 3.10

From the information above and elsewhere in the book, together with your own knowledge and experience, draw up a chart which shows visually:

(i) possible mediums of communication.

(ii) the value of each (bearing in mind accuracy, cost, effectiveness, etc.).

Then, working from this, draw up a list of situations where writing will be the best means of communication, seeing who can suggest most situations.

WRITING FOR A LIVING

EXERCISE 3.11

Here are several people who make their living by writing. Read the different accounts and then, in small groups:

1 *Discuss which writing abilities each job is likely to require.*

2 *Draw up a list of other jobs where writing is likely to be important – perhaps as a means to getting a job done rather than as an end in itself.*

THE COPYWRITER

Lorna Murrell, 22, is a copywriter at Saatchi and Saatchi – one of the top advertising agencies. It's been known to give people, as well as products, a glossy image: the Prime Minister numbers among the agency's past clients. The copywriter comes up with the slogans for adverts.

Lorna joined in November. After doing a copywriting course at Watford College, she did a series of attachments. "It's a way of gaining experience. You turn up at agencies and see someone with your portfolio (a folder showing examples of your work). If they like it, they may give you work for a few weeks – often unpaid. The idea is to get a permanent job.

There are some strange terms in the advertising business. Lorna starts off as a junior copywriter.

"Then you become a light weight copywriter, then a middle weight, and then you become . . ."

"Frank Bruno," puts in Steve, the photographer.

"Well, no," says Lorna, "group head."

Lorna shares her office with an art director, Linda Cash. Together they think up ideas for advertising campaigns. "Once the idea's been approved, I write the copy and Linda decides on the look. The time we're given to do it can vary from a month to a few days."

They work well as a team, "though it's very difficult because you're sitting in a room with someone all day." They've done radio commercials, promoted airlines, charities and government schemes. Coming up with ideas is always the toughest part. "As you get more experienced it becomes easier, you learn a lot as you go along. You have to think around the subject a lot and it helps if you can find out as much as possible about the product."

Copywriting is regarded as a useful training for writers. "At college they said it was a very good discipline if you want to do any other sort of writing. You have to be very economical with words and you have to get your point across really quickly. You can't waffle at all."

If Lorna and her partner do not believe in a product, they can refuse to work on it. They rarely have to make compromises. "We've had problems with things where we've been filled with enthusiasm until we've researched it and found it wasn't such a good thing after all."

She feels a great sense of achievement when she sees her work up in print. She's also given a lot of freedom in her job – and the money is good too. "It's supposed to be one of the top stress industries, along with dentists and the army, or something. But I'd rather have a stressful, exciting day than be bored out of my mind. There's nothing else I want to do."

THE NOVELIST

Tom de Haan's first novel (*A Mirror for Princes*, published by Cape, February '87) is set in an imaginary country in medieval times. It's a family saga on a grand scale. He wrote it two years ago, when he was 22, but he had the original idea for the book long before.

"It was my fantasy world when I was little. The country and its history is very clear in my mind. The characters are very much alive in my imagination. I dream about them sometimes. The sort of books I used to like are ones which take you out of ordinary life. In a way it's a very easy way of writing – to create a world of your own and put people in it so that you can explore their emotions and their feelings."

He's been writing since he was eight or nine. At home he has suitcases full of stories. He says he writes like a maniac. "I actually find it very difficult to stop writing. Once I start I want to go on and on and on. Writing that book was one of the happiest times I ever spent."

He writes under a pseudonym; he's very keen to keep his true identity secret. He does not want his colleagues at work to know about the book – "They might not take me seriously" – only his parents and a couple of friends know of its existence.

The book has no particular message. "That's where I have my problem," he says frankly. "It's just an exercise in storytelling. I worry about that a lot. But you can't possibly write about things outside your experience, real or imaginary, when you're younger."

The first publishers he approached rejected the novel. "It is the most depressing thing when you get this enormous parcel back in the post with a little letter attached to it." Then he sent the book to an agent and it was swiftly accepted by Cape.

"I didn't think it was very likely that the book would be published. The original version was very long and rambling. Cape in fact asked me to cut a great deal, which was painful. But don't mistake me, I have a very high opinion of what I write. At the same time, I didn't think people would enjoy it. The main character is an enormously disappointing selfish person."

He is now writing his second novel, with high hopes. "I have the desire to be rich and for my books to be famous. I want people to read them, yet at the same time there's this awful moment of baring your soul."

THE REPORTER

When Mark Stokes, 22, left school, he wrote to the editor of the *Kentish Gazette* criticising the paper's county cricket coverage. "I asked if I could do some reports for them. When a vacancy came up they offered it to me. I hadn't given my career much thought till the 5th year at school, when I realised that I wasn't any good at maths or physics."

He was taken on as a trainee. "The editor gets job applications from all over the country, I was very lucky to live nearby and be on the doorstep. It's a good place to get your groundwork." For the first six months he was on probation. "I got all the grotty jobs – Women's Institute meetings and church fetes, not to mention having to run next door to the supermarket for ice-creams."

Then he had to serve indentures for $2\frac{1}{2}$ years and pass the NCTJ (National Council for the Training of Journalists) exams. He qualified this month and has just been made a senior reporter. He's gained a lot of confidence since he first arrived. "I was timid and meek. You're chucked in at the deep end and have to pick things up as you go along. I used to ponder for about half an hour over a simple wedding report.

That's the trouble with this trade – when you think you've hit on a really imaginative idea, it's probably been done by someone somewhere else. When you do come up with something, they normally say, 'Oh, where did you read that?' I enjoy writing, I'd like to do more features, but there's not much time for that.

"We're office bound most of the time. This picture that people get of journalists sitting down and thinking, Now, where can I rustle up a story? is a bit of a myth really. Certainly here. When I come in on a Monday, everything I've got to do will be entered in the diary – you don't get any say. You don't actually go out and happen to see a mugging as you're walking down the street, or anything like that."

He hates covering inquests most of all. "It's in a really morbid place. I don't really enjoy that, especially the grieving relatives." He would like to specialise in sport and is thinking of

doing an NCTJ course. "That's probably the next stage.

"It sounds corny, but you meet a lot of people in this job. Your face gets to be known in town as well, which is nice. You never go short of a drink in the pub."

THE FREELANCE JOURNALIST

Ro Newton, 21, writes regularly for *Just Seventeen* and is also a presenter on *Whistle Test*. She left school in Cheshire when she was 18 with 'A' levels in English and Sociology and came to London to do a one-year course in magazine journalism at the London College of Printing. She was flung in at the deep end: "For my first project I had to interview people on their first sexual experience!"

While at the college she did two attachments (work experience directly relevant to journalism). "One was on a local newspaper – all births, deaths and marriages. But I was always into music and I pestered the music papers for an attachment. After that I started writing freelance features and it went from there. Talk Talk was my first interview.

"After the course I went home and was on the dole for nine months (I was 19), but I was also sending in freelance pieces – reviews mainly – and I'd write up features on local bands. Because the papers I was writing for weren't that well known (*Zig Zag*, *Jamming* etc.), they'd give you a full page and print the whole feature, which was good.

"From there I started helping one of the DJs at the local radio station voluntarily and got interviews through him."

A radio journalism course at the National Broadcasting School (now closed) inspired Ro to write to *Whistle Test*, who luckily were looking for a new presenter. It was co-presenter David Hepworth (Editorial Director of *Just Seventeen*) who put her on to the magazine, and her mixture of enthusiasm and good writing has kept her in regular work ever since.

London College of Printing, Elephant and Castle, London SE1. Tel: 01-735 8484.

from Just Seventeen

4 Reading and Responding

When I test the accuracy and speed of reading of students in my classes I usually find that I can read *two or three times faster* than they can, yet still get as many correct answers. This is true even with, for instance, BTEC National Diploma Classes. Now obviously this has advantages for me: I can choose either to do more work in the same time as them, or to do the same work and have more spare time. Either way I benefit. Yet they – and you – could be in the same position if you improve your reading skills. If you are interested, read on.

An efficient reader can read 500 words a minute – what is your reading speed?

How to read faster

(This applies especially to everyday material, which is not particularly difficult, and doesn't need special study.)

A Widen your eye span to take in more words: don't 'fixate' on every word – take in small groups of words at a time. (To help you do this – don't move your head as you read – and don't follow individual words with your finger or pencil.)

B Don't regress, i.e. don't go back over material you have just read – keep on reading. (To help you do this put a card over the material you have already read and move it along accordingly.)

C Don't subvocalise, i.e. don't mouth the words silently to yourself – your eyes and brain can move faster than your lips.

D Try to achieve a *reading rhythm*.

E Just try *aiming to read faster* (willpower?).

How to read better

A Ask yourself *why* you are reading. (This will help you decide what to look for and remember, and what you don't need to worry about.)

B Choose a place it is easy to *concentrate* in. (Otherwise you will be distracted – and you can't do two things at once.)

C (A long-term aim) *Read widely* to increase your knowledge and vocabulary. (Practice makes perfect – and the more you know the less chance there is of being confused by difficult new words, which slow you down.)

D Try to *anticipate* and *read critically*. Don't just accept what you read. Ask yourself questions about it, such as 'Can the writer prove this?' 'Whose side is the writer on?' 'Is he being serious here?', etc., etc. (Be an *active* not a passive reader.)

E Look for the *main points* (often the writer will help you by using **headings**, subheadings, or BLOCK CAPITALS, or by underlining words or putting them in *italics*). Sometimes the main point will be expressed in the first sentence of a paragraph and the rest of the paragraph will simply illustrate this main point.

F *Test your comprehension* as you read. Mentally summarise what you have read. Ask and answer questions. (If you are working with a friend test each other – or discuss what you have read.)

G *Relate what you read to your own experience* and *draw your own conclusions*. Make the material your own – something you know and have views on, a part of you. Again – be an *active* reader.

H Above all *read for enjoyment*. Choose books on topics you are interested in. One topic may lead to another. The more you read, the more reading will become a pleasant habit and the less effort it will seem or be. Are you really enjoying that TV programme? If so, fine, keep watching. But if not, pick up a book. Remember: libraries are free, there is no book licence, and books can be taken anywhere to be read.

Reading: the 'gears' or speeds

Some reading is more difficult; some is more important. Adjust your reading speed and technique accordingly. Experts identify four main 'gears'.

First: Study Reading (up to 150 words per minute)

For difficult and/or important material: Skim read/Re-read/Note/Revise/ Think about and make connections.

Second: Slow Reading (150–300 w.p.m.)

For quite difficult material or to ensure 100 per cent *comprehension*. This is how most students read if they haven't improved their reading skills: for them it is 'normal' speed.

Third: Rapid Reading (300–800 w.p.m.)

For average or easy material where the aim is to have a general, but not necessarily 100 per cent, understanding.

Using the techniques suggested in 'How to read faster'.

Top: Skimming/Scanning (800 + w.p.m.)

Reading rapidly for general impression or to locate specific information.

This technique pays particular regard to *cues* such as headings, first sentences, etc. (See 'How to read better', point **E**.)

An example would be looking through a telephone directory to find a name – you only read what is absolutely necessary.

Where can I find out more about reading? _____

You have just read a very brief summary. You will find more information, examples, tests and explanations in books like these, which your local or college library may well have:

Read Better, Read Faster by M. and B. De Leeuw (Pelican)
Use Your Head by Tony Buzan (BBC)
Rapid Reading Made Simple by G. R. Wainwright (W. H. Allen)

EXERCISE 4.1

1 Follow-up work

(i) *Look back through the advice on reading and draw up a checklist of techniques you have not used so far. Each time you come to a new piece of reading (for example, a textbook in another subject, or a novel or short story read for pleasure), try to use some of the appropriate techniques from your checklist. When you find yourself using a technique regularly, cross it off the checklist. That will leave only those techniques you seldom or never use. In friendly competition with a friend see who can reduce their checklist the more quickly.*

(ii) *Keep a daily log of all materials you have read – including books, magazines, letters, newspapers, handouts from your teachers, etc. By each entry put down which 'gear' you read it in. At the end of the week discuss your findings with fellow students.*

2   Selecting and reading the right information

First you will need a good selection of travel brochures from local travel agents.

You are working in a travel agents' and receive a letter asking for details of holidays to fit the following requirements:

- *for two adults and an eight-year-old child.*

- *at San Antonio in Ibiza.*

- *for two weeks.*

- *between mid-July and mid-August.*

- *preferably costing no more than £400 per adult and with at least a 20 per cent discount for the child.*

- *departing from Birmingham Airport.*

- *with a guarantee that prices will not be affected by any change in the value of the pound.*

- *with the option of cancellation if there is any major change by the travel company, such as change of UK airport or a change of accommodation to a lower level of rating.*

- *with information about car hire charges.*

Look through the assorted travel brochures to find the relevant information, and:

(i) *List holidays which cover the points required.*

(ii) *Write to the customers on behalf of the travel agent, advising them of the possible holidays they should consider and suggesting which seems to offer the best value.*

(If there is no holiday giving all the points required, please indicate:

- *the other holiday in this price range which has most of the stated requirements, and*

- *the holiday with all the points required which exceeds the cost limit by the smallest amount.)*

Comprehension

There are too many words I can't understand _____

Here you have several alternatives:

A *Read widely throughout your course* – not just books, but magazines and newspapers, not just fiction but non-fiction too. The more you read, the more words you will come across, and in different contexts. If you take the trouble to look up new words in your dictionary and to make a note of new words (including those in other subjects you are studying), this will help increase your vocabulary. It's common sense – the more words you know, the lower the chance of coming across words you don't know. Try setting yourself a target – to learn and use twelve or twenty new words a week (more if you can). Just twelve new words a week (and you would try to learn more than that if you were learning a *foreign* language) will give you more than *400* new words over an academic year. Informal competition with a friend or group of friends can help here.

B *Deduction!* Do you know what *samphire* is? Don't worry if you don't; I didn't know either for a long time. But let's suppose you came across the word samphire in a passage on wild plants you can eat, and the actual context was this:

> The first time I was offered a whole dish of wild vegetables I was frankly scared. The plant was marsh samphire, a skinny little succulent that grows abundantly on saltings. It lay on my plate like a mound of shiny green pipecleaners . . .
>
> *from* Food for Free *by Richard Mabey*

After reading this you should not only be able to tell me what samphire is, but also where it grows, what colour it is, what it looks like, and whether you can eat it. Not all words, of course, will have quite such a helpful context, but many new words can be worked out with a bit of thought.

C *Ignore!* Not all words are equally important. When you send a telex or telegram you usually miss out a lot of words – but it can still be understood. If the words you don't know are not especially important you can, in emergency, simply pass over them. Let us take that word samphire as an example again. Suppose that the first time you met it was in this extract from Shakespeare's play *King Lear*:

> Half way down [the cliff]
> Hangs one that gathers samphire, dreadful trade!
> Methinks he seems no bigger than his head.
> The fishermen that walk upon the beach
> Appear like mice

In fact, even here, we get some clues as to what samphire is (the fact that men gather it from the sides of cliffs). But even if we still don't know exactly what it is this doesn't really matter. In this play the samphire is just an incidental descriptive detail and does not have any effect on the main characters or the action of the play. As such it can, if necessary, be ignored. (This, incidentally, contrasts with the previous passage from *Food for Free*. There, the subject of the passage was edible wild plants – and so samphire was, in a sense, a major character, and not to be ignored.)

'I can't follow the argument: what's the writer trying to say?'

Try looking for *cues*. These are words (or other aspects of the passage, such as <u>underlining</u>, BLOCK CAPITALS etc.) which give you a clue, or act as a signal:

- to tell you *what order* events happened in, e.g.

  first/first of all/at first/in the beginning
  before that/earlier/previously
  at the same time/meanwhile/simultaneously
  then/next/secondly/afterwards
  finally/at last/eventually.

- to tell you what are *main points* and what are examples or illustrations of these points.

  (i) Often the first few lines of a paragraph contain the main point, and the rest of the paragraph just gives further information in the form of examples or illustrations emphasising the original point.

  Sometimes examples are signalled by phrases like:

  such as/for instance/for example.

  The opening lines and the closing lines of a passage are particularly likely to contain main points.

  (ii) **HEADLINES**, <u>underlining</u>, BLOCK CAPITALS, etc. are all ways of drawing your attention to main points. Never forget the importance of the *title* of the passage you're reading.

- to tell you the writer is *changing his or her point of view* and looking at *the opposite side of the argument*. Words like:

however/on the other hand/despite this/but,

particularly coming at the start of a new paragraph, usually signal a change of direction in the argument.

● to indicate *cause and effect*: that one thing has caused something else to happen. Words to look for here are:

as a result/therefore/thus/consequently/because/since.

EXERCISE 4.2

To check if you understand this, read the following passage:

Why go to Polytechnic?

Why do some students go to poly-technics while others go to other institutions of post-school education? If a student is going to study an HND course or any other non-degree course then the answer will generally be that that particular polytechnic is providing the best course available. However, many students who study for a degree, including myself, only came to a polytechnic because they failed to obtain a place in a university and indeed in my case, not only did I come to polytechnic as a second choice, I am studying for a course that I originally did not want to study.

Such an attitude is unfortunate but it is true to say that many if not the majority of students studying for a degree at a poly are at a poly for the same reason. Polytechnics are regarded by many, including careers masters, as second-class universities and yet there are many advantages in studying at a poly.

Firstly, polys have a far wider level of education to offer.

Secondly, if a student is studying for a degree then that course will probably have been validated by the Council for National Academic Awards (CNAA), a body which is far more prepared to innovate compared with Universities who validate their own degrees.

Thirdly, courses at polytechnics tend to be more vocational than university courses and for many people this is of crucial importance.

Fourthly, poly courses tend to be 'student' centred compared with universities which tend to place far greater emphasis on the course than the student that takes it.

There are, however, very serious problems relating to polytechnic education. Most important is that polys have since their foundation suffered from cash problems. Library facilities, for instance, are in most cases not only overcrowded but also lack all but the most basic facilities. Many polytechnics are multisite institutions and the concept of a corporate institutional identity does not exist.

In London, Thames Poly has a site in West London, a site in South East London and a Teacher Training site in Kent with over 20 miles between them.

In the earlier part of this article I compared poly education with university education. The reason for this is that the majority of those who read this will be trying to decide which college to study at. However such a comparison is incongruous. The roles of polys and universities within the education system are different.

Why were the polys created? They were founded because of Harold Wilson's idea that Britain was in need of the 'White Hot Heat of the Technological Revolution' and were seen as institutions that could provide the 'white hot technocrats' who would run this revolution and the courses would give training for Britain's future engineers, accountants, surveyors etc. This did mean that the nature of post-school education would have to change. Universities were seen as giving 'an education for life' with specific vocational training given in only a few specialist subjects such as medicine. Polytechnics were to be financed by Local Education Authorities, to ensure that these institutions would keep to this vocational ethos. Polys are also supposed to be sympathetic towards the needs and aspirations of the local community.

from Focus *by R. B. Taylor*

Now answer these questions on it.

1 *What do you think is the main point of the passage, and what clues suggest this?*

2 *After saying (in the second paragraph) 'Polytechnics are regarded by many, including careers masters, as second-class universities', what one word signals that the writer is now going to take a different point of view?*

3 *After spending the third, fourth, fifth and sixth paragraphs describing the advantages of polytechnics what one word, early in the seventh paragraph, signals that the writer is now going to look at the opposite side of things (namely the problems of polytechnics)?*

4 *The third, fourth, fifth and sixth paragraphs each deal with a separate advantage of polytechnics. How (apart from giving each point a separate paragraph) does the writer signal that a fresh point is being made in each case?*

5 *Look at paragraphs seven and eight. The writer makes two specific points about polytechnics and gives a specific example of each point. What are the points, and what are the examples?*

6 *What example of 'cause and effect' occurs in the first paragraph? What word links the cause and the effect?*

7 *Can you find a parallel example of 'cause and effect', using the same linking word, in the last paragraph?*

8 *Sometimes a writer will indicate that he or she is 100 per cent sure about something, for example by using absolute terms like:*

   always, never; will, will not; must, must not.

However, life isn't always so straightforward. Often the most that a writer can say is that most of the time something is true. If the writer can't be 100 per cent sure, he or she will tend to use words and phrases like:

   usually, generally, most of the time, in most cases, as a rule, in general.

And if the writer's even less sure he or she may have to use words like:

   probably, possibly, perhaps, may, might, sometimes.

Now, look back through the passage and find any words or phrases that signal that what the writer is saying isn't 100 per cent true (not because he's lying but because what he's writing about isn't straightforward – he realises that there may be exceptions to what he's saying).

'The sentences confuse me. They're so long and complicated.' ━━━━━━

Take a look at this sentence – all 95 words of it:

> In the event of loss or damage to this product caused by burglary, theft, or accidental means within 3 (three) years from the date of delivery, or in the event of any fault occurring in the product resulting in the malfunctioning thereof within the same period the manufacturer or the company's accredited retailer from whom the product was purchased will replace such product if it has been lost, repair it if it has been damaged or rectify such faults as have occurred therein, in every case free of charge subject to the undermentioned conditions.

All those words crammed up together do look a bit overpowering. (Incidentally, if you're one of those students who tends to use commas instead of full stops let this be a warning. Full stops give the reader a chance to catch his or her breath, physically and mentally, and follow what you're saying.)

Don't panic. Try the flow chart approach. You should end up with something like the illustration shown opposite.

If you've used flow charts before, this should be fairly easy to follow. If you haven't, there's always a first time.

Flow charts, incidentally, have many uses. In one experiment newly qualified doctors used flow charts when diagnosing the symptoms in suspected appendicitis cases. With the help of the flow charts it became much easier to decide who actually had appendicitis.

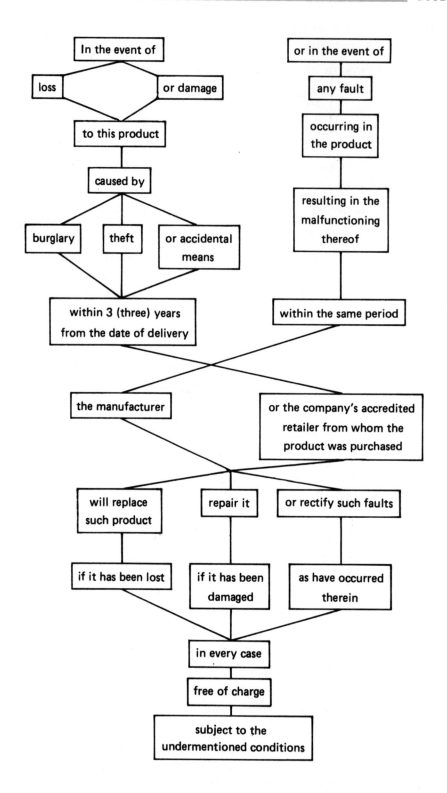

EXERCISE 4.3

> *How many areas can you think of where a flow chart approach could be useful? Take your own studies as an example. Prepare a flow chart showing how you would tackle a comprehension.*

WHY 'IN YOUR OWN WORDS'?

Why do so many comprehensions require you to answer 'in your own words'? Why don't they let you use the words of the original passage?

In case you ever wondered what was so important about 'in your own words', here is a short exercise.

EXERCISE 4.4

> *Read the passage and then answer the questions that follow:*

> 'LONDON. Pugglemess term lately over, and the Lord Tinslebore sitting in Rinlonks Inn Hall. Immucable November weather. As much mud in the streets, as if the waters had but newly formed from the face of the earth, and it would not be wonderful to meet a seggumpalot, forty feet long or so, doddlebing like an elephantine zig pod up Thursdrible Hill. Smoke gingling down from the chimney pots, making a soft black siffle with sprokes of tooze in it as big as full-grown snowsprokes . . .'

> **1** *What has just finished?*
>
> **2** *Where is the Lord Tinslebore sitting?*
>
> **3** *What is the weather like?*
>
> **4** *What might the seggumpalot be doing?*
>
> **5** *What is it compared to?*
>
> > *from* Teaching English as a Second Language *by J. A. Bright and G. P. McGregor*

As you will have guessed the passage was half nonsense. (It is, in fact, the opening of *Bleak House* by Charles Dickens, with all but the simplest words made into nonsense words.)

Yet it was possible to gain 100 per cent by answering the 'nonsense' questions with 'nonsense' extracts from the 'nonsense' passage. In other words, *simply using words from a passage is no guarantee that you understand them.* This is a pity as it means that, to avoid this, some comprehensions become a sort of paraphrase or translation exercise – which is only a part of comprehension (understanding). But how otherwise can your comprehension be checked?

WHAT CAN COMPREHENSIONS TEST?

Let us start by listing possible *skills* or *knowledge* a comprehension may be trying to test:

- *Selective reading* – searching quickly for particular pieces of information, such as a name in a telephone directory or a time on a railway timetable.

- *Deduction of meaning from context* – working out the meaning of words you don't know from clues in the other words around them.

- *Existing vocabulary* – knowing what a word means, even without clues from the context.

- *Summary* – ability to select main or important points and discard examples, repetition, 'padding', etc.

- *Evaluation* – giving an opinion about what is written, for example, agreeing or disagreeing with it.

- *Analysis* – being able to see what is fact and what is opinion, what is important and what is not, what the writer's attitude is etc.

- *Inference* – seeing what the passage is suggesting or implying, even if the point is not stated directly or explicitly.

- *Technique of writing (organisation of information)* – analysing whether the passage works by listing events in the order they happened in, by comparing and contrasting, by showing cause and effect, by classifying material into different types, by literal description or imaginative comparison, etc.

- *Information transfer* – can you transfer information from one form to another (for example, from a graph or chart to continuous writing, from a magazine article to notes, from a phone message to a memo, etc.)?

- *Response to language* – appreciation of tone and register, of levels of formality, of use of dialogue, of prosaic or poetic features, etc.

- *Appreciation of purpose* – being able to see what the writer is aiming to achieve (for example, is he or she writing to persuade, to inform, to entertain, to condemn, to express feelings and emotions, to describe, to amuse, to evoke an atmosphere, etc.)?

- *Overall understanding* (all the above, as necessary).

DIY COMPREHENSION

EXERCISE 4.5

Now that you have had a brief introduction as to why comprehensions are set, here is a chance to make one yourself. A passage is provided. Work out eight or ten questions which you feel are a full and fair test of overall understanding. Then exchange questions with another student; he or she tries to answer your questions, you try to answer his or hers. Afterwards discuss how similar or different your questions were, and what this suggests. Is working out a good comprehension easy?

This is an extract from Colin Turnbull's book The Forest People, *which describes his experiences while living with a tribe of pygmies in Africa.*

He asked me which of the two girls I thought looked the more attractive. I said Amina, without a doubt, because she was the most beautiful girl I had seen in a long time, and the BaBira are not noted for their good looks by any means. Amina was tall and a warm brown in colour, her eyes were deep and thoughtful, her expression was kind and gentle. Yes, by all means she was the more beautiful of the two. Kenge nodded thoughtfully and changed the conversation.

That night I sat up late with the men, and when I went back to my hut I was surprised not to see any bachelors sleeping on the floor as they usually did. But three logs were placed beside the bed, and were glowing cheerfully. I sat down on the edge of the bed and found, as I had expected, that Kenge had decided it was too cold to sleep on the ground all by himself, so he had curled up in my blanket. He was considerate enough, on such occasions, not to take my blanket on to the floor, but rather to take half of the bed. So I crawled in beside him and was about to say something when I realized that the body beside me was considerably taller than Kenge, and very differently shaped. It was Amina.

It was a difficult moment, but I could see the whole situation at once . . . I had become the centre of a nice political manoeuvre. The Chief had sent his daughter, not to win the pygmies by her gifts of plantains and manioc flour, but to win them by winning me. The pygmies, anxious to get what they could out of the situation, liking Amina anyway, but having some consideration for me, got Kenge to find out which of the two girls I preferred. That, evidently, was to be the limit of my choice in the matter. I confess I was glad I had chosen Amina, but I could see all sorts of difficulties arising if I were to take advantage of the situation. No doubt the Chief had in mind the considerable bride-wealth he could demand should, by any chance, his daughter bear a mulatto child. Still, it was good of him to send his prettiest daughter.

I considered for a minute or two and then said, 'Amina?' very quietly. It had begun to rain, and I half hoped she would not hear me. It would be a terrible disgrace to her – and to me – if I turned her out, yet I wanted no part of a lengthy and costly dispute over bride-wealth. But Amina was by no means asleep. She laughed lightly and made fun of my KiNgwana name, which means 'the long one'. So I said, 'Amina!' once again, a little more sharply, still trying to think what a supposed gentleman and scholar should do under such circumstances. But Amina was not helping. She just snuggled closer and said, 'Yes, tall one?' Then in a moment of inspiration I simply said, 'Amina, the roof is leaking.' And with masculine authority I added, 'Get up and fix it.'

Without a word she got up and started searching for the leak, pulling at the leaves until a steady trickle of water came down, splashing on the floor beside the bed. By the time she had repaired the damage and checked the whole roof with womanly efficiency I was asleep – at least so I pretended. With a sigh she pulled the blanket from me and also went to sleep – or perhaps she, too, was pretending. But it was a solution, if a chilly one, and my last thoughts that night were that Kenge would at least have left me some of the blanket, no matter how annoyed with me he was. These villagers – they were just animals.

When I woke in the morning I hardly dared open my eyes; but a tentative exploration proved that the other half of the bed was empty. I thought that all was well after all. Amina had cut her losses and left at dawn. But when I had put my trousers on and stooped through the low entrance of the hut into the camp, there she was. She was sitting on a log beside the hut, quietly fanning the fire and cooking my breakfast, just as every other wife was doing for her husband. Kenge was making it very obvious to everyone that he was eating with the bachelors, and they were making it obvious that they had not slept in my hut that night. Everyone else studiously ignored my appearance except old Moke, who was walking past on his way to the stream to bathe. He looked at me sideways, shook his head and gave a little knowing old laugh. And as he walked on he shook his head all the more vigorously and laughed all the louder.

I was about to go after him, thinking that at least I could ask his advice, but Amina caught hold of my trouser leg and said, 'There is no need for you to go the stream to bathe, I have brought you water – behind the hut.' So I went behind the hut and washed, and then sat down and had breakfast while Amina went to join the other women and chat to them. While she was gone Kenge strolled by and elaborately asked me if the food was all right. He also asked me, rather loudly, if I had slept well, and Amina answered from across the camp, 'Yes, he told me to mend the leak in the roof!' This proof of domestic bliss brought howls of mirth from all around, the more infuriating because I could not see what was funny about it. Then Kenge told me that this was what men always said to their wives when they wanted to be allowed to sleep in peace.

That night, Amina and I came to agreement. She was to stay with me and cook my food . . . and mend leaks in the roof every night. This way she preserved her reputation and I mine, and there would be no complications. And so it was. I grew very fond of Amina, and later on, when I was in a village and became very ill, she walked ten miles every day to see me, and ten miles back. And she brought me refreshing fruits and sweet-smelling plants and flowers, and sat beside my bed without saying a word.

EVALUATING A COMPREHENSION

A lot of students seem to do comprehensions without realising why (except that one or more will 'come up in the exam'). Yet comprehensions, as I have suggested, are set to test certain skills and it helps to be aware of this. Not all comprehensions are good tests, but even with these it usually helps to know what they are *trying* to test.

EXERCISE 4.6

Look at the following comprehension test.

First of all, read it and answer the questions, as you would in an exam.

Then, look back at it, and ask yourself how well or how badly this particular test actually revealed your understanding of the material. In particular look back at the section on 'What can comprehensions test?', and check how many skills the comprehension was trying to test. Consider too whether the questions set were a fair test. Would they have been better worded another way, or left out altogether? Can you think of questions that should have been asked but weren't?

In conclusion – is this a fair comprehension exercise?

Read items (a), (b) and (c), which all relate to the questions which follow. Then answer the questions in your own words as far as possible.

Dictionaries may be used.

a)

NORTHUMBRIA POLICE
CRIME PREVENTION BULLETIN

Dear Ratepayer,

Burglary now forms the largest proportion of crime that is committed in our region.

In the **NEWCASTLE** area burglary figures have risen considerably yet people continue to make things easy for the thief, **WHY ! ! !**

We need your help **NOW** in preventing this sort of crime.

Your premises can be made much safer by taking the following crime prevention measures. . . .

1. Fit window locks to all ground floor windows.

2. Make sure that exterior doors are fitted with good quality 'deadlocks'.

3. If you see anything suspicious, telephone the POLICE at once.

DON'T FORGET ! ! !

If you need further advice about locks, burglar alarms, cash carrying or any other aspect of security, then telephone **NEWCASTLE 323 451** and ask for the **CRIME PREVENTION OFFICER HIS ADVICE IS FREE**

Northumbria Police Printing Department, Force Headquarters, Ponteland

b)   **Do better locks really stop burglars?**

Have you taken to heart all those warnings to "Lock It"? Have you put strong locks and bolts on your doors and windows and do you make sure they are all secure whenever you go out? Well the Home Office, the government department in charge of these crime prevention campaigns,
5   has got news for you. It has decided that it is not going to make much difference to your chances of being burgled. The revelation comes in a new study from the department's research and planning unit: *Residential Burglary* by Stuart Winchester and Hilary Jackson. Its principal conclusion, which will embarrass the Home Office officials responsible for

10 crime prevention policy, is that good security is a poor deterrent to burglars.

The Report says that the most important influence on a burglar's choice of target is the ease with which a house can be approached unobserved. The most vulnerable houses are set well back from the road, those

15 hedges, shrubs and fences that people put up to give themselves privacy also assist burglars.

The other key factor is whether the house is occupied. Four out of five daytime burglaries and 19 out of 20 evening break-ins take place when there is nobody in. Only at night is the burglar likely to call when you

20 are at home, but night-time burglaries account for only 15 per cent of break-ins.

When the burglar has got both time and privacy in which to work, only the toughest security measures will be effective. Most burglars are willing to force a door or window and to break glass to get inside. Only

25 iron bars or steel doors seem to be able to withstand a determined burglar. This means, say the Home Office researchers, that to concentrate crime prevention resources in the present way, on what is called "target hardening", can make only a small impact.

Burglary is one of Britain's commonest crimes – the average household

30 now has a one in 35 chance of being burgled in any one year. About half a million homes suffer every year and though the cash value of what is stolen is frequently small the psychological impact of the crime is often severe.

It is difficult to catch burglars because they rarely leave fingerprints

35 and are almost never seen by their victims. Official figures claim that just under a third of burglaries are eventually cleared up, but when un-reported burglaries are included, the true figure is probably nearer to a sixth. As a result, the police and Home Office concentrate on preventive measures. The Home Office runs national crime prevention publicity

40 campaigns, while at local level there are some 500 full-time police crime prevention officers. The new study – in a thriving tradition of Home Office research that pours cold water on official policy – challenges the underlying rationale of this work.

One useful innovation might be burglary squads – either of police or

45 local residents – on patrol. This method has produced good results in Seattle, USA, but a disadvantage is that people tend to lose interest, especially when the rate of burglary is as low as it still is in most parts of Britain.

c) **Burglary rate per 1000 households by tenure, type of accommodation and age of head of household**

Great Britain, 1979 and 1980 combined

Tenure	Burglary rate per 1000 households
Owner occupied, owned outright	20
Owner occupied with mortgage	22
Rented with job or business	28

Rented from local authority	38
Rented from housing association	29
Rented privately, unfurnished	24
Rented privately, furnished	72

Type of accommodation

Detached house	25
Semi-detached house	22
Terraced house	27
Purpose-built flat	38
Converted flat	47
With business premises	78

Age of head of household

16–24	90
25–29	50
30–44	27
45–59	29
60–64	22
65–69	20
70–74	17
75–79	21
80 or over	23

from General Household Survey, *1980 (HMSO)*

Questions

1. According to Item (b) why does a burglar choose a particular house to break into?

2. What do you understand by the phrase "target hardening" in l. 28 of Item (b) and why do you think it is in inverted commas?

3. What are the two main "preventive measures" (ll. 38–9, Item (b)) which the police and the Home Office concentrate upon?

4. Item (a) is a leaflet sent to Newcastle householders with the annual Rate demand. By what means does it try to put over its message forcefully?

5. Look carefully at items (a) and (c), identify the households most at risk of being burgled, and consider reasons why this might be so.

Then use your material to write a newspaper article under the heading: "Who is most at risk?"

6. Summarise, in the form of a confidential checklist for the information of your local crime prevention officer, your own security arrangements against burglary, and briefly evaluate their possible effectiveness. (You need not limit yourself to your actual situation, but may alter or invent details as you wish.)

7. (You are advised to spend about 50–60 minutes on this question.)

Assume that you have been burgled and your property has been vandalised. You have already informed the police.

(a) Write a letter to your insurance company giving the relevant details of the burglary and asking for advice on what to do next,

and

(b) Write a personal letter to a friend giving an account of how this burglary happened and your reactions to it.

A specimen GCSE paper produced by the Northern Examining Association for Syllabus C – English for Mature Students

VISUAL COMMUNICATION – CHARTS, GRAPHS AND DIAGRAMS

A mass of figures, instructions and information tends to put some people off reading an item. Pictures, charts, graphs and diagrams are often easier to read and can be understood more quickly – provided they are well presented.

EXERCISE 4.7

Find an example of each of the following: a line graph, a bar chart, a pie chart, a pictogram and a flow chart. Some of the textbooks in your other subjects, such as geography, may contain examples.

Now consider why each is used and what makes an effective chart, graph or diagram. The following questions should help:

1 *Does it catch and keep your attention and, if so, how?*

2 *How easy is it to understand?*

3 *How much information can it present without beginning to appear cluttered or confusing?*

4 *Does it give a quick impression of comparisons and relationships?*

5 *How accurate and precise is it – or is the main value in communicating an overall impression?*

6 *Is it more useful for presenting short-term figures rather than illustrating the position over a longer period?*

Look back at the examples you have found to help you answer these questions.

To help you consider how to present an effective chart, graph or diagram yourself, read the following advice:

A A *key* helps, especially when the symbols on the chart, graph or diagram are ambiguous, or you have unimaginative readers.

B *Big is best.* A larger chart or diagram is easier to read than a small one. It has more impact too. It is also worth using the largest units possible (hours rather than minutes, for instance). What you lose in precision you will gain in readability and ease of understanding.

C If you are using pictures or symbols try to keep each picture or symbol the same size. Then the *number* of pictures or symbols will be an accurate guide, without the reader trying to work out whether size and volume are also significant.

D On charts and graphs horizontal writing is easier to read than

```
v   w
e   r
r   i
t   t
i   i
c   n
a   g
l   !
```

E Different colours or patterns can help separate out the different elements on a chart or diagram. Again, this helps readability.

F Edit your chart or diagram. Be ruthless. Cut out all unnecessary lines, numbers or words. *Keep it simple.*

EXERCISE 4.8

Examine the two examples which follow and consider their effectiveness. Bear in mind the points outlined above.

a

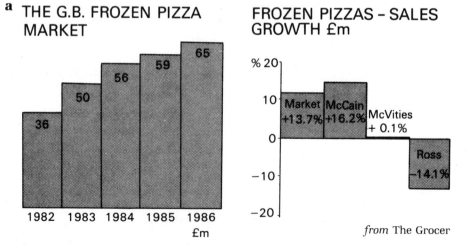

THE G.B. FROZEN PIZZA MARKET

FROZEN PIZZAS – SALES GROWTH £m

from The Grocer

b
Things in the retail price index

The size of a slice shows the relative importance given to that particular group of things. Inside each slice, you'll find examples of the main things included.

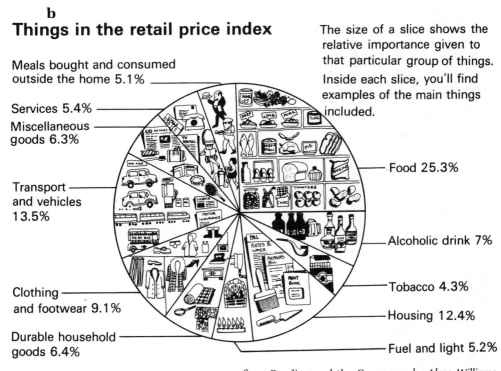

Meals bought and consumed outside the home 5.1%

Services 5.4%

Miscellaneous goods 6.3%

Transport and vehicles 13.5%

Clothing and footwear 9.1%

Durable household goods 6.4%

Food 25.3%

Alcoholic drink 7%

Tobacco 4.3%

Housing 12.4%

Fuel and light 5.2%

from Reading and the Consumer *by Alma Williams*

EXERCISE 4.9

1   *Research and prepare an illustrated guide to bar charts, pie charts and pictograms for college students. Try to choose or create examples which will be relevant to students taking GCSE subjects.*

2   *In groups of four or five students, choose a product which is in everyday use and which you can bring into class. Examples could include chocolate or snack bars, deodorants, pocket calculators and make-up.*

Arrange to bring in and test examples of your chosen product, devising at least five tests for each product. Your ultimate aim should be to present your findings in a visually interesting and understandable format.

The comparison of styling mousses on page 86 is an example of one approach. Try to find a different way of presenting your findings.

SUMMARY WRITING

Only the main points of a passage are needed in a summary. Recognising the difference between main points and illustrative examples, anecdotes, 'padding', etc. is therefore a vital skill.

TRIED AND TESTED

WE ASKED, WAS THE MOUSSE...

Question	Wella Stylite Conditioning Styling Mousse, Normal Hold (£2.00 for 125ml)	Vidal Sassoon Styling Mousse Extra Control (also in Light Control Formula) (£2.55 for 150ml)	Sunsilk Styling Mousse, Regular Hold (also in Extra Hold) (99p for 90ml)	Roger & Gallet Tenax Styling Mousse (£1.95 for 200ml)	Revlon Flex Body Building Styling Mousse, Regular Control (also in Extra Control) (£2.39 for 150ml)	Jo Ba Styling Mousse (one type only, gives Normal to Strong Hold) (£1.79 for 150ml)	Boots System 1 Protect Protein Styling Mousse (99p for 100ml)	Boots Country Born Conditioning Styling Mousse, Extra Hold (also in Normal Hold) (£1.25 for 150ml)	Alberto VO5 Styling Mousse Extra Control (also in Normal Control) (£1.20 for 100ml)	Comments
In an attractive can?	•••	•••	••	•••	•••	•••	•••	••	•••	"Boots System One should have a different can as it looks quite cheap, but worked well." *Hannah*
Nicely perfumed?	•••	••	•••	•••	•••	••	•••	•••	••••	"Tenax smelt more like something for men, though it wasn't over-strong on my hair." *Julie*
Firm and easy to put on?	•••	•••	•••	•••	•••	••	•••	•••	•••	"Vidal Sassoon shot all over the place and L'Oréal didn't come out very easily as it was so firm." *Hannah*
Easy to style, body-giving?	•••	•••	•••	•••	•••	•••	•••	•••	••••	"Tenax and Alberto added tons of body, made my hair look about twice as thick!" *David*
Going strong at lunchtime?	•••	•••	•••	•••	•••	•••	•••	•••	•••••	"Country Born held my hair well but none of them were strong enough for me – I usually use something more like araldite gel." *Jo*
... at 9pm?	•••	•••	•••	•••	••	•••	•••	••	••••	"My hair did go pretty floppy with Flex, but I only had to zap it up with a splash of water and it was fine again." *David*
All gone in the morning?	•••	•••	•••	•••	•••	•••	•••	••	••••	"When I woke up the morning after using Tenax the day before, my hair felt completely back to normal – great!" *Jo*

from Looks

Once you have this skill, writing within the number of words required is no longer a problem. Indeed, you may feel that you don't even need the number offered.

To take a rather exaggerated example, read the following passage about the Peter Principle (which states that 'every employee tends to rise to his level of incompetence').

The Peter Principle: an introduction

As an author and journalist, I have had exceptional opportunities to study the workings of civilized society. I have investigated and written about government, industry, business, education and the arts. I have talked to, and listened carefully to, members of many trades and professions, people of lofty, middling and lowly stations.

I have noticed that, with few exceptions, men bungle their affairs. Everywhere I see incompetence rampant, incompetence triumphant.

I have seen a three-quarter-mile-long highway bridge collapse and fall into the sea because, despite checks and double-checks, someone had botched the design of a supporting pier.

I have seen town planners supervising the development of a city on the flood plain of a great river, where it is certain to be periodically inundated.

Lately I read about the collapse of three giant cooling towers at a British power-station: they cost a million dollars each, but were not strong enough to withstand a good blow of wind.

I noted with interest that the indoor baseball stadium at Houston, Texas, was found on completion to be peculiarly ill-suited to baseball: on bright days, fielders could not see fly balls against the glare of the skylights.

I observe that appliance manufacturers, as regular policy, establish regional service depots in the expectation – justified by experience – that many of their machines will break down during the warranty period.

Having listened to umpteen motorists' complaints about faults in their new cars, I was not surprised to learn that roughly one-fifth of the automobiles produced by major manufacturers in recent years have been found to contain potentially dangerous production defects.

Please do not assume that I am a jaundiced ultra-conservative, crying down contemporary men and things just because they are contemporary. Incompetence knows no barriers of time or place.

Macaulay gives a picture, drawn from a report by Samuel Pepys, of the British navy in 1648. 'The naval administration was a prodigy of wastefulness, corruption, ignorance, and indolence . . . no estimate could be trusted . . . no contract was performed . . . no check was enforced . . . Some of the new men of war were so rotten that, unless speedily repaired, they would go down at their moorings. The sailors were paid with so little punctuality that they were glad to find some usurer who would purchase their tickets at forty per cent discount. Most of the ships which were afloat were commanded by men who had not been bred to the sea.'

Wellington, examining the roster of officers assigned to him for the 1810 campaign in Portugal, said, 'I only hope that when the enemy reads the list of their names, he trembles as I do.'

Civil War General Richard Raylor, speaking of the Battle of the Seven Days, remarked, 'Confederate commanders knew no more about the topography . . . within a day's march of the city of Richmond than they did about Central Africa.'

Robert E. Lee once complained bitterly, 'I cannot have my orders carried out.'

For most of World War II the British armed forces fought with explosives much inferior, weight for weight, to those in German shells and bombs. Early in 1940, British scientists knew that the cheap, simple addition of a little powdered aluminium would double the power of existing explosives, yet the knowledge was not applied till late in 1943.

In the same war, the Australian commander of a hospital ship checked the vessel's water tanks after a refit and found them painted inside with red lead. It would have poisoned every man aboard.

These things – and hundreds more like them – I have seen and read about and heard about. I have accepted the universality of incompetence.

from The Peter Principle *by L. J. Peter and R. Hull*

There is really only one main point in this whole passage. As the writer says, 'men bungle their affairs'. The rest of the passage simply illustrates this point. Generally speaking each paragraph simply offers a fresh illustration.

A paragraph by paragraph analysis would go something like this:

1st paragraph. The writer's wide experience.
2nd paragraph. Leads him to believe 'men bungle their affairs'.
3rd–8th paragraphs. Modern examples of this.
9th paragraph. Not just a modern problem: happened in the past too.
10th–15th paragraphs. Historical examples of this.
16th paragraph. Leading to the conclusion – 'I have accepted the universality of incompetence'.

Now read the following passage:

Bones

Just how much sex is there in a skeleton? When archaeologists state categorically that half a femur comes from a twenty-year-old woman we are impressed with their certainty, not the less so because the statement, being a guess, is utterly unverifiable. Such a guess is as much based on the archaeologists' assumptions about women as anything else. What they mean is that the bone is typically female, that is, that it ought to belong to a woman. Because it is impossible to escape from the stereo- typed notions of womanhood as they prevail in one's own society, curious errors in ascription have been made and continue to be made.

We tend to think of the skeleton as rigid; it seems to abide when all else withers away, so it ought to be a sort of nitty-gritty, unmarked by super- ficial conditioning. In fact it is itself subject to deformation by many influences. The first of these is muscular stress. Because men are more vigorous than women their bones have more clearly marked muscular grooves. If the muscles are constrained, by binding or wasting, or by continual external pressure which is not counter-balanced, the bones can be drawn out of alignment. Men's bodies are altered by the work that they do, and by the nutriment which sustains them in their growing period, and so are women's, but women add to these influences others which are dictated by fashion and sex-appeal. There have been great changes in the history of feminine allure in the approved posture of the shoulders, whether sloping or straight, drawn forward or back, and these have been bolstered by dress and corsetting, so that the delicate balance of bone on bone has been altered by the stress of muscles maintaining the artificial posture. The spine has been curved forward in the mannequin's lope, or backwards in the S-bend of art nouveau or the sway-back of the fifties. Footwear reinforces these unnatural stresses; the high-heeled shoe alters all the torsion of the muscles of the thighs and pelvis and throws the spine into an angle which is still in some circles considered essential to allure. I am not so young that I cannot remember my grandmother begging my mother to corset me, because she found my teenage ungainliness un- attractive, and was afraid that my back was not strong enough to maintain my height by itself. If I had been corseted at thirteen, my ribcage might have developed differently, and the downward pressure on my pelvis would have resulted in its widening. Nowadays, corseting is frowned upon, but many women would not dream of casting away the girdle that offers support and tummy control. Even tights are tight, and can cause strange symptoms in the wearer. Typists' slouch and shop-girl lounge have their own effect upon the posture and therefore upon the skeleton.

Most people understand that the development of the limbs is affected by the exercise taken by the growing child. My mother discouraged us from emulating the famous girl swimmers of Australia by remarking on their massive shoulders and narrow hips, which she maintained came from their rigorous training. It is agreed that little girls should have a different physical education programme from little boys, but it is not admitted how much of the difference is counselled by the conviction that little girls should not look like little boys. The same assumptions extend into our suppositions about male and female skeletons: a small-handed skeleton ought to be female, small feet are feminine too, but the fact remains that either sex may exhibit the disproportion.

from The Female Eunuch *by Germaine Greer*

The first third of this passage contains developing argument and changing information. Even so we could probably summarise the first **238** words something like this:

When archaeologists tell us what sex a skeleton is they are working from a set idea of what a female skeleton *should* look like. Yet skeletons are not a fixed shape. Muscular stress is just one factor that affects their shape, and this stress can be created by the work people do or the fashions they wear. [*57 words*]

The next third (about 237 words) doesn't, however, so much add new ideas as illustrate the points already made. It could perhaps be summarised as:

Fashion changes, past and present, have affected, variously, the shoulders, back, spine, thighs and pelvis. [*15 words*]

The last paragraph does at least add a new point, which could be summarised thus:

It is not always recognised that the exercises children are encouraged to do are those which will produce the limb development considered appropriate for their sex. [*26 words*]

This clarifies an earlier point:

Ideas of what each sex *should* look like affect ideas of what sex skeletons are but don't *prove* that sex. [*20 words*]

Put the bracketed parts together, incidentally, and you have a 118 word summary of a 598 word passage, that is, a summary about *one-fifth* the size of the original passage.

Notice some of the summary techniques used above.

● *More time was spent summarising the ideas* – e.g. in the first third of the passage – than the examples and illustrations – e.g. in the second third.

● *Generalisations replaced specific details* – e.g.

that half a femur comes from a twenty-year-old woman

became

what sex a skeleton is

and

If the muscles are constrained, by binding or wasting, or by continued external pressure which is not counterbalanced, the bones can be drawn out of alignment.

became

>   muscular stress . . . affects their shape.

● *Simple language should replace complicated* – e.g.

>   the stereotyped notions of womanhood as they prevail in one's own society

could have been replaced by

>   a set idea of what a female skeleton *should* look like.

EXERCISE 4.10

Look at the 'persuasive writing' passages at the end of Chapter 5 and try to summarise those you find most interesting. Aim to produce a summary no more than one-third the original length.

Varieties of tone and register

LEVELS OF FORMALITY

We can all see the difference between formal and informal language, between for instance:

>   Bring it back if anything goes wrong.

and

>   Should this product or any part of it become defective under normal use within 12 months of the date of purchase, the defect will be rectified and any defective component parts repaired or replaced.

Partly this is a difference of words, and partly it is a difference of precision. Informal language tends to be used between people who know each other and who can therefore take a lot for granted. Formal language is more often used in forms and documents where the exact meaning of the words needs to be clear – even if this means more words and longer words. It's a bit like the difference between talking and writing seen in Chapter 1. Each has its uses.

EXERCISE 4.11

Sort out the words in the list below into pairs with similar meaning. Then put them into columns marked **informal** *and* **formal***.*

start	*let*	*wide*
question	*help*	*despatch*
extensive	*commence*	*purchase*
permit	*send*	*pulchritude*
beauty	*food*	*buy*
interrogate	*assist*	*nutrition*

Here is an example:

Informal	Formal
buy	*purchase*

However, language isn't just formal or informal – it's all sorts of shades between. Asking someone to close the door, for instance, could be done at various levels.

Fairly formal   Could you possibly close the door please?
Would you mind closing the door?

Semi-formal   Could you close the door, please?
Close the door, please.

Fairly informal   Close the door.
Shut it.

without even considering more formal flights of fancy, such as:

The closure of the portal in closest proximity, if graciously undertaken by your estimable self in the interests of air current exclusion, would merit my heartiest and most sincere appreciation.

EXERCISE 4.12

1   *Try this yourself. Find as many ways as possible to express the following, and indicate what level of formality each example is:*

   (i) Asking someone to be quiet.

   (ii) Asking someone to marry you.

   (iii) Complimenting someone on what he or she is wearing.

   (iv) Describing the look on someone's face.

EXERCISE 4.13

1   Copy the table below and fill in the gaps (where possible), and then continue the table by adding a further five examples of your own.

Rather formal (posh)	Standard English (semi-formal)	Colloquial (fairly informal)	Slang (very informal)
exhausted	tired	all in	knackered
victuals			
	work hard		
		walkover	
			pissed off
		copper	
	kill		
infatuated			

Now, briefly explain when *and* why *it would be appropriate (if at all) to use each of the varieties of English indicated on page 93.*

2   *Make a list of the people you have spoken to today and for each explain which level of formality you used.*

WHICH LEVELS TO USE WHEN – AND WHY

Rich young man: [to beautiful girl drinking Campari at sun-soaked resort]
Were you truly wafted here from Paradise?

Girl: No. Luton Airport.

These days there isn't much of a case for very formal English. It's true that business documents need to be carefully worded. Claims can be made under them or against them amounting to thousands or even millions of pounds, so they need to be able to stand up to close legal investigation of every word. Formal English tends to be more precise than informal so is often used in documents. Even so, semi-formal or standard English is usually enough. Quite simply, it is easier for most people to understand. Over-formal English, on the other hand, can lead to cases like this.

A visitor to a government building in Washington DC found a door with this imposing sign:

> **4156**
> **General Services Administration**
> **Region 3**
> **Public Buildings Service**
> **Building Management Division**
> **Utility Room**
> **Custodial**

On asking what it was, he discovered it was a broom cupboard.

Over-formal language, in the shape of official forms, also confuses thousands of ordinary people each year. For example, a question on a form issued by a Yorkshire local authority to its council house tenants asked for 'length of tenancy'. One resident replied. 'Approx. 38 feet'. To meet this problem a group of people have set up a 'form factory' just to simplify official forms and make them more readable. Now try this yourself.

EXERCISE 4.14

1 *Take the following extracts and rewrite them in a less formal style – as if you were writing them for a friend:*

a Possession of such a letter is not obligatory but should greatly facilitate entry.

b Small dogs may, at the discretion of the conductor and at the owner's risk, be carried without charge upon the upper deck of double-decker buses or in single-decker buses. The decision of the conductor is final.

2 *Now collect five different examples of 'official English', such as notices in the school or college, on public transport, official forms, regulations, etc. Then produce more informal versions of the five you have found. Then discuss whether the versions you have produced are better than the originals.*

If over-formal English can cause problems, so too can informal English. Sometimes informal English can be *too* personal, as we might find if we tried replacing

> **NO ENTRY**

signs by ones reading

> **YOU CAN'T COME IN**

It can also be too casual, and thus either offend, mislead or cause extra work for the reader. For instance, writing to a friend you could say, 'about that money you lent me' and (unless you are in the habit of borrowing money from your friend – in which case he or she might not be a friend much longer) your friend will understand what you are referring to. Writing to a bank, however, where you are just one of many customers, and where many loans are made, you would probably need to be more specific – for instance, 'Last August I borrowed £1000 to buy a new motor bike.' Remember that one of the advantages of more formal language is that it is often more precise.

EXERCISE 4.15

To show some of the dangers of casual or informal language, read the following and then explain how each could be understood in two ways.

a) *You will be lucky to get this student in your class.*

b) *If I said you had a beautiful body, would you hold it against me?*

c) *Well Margaret, if you've nothing on, why don't I come over?*

d) *[To a class of students] I don't think you lot were all there yesterday.*

e) *We shall waste no time in dealing with your complaint.*

For everyday business purposes, then, a *semi-formal tone* is probably best. It avoids the confusions caused by both over-formal and over-casual language and is more universally clear and understandable.

To remind you of the shades of formality, however, and that each has its place, try this exercise.

EXERCISE 4.16

1   *Consider David Barnes, aged 68, a retired army major, with three children and a granddaughter.*

   In the course of a normal weekday, how many different ways might he be addressed – both in speech and writing? (For example, would his children address him in the same way as an assistant at the local post office?)

2   *Now do the same for Christine Ellis, aged 32, a primary school teacher, married with one child.*

   (You should be able to think of at least eight different forms of address for each.)

EXERCISE 4.17

RSVP

The following extracts from messages all have something in common. In one way or another they all 'request the pleasure' of someone's company – some more forcibly than others. Who is doing the requesting in each case, and how forcibly or persuasively?

In what ways do these messages differ? Consider especially the different varieties of English involved, and:

   (i) how you would feel receiving each of these messages.

   (ii) how far the level of formality would be responsible.

   (iii) whether the level of formality was appropriate.

a)

INFORMATION has this day been laid before me,
the undersigned Clerk to the Justices,
by EDWARD PETER BAINES, Chief Constable of the
Newtown Police, for that you,
at Newtown
on the 2nd day of November 1986
did drive a motor vehicle, namely, a motor car
on a restricted road called Waterloo Road
at a speed exceeding thirty miles per hour,
contrary to Road Traffic Regulation Act, 1967, section 71, 74, 78
YOU ARE THEREFORE HEREBY SUMMONED to appear
before the MAGISTRATES' COURT, sitting at

Simon Road
Newtown

on the 15th day of April 1987 at the hour of
10.00 a.m. in the forenoon, to answer to the said information.

b)

Dear Mr
Thank you for your application for the post of   . The
Selection Panel would be very pleased if you could join the
short list of candidates who are being invited to come here for
an interview. In order to be briefed before meeting the panel
you are asked to report to   at   on
           at   and I should be grateful if you would
telephone my secretary at the above number to say whether or
not you can attend.
The interviews for this post are timed for
                                        in

c)

CHANCE ENCOUNTER
Soft glow kindles
Sparks of fire leap
Your body next to mine
Tender touch
Taut desire
Alike, unlike, attract, embrace
Mystery and fascination of a chance encounter
Weave spells
For you
For me
For us?

d)

Lady young, Lady fair
Answer this fond lover's prayer
Box B501

TONE AND REGISTER

EXERCISE 4.18

There follows a variety of extracts. Read each one and then answer the following questions about each.

1 *Is this intended to be read or listened to?*

2 *What kind of person is speaking or writing?*

3 *What reader or listener does the person have in mind?*

4 *What purpose does the person have in mind?*

5 *Is the person writing or speaking a man or a woman – or could it be either?*

6 *Is this modern English, and if not, of what period is it?*

7 *Is this 'Standard English' (BBC English), and if not, what variety is it?*

8 *Considering the levels of formality mentioned earlier in this section how would you rate this extract?*

9 *How serious is the extract and how can you tell?*

10 *How appropriate is the language in this extract?*

(For all the above try to point to particular words, phrases, or features which illustrate your answer.)

a) **Rabies** – of all communicable diseases, rabies is probably the most unpleasant. The vaccine in the past had a deservedly dubious reputation because of its side effects. However, the current vaccine is entirely safe and provides a good level of antibody. Anyone on a zoological expedition should certainly be vaccinated, and it is strongly recommended for anyone spending time in rural communities. Even with a vaccination, if a person is bitten by a rabid (or even suspected rabid animal), they should seek medical help and request hyper-immune globulin and post-exposure vaccination.

b) 1 The Lord is my shepherd, I shall not want.

2 He maketh me to lie down in green pastures: he leadeth me beside the still waters.

3 He restoreth my soul: he leadeth me in the paths of righteousness for his name's sake.

4 Yea, though I walk through the valley of the shadow of death, I will fear no evil: for thou art with me, thy rod and thy staff they comfort me.

5 Thou preparest a table before me in the presence of mine enemies: thou anointest my head with oil, my cup runneth over.

6 Surely goodness and mercy shall follow me all the days of my life: and I will dwell in the house of the Lord for ever.

c)

Is crime getting worse?
(do I believe the Daily Express?)

Firstly, you can't really say crime is getting worse 'cos can't tell how much crime there is:

* Official stats count odd things like who was found guilty, how many cases were 'cleared up' etc. but lots of crime is undetected, unsolved, unnoticed etc.

* Classifications differ - e.g. definitions of homosexuality & larceny. The police try less hard, the public care less.

NOT NO CRIME? * lots of things don't count as crime - e.g. Students smashing up their college isn't the same as Chelsea fans smashing shops & white collar crime is widespread but not detected (READ SUTHERLAND)

Secondly, even if you know how much crime, you don't know why:

* What is crime?

d) Don't you care for my love? she said bitterly.

> I handed her the mirror, and said:
> Please address these questions to the proper person!
> Please make all requests to head-quarters!
> In all matters of emotional importance
> please approach the supreme authority direct! –
> So I handed her the mirror.
>
> And she would have broken it over my head,
> but she caught sight of her own reflection
> and that held her spellbound for two seconds
> while I fled.

e) In the last year he had rendered two opponents totally senseless for over fifteen minutes, and maimed a third. He hit the fourth and last with a rare, double-fisted technique, simultaneously on each temple, causing blood to gush from the ears as well as the nostrils. Next year, to his great and ill-concealed chagrin, he was unopposed and had to content himself with a demonstration in which he uprooted a medium-sized tree, kicked a hole six inches above the ground through a mud wall, and in the culmination felled a diseased water buffalo with a single, crushing hammer-fisted blow on the skull.

f)

g)

SNOOZLER SOFA

(three seater, convertible to double bed)

Model no: 123/zzz
Made in England by CA Snoozler Limited, 3 Dovetail Road, Carving, Beds. Tel Carving 1234.

Price £200. *Credit sale*: deposit £40, 24 monthly payments of £8.00 – true rate of interest 18.2%. Total credit price £232.

Size height 91 cm (36 in.), width 178 cm (70 in.), depth 94 cm (37 in.), seat height 41 cm (16 in.). Converts to bed 137 cm (54 in.) wide by 183 cm (72 in.) long.

Construction upholstered in *Snuglon* (90% acrylic, 10% wool) or *Slideon* (a PVC-coated cotton/polyester)

polyether foam-filled mattress/seat and reversible back cushions (non-removable covers)

supported on rubber webbing

teak veneered wooden frame coated with polyurethane

steel extending bed frame

Colours blue, brown, red

Care gently brush or vacuum soft upholstery regularly. Wipe over wooden frame with damp cloth rinsed in warm water; do not use a wax polish; do not place sofa close to direct heat. Avoid contact with hair-oil and other sorts of grease.

Snuglon – dry clean only, but occasional grease marks may be removed with a stain remover (follow instructions carefully).

Slideon – wipe over with a damp cloth rinsed in warm soapy (not synthetic detergent) water; repeat with cloth rinsed in clean cold water. Dry thoroughly.

Wear SNOOZLER is made to BS 4875: Part 1 – strength rating 2: suitable for normal domestic use.

Snuglon – made to BS 2543 (specification for woven upholstery fabrics); this means it's colour fast to light, water and rubbing. Moth-proofed.

Slideon – made to BS 4216 (specification for PCS-coated knitted fabrics) Grade V; this means it's lightweight and recommended for domestic upholstery and that it's colourfast to daylight and rubbing.

h)

AVON
The Beauty Business

Hello,
I'm _____Angela_____, your Avon Representative. I called today with our latest Brochure/Sample. Please take a look and when I call back on ___Tue/Wed___ at ___p.m.___ I'll be happy to give you more information about our wide range of products and special offers.

Looking forward to meeting you.

i) A number of experiments have tried to find out what makes people fall in love. Physical attractiveness is most important, particularly in the early stages. Parental interference tends to strengthen attraction – the 'Romeo and Juliet' effect. Playing hard to get doesn't work very well, but those who seem to be hard for others to get are found attractive. People high in internal control are less likely to fall in love. And the variables discussed for friendship also affect love – similar attitudes, being liked, and so on.

Love goes through a number of stages. As we have seen, sexual attraction is signalled by non-verbal cues – facial expression, gaze, etc – as for friendship, but also including touch and pupil dilation. The process of falling in love is probably due to massive reinforcements, and a sudden upward surge of interaction and liking. This makes increased demands for synchronizing and mutual adjustment, and inevitably the scope for conflict and disagreement is greatly increased – while each partner is also very dependent on the other for rewards received. This has the properties of an approach-avoidance conflict and would be expected to lead to an oscillation of intimacy–withdrawal, until smoother synchronizing is attained. The periods of the engagement and honeymoon appear to be designed to help this process to happen. It is interesting that in the U.S.A. honeymoons are often found stressful, and that honeymoon couples often seek out the company of other such couples and return home earlier than planned (Rapoport and Rapoport, 1964).

j) TO: NOMZAMO WINNIE MANDELA
      802 BLACK VILLAGE
      BRANDFORT

NOTICE IN TERMS OF SECTION 20(a) OF THE INTERNAL SECURITY ACT, 1982 (ACT 74 OF 1982)

Under and by virtue of the powers vested in me by section 20(a) of the Internal Security Act, 1982 (Act 74 of 1982), I hereby prohibit you for the period from 2 July 1983 to 30 June 1988, both dates inclusive, from attending within the Republic of South Africa –

(1) any gathering as contemplated in subparagraph (i) of the said section 20; or

(2) any gathering as contemplated in subparagraph (ii) of the said section 20, of the nature, class or kind set out below:
    (a) Any social gathering, that is to say, any gathering at which the persons present also have social intercourse with one another;
    (b) any political gathering, that is to say, any gathering at which any form of State or any principle or policy of the Government of a State is propagated, defended, attacked, criticized or discussed;
    (c) any gathering of pupils or students assembled for the purpose of being instructed, trained or addressed by you.

Given under my hand at Cape Town this 18th day of June 1983.

L. LE GRANGE
MINISTER OF LAW AND ORDER

Note: (1) The Magistrate, Brandfort, has in terms of section 20 of Act 74 of 1982 been empowered to authorize exceptions to the prohibitions contained in this notice.

(2) In terms of section 25(2) of the said Act you may, at any time within a period of fourteen days as from the date on which this notice is delivered or tendered to you, make written representations to the Minister of Law and Order relating to the prohibitions contained in this notice and you may also, within the said period, submit in writing any other information relating to the circumstances of your case. You may also, in terms of section 38(4) of the Act, apply in writing to the Board of Review to present oral evidence before the Board of Review. The address of the Board of Review is: The Secretary of the Board of Review, Private Bag X655, Pretoria, 0001.

EXERCISE 4.19

1   *You have lent a friend, who has since left the area, a substantial amount of money – but now need it repaying.*

   (i) *Ring your friend and raise the matter. Write down what you would say to him or her over the phone.*

   (ii) *Six weeks and several fruitless phone calls later (by which time you need the money urgently) write to your friend, again seeking repayment, and using whatever tone you consider most appropriate.*

2   *You are a bank manager and have a customer who has just become £100 overdrawn.*

   (i) *Send the customer a routine first letter informing him or her that he or she is overdrawn and suggesting repayment.*

   (ii) *Six weeks later, the customer has not only ignored your first and subsequent letters but is now £200 overdrawn. Write an appropriate letter.*

PERSUASIVE WRITING – ADVERTISING

Millions of pounds are spent every day on one particular type of persuasive writing – advertising. Whether the words are intended for use on a radio or television commercial or as part of a newspaper or magazine advertisement the aim is the same: to persuade you to buy or support something. (The 'something', incidentally, could be anything from a can of soup to a political party, from a new car to a charitable cause.)

To help you understand the way advertising works, read the following questions. Can you think of any advertisements you have seen recently which have some of these features?

A Does the advertisement:

- present simple information, as in a classified advertisement or many advertisements in specialist magazines?

- rely largely on a picture to suggest the benefits of the product, perhaps using an elegant, exotic or luxurious setting to suggest its quality?

- appeal to hidden or subconscious feelings by using dream-like or fantasy elements?

B Does the language of the advertising (including the brand name):

- have the characteristics of popular journalism, such as short sentences, short paragraphs, simple language and headlines?

- have associations of warmth, status, luxury, mystery or the exotic?

- include one or more of the following adjectives: new, fresh, clean, better, easy, bright, beautiful, classic, good, special, extra, rich, golden?

- operate in a colourful, imaginative or figurative way (for example 'Beanz Meanz Heinz')?

C Is there an appeal or reference to one or more of the following elements?

A happy family	Success in a career or job
Love and romance	A nostalgic view of childhood
Experts	Famous or important people
Unspoilt nature	A rich and luxurious life style
Beautiful women	Exotic or glamorous locations

D Are any of the following techniques used?

The idea that the product is new
An element of drama or storytelling
Words spelt wrongly to attract attention
A 'before and after' demonstration of the product's use
An interview with a 'man or woman in the street'
Sophisticated photography
Repetition (especially of slogans)
Exploitation of feelings of worry or inadequacy
Comedy and humour

E   Are the people who appear in the advertisements usually:

> children, adult, middle-aged or old?
> men or women (and in what roles)?
> black or white (and in what roles)?
> attractive, of average appearance, or unattractive?
> at work or at leisure?

Which particular types of people tend to be seen advertising which particular types of product?

F   Does the advertising follow the AIDA principle? i.e.

> first attract the *attention* of potential customers
> so as to arouse their *interest* in the product
> then create a *desire* for its benefits
> and finally encourage *action* from potential customers.

A request for more information about the product would be one kind of action – with actually buying the product being the ultimate action hoped for.

How *exactly* does each advertisement try to attract attention, arouse interest, stimulate desire and encourage action?

EXERCISE 4.20

Now look at the advertisements which follow and ask the same questions.

Hitting our target is tougher than you think.

Because the Royal Marines Commandos have such a special job to do, we are looking for people with very special qualities. If you think you've got the determination and you are fit, over 16 and under 28, and over 162.7cms (5' 4"), call in at any RN and RM Careers Information Office, or fill in the coupon.

Send to: Major A C S Chibnall RM, PO Box 2, Liverpool L4 1UR.

Name_____

Address_____

_____ Postcode_____

Telephone_____ Date of Birth_____

Normally you should have been a UK resident for the past five years.

ROYAL MARINES COMMANDOS

You can't appreciate good wine unless it's in the blood.

And when it comes to good wine, you'll be hard pressed to find a more enjoyable drink than Bulls Blood. Or as the Hungarians would say, Egri Bikaver.

The bouquet is fresh, clean and wholesome. The flavour is smooth, full and straightforward.

And the history is rather interesting. We go back to the 16th Century with the Turks invading Hungary.

Outnumbered 50 to 1, the defending Hungarians downed copious draughts of Egri Bikaver to sustain themselves in the midst of battle.

So fierce were they in the defence of their town, that the Turks concluded the Hungarians must be drinking the blood of bulls.

Needless to say, the Turks fled – sour grapes on their part no doubt, and the Hungarians celebrated with yet more Bulls Blood.

You too can enjoy the same. Bulls Blood has since earned itself the "Minosegi Bor." That's Hungarian for Appellation Contrôlée.

Every bottle carries its own designation of vintage – a fair mark of its quality. And quality fairly oozes out of the grapes that go into the making of Bulls Blood.

There are four of them. Kekfrankos, a red wine grape rarely grown outside Hungary, Oporto, Cabernet Sauvignon and Medoc Noir.

Once picked and pressed, the young wine is left in oak casks to mature for at least two years.

These large casks are stored in the very tunnels that the Hungarians had built to mount their ambushes on the luckless Turks. The result is a pleasant, clean, easy to drink wine.

And that's no bull.

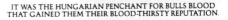

IT WAS THE HUNGARIAN PENCHANT FOR BULLS BLOOD THAT GAINED THEM THEIR BLOOD-THIRSTY REPUTATION.

If you had visited Chernobyl on Friday 25 April, you would have seen a clean, safe nuclear plant.
After Saturday 26 April, if you lived up to 100 miles from Chernobyl you would have been evacuated, or worse.
What does a visit to Sellafield really prove?
GREENPEACE
TO ENCOURAGE A FULL DEBATE ON NUCLEAR POWER THEY LET YOU SEE THIS COMMERCIAL.
AND BANNED OURS.
We believe there should be a full and open debate on nuclear power. (Especially after the horrific accident at Chernobyl.)
But it appears the authorities don't share our view.
Perhaps they're afraid you'll want to close down places like Sellafield.
Certainly, that's the only reason we can see for banning our commercial.
While allowing millions of people to see the one from British Nuclear Fuels PLC.
We don't want to stop you going to see an exhibition at Sellafield. And we wouldn't dream of preventing BNFL from putting their case for nuclear power.
But we do object to being prevented from putting our case too.
If you'd like a full debate on nuclear power, rather than a one-sided campaign from British Nuclear Fuels, write to your MP now.
Or fill in the petition below.
STATEMENT OF CONCERN
We, the undersigned, wish to express our deep concern over the Independent Broadcasting Authority (IBA) ruling which permits pro-nuclear television advertising by British Nuclear Fuels PLC while denying access to the same medium to the environmental pressure group Greenpeace, which has expressed opposition to nuclear power on environmental, safety and economic grounds.
In the interests of a fair debate, a one sided presentation of the case for nuclear power, however discreetly it is portrayed, should not be permitted.
Name
Address
Tick box if you would like to receive information about Greenpeace including the broadsheet, Facts you should know about nuclear power.
Please send this coupon to
GREENPEACE
36 Graham Street, London N1 8LL.

EXERCISE 4.21

1 *Choose* either *a series of television advertisements (if you have access to a video recorder, try recording about four minutes of advertisements),* or *a number of advertisements from a magazine.*

Now ask the questions listed on pages 104–5 about the advertisements you have chosen and make notes on the answers.

2 *Discuss your findings with a group of four or five other students, looking in particular for the number of similarities between advertisements and the number of differences. Explain the differences and indicate which were the most effective advertisements.*

EXERCISE 4.22

1   Draft a full page advertisement to appear in a magazine of your choice. The advertisement could be for a product, a service, an organisation, or a particular cause (such as a charity or a political party).

Think carefully about who your readers will be. How will you attract their attention, arouse their interest and create the desire to respond to your advertisement? What benefits will your advertisement offer?

Remember the techniques discussed earlier in this section.

2   In groups of four or five circulate and discuss each draft in turn. Note any constructive suggestions made about your draft.

3   Now produce a final version of the advertisement, incorporating the best of your original material together with the best of the suggestions made by your fellow students.

EXERCISE 4.23

Research an aspect of advertising which particularly interests you. Then produce a report, outlining what you were researching, how you went about it, what you found out and any conclusions you came to. Aim to write about 500 words. If you need any help organising your material, check the section on report writing in Chapter 6.

If there isn't an aspect of advertising which especially interests you choose one of the following:

Women/men in advertisements
An advertising campaign
Television advertising
Newspaper advertising
The work of an advertising agency
The advertising approach of a particular company or organisation
The price of advertising
The language of advertising
Images of the family in advertising
The story element in advertising
Young people in advertisements

REVIEWS

Reading a review can help you decide whether or not to read a particular book, go to see a particular play or film, or watch a particular TV programme. That's because, generally speaking, they are written by people who have read them or seen them, for the benefit of people who haven't. They try to give a good idea of what the book or film or whatever is like – but without spoiling the story.

Book reviews

These can be very short. Look at these, for instance:

Woman of the Century

It made me laugh, it made me cry, it made me care – what more can you ask? *The Century's Daughter* by Pat Barker (Virago hardback, £9.95, paperback, £3.50) is a work of imagination, but so deeply rooted in truth, so vivid and compassionate, that it enlarges rather than reflects reality.

It's the story of Liza Jarrett, born at the turn of the century. She lived through two world wars, brought up her children during the depression, was deserted by her husband, and then widowed. Now in the 80s she's sticking it out defiantly in her own home when the rest of the street is empty and condemned.

It's the story too of Stephen – homosexual, alienated from his working-class parents by higher education – the social worker who must persuade Liza to move into sheltered accommodation but in an unexpected reversal of roles finds himself drawing from her resilience and humour the strength he needs to cope with his own troubles.

Inspector Thanet Investigates

There's nothing quite like unravelling a fictional crime step-by-step with a really painstaking and persistent detective, and of all those around today few give more satisfaction than Dorothy Simpson's Inspector Luke Thanet of Sturrenden CID. It's a combination of the skill and determination with which he goes about his grisly business, the depth of his understanding of the offender's mind plus his own family-man image. In his latest case, *Dead on Arrival* (Michael Joseph, £9.95), he must find out who "done in" Steven Long, a youngish man separated from his wife and at odds with relations, living alone, yet on the night of his death mysteriously visited by several people. Now which of them hated him enough to kill him, and why?

Even an over-bossy boss and threats of an official complaint fail to deflect Thanet, and what's more, loose ends are tied up in time for him to attend his daughter's all-important cookery competition and see her win first prize.

French Kisses

First it's necessary to accept that a French girl of aristocratic birth, who in 1944 was an active member of the Resistance, working and longing for the liberation of her country by the Allies, could fall in love and allow herself to become pregnant by a German army officer. But believe that and the rest of *Never Leave Me* by Margaret Pemberton (Macdonald, £10.95) takes off passionately, unstoppably and as near as dammit tragically. Dieter Meyer, Lisette de Volmy's lover meets a violent death just after the invasion begins. Two other men – one English, one American – long for her, she chooses the American, Greg Dering. They marry, and eventually he takes her home to a rich and glamorous life in San Francisco. But she lacks the courage to reveal that he is not the father of her son, and gradually the strain of deception corrodes their relationship, leading to a devastating climax which nearly destroys both them and their family. Turbulent stuff with lots of love and longing, misunderstanding and jealousy, tears but eventual happiness.

from She

As you can see, even a short review can tell you quite a lot. However, it has to leave a lot unsaid and we have to take the writer's word for a lot of things. There just isn't room for more detail or examples. Usually, therefore, a book review will need more detail – and thus be much longer. Have a look at this one, for instance. It appeared in a local newspaper. How much does it tell you about the book? Does it encourage you to want to read it?

Recalling the Years of Change for All

Compulsive. One word that spells the very essence of a good book. And speaking as one who digests around 60 a year, coming across the sort which causes pans to burn and unwashed dishes to pile up is indeed a rare event.

I have sometimes found this literary quality in a factual book. Never in a novel – until ten years ago when I read a book by Kathleen Conlon. It was her first novel and it was called *Apollo's Summer Look*.

I picked it up, and couldn't put it down again.

Four days ago I repeated this experience when I received a review copy of a book called *A Move in the Game*. First inclination was to relegate it to third place on my current book list, but the author's name – Kathleen Conlon – rang a distant bell of a decade ago and, to put it succinctly, I got stuck in!

For seven hours I was immovable. Colleagues thought I was skiving. Usual routine interruptions took on the proportions of major disasters and, 355 pages later, my list of folk to phone had grown alarmingly.

To describe *A Move in the Game* as eminently readable doesn't really do justice to either the book or its extremely talented author.

The fact that she's a local woman – she lives in Birkdale – is almost irrelevant, except for the fact that Southport is so much richer for her work.

A Move in the Game begins one September day in 1960 when a coach crash wiped out most of the high school sixth form in a small country town.

Linked thereafter were three very different girls, Beatrice, Joanna and Madeleine.

For the next 17 years their lives, and those of their men, formed a complex ever-changing pattern as they pursued careers, or opted out of the rat-race, married, remained uncommitted, had children and love affairs, and ultimately found themselves.

But what they found was not always what they expected, and there lies much of the compulsive fascination of this very skilfully constructed novel, which is a detailed, yet subtle evocation of the years 1960–77, which brought about so many changes in the lives of Kathleen's three characters, and indeed, in all our lives.

One specific sentence for me, forms the crux of the book and it is this: "If I could only go back and stand beside the me of that time, and try to understand how I felt, how I saw things, then I might begin to know what I'm all about."

Overheard conversations, drawing on her own experiences and those of others, plus a remarkable insight, sensitivity and understanding of life and of women, have combined with the author's imagination to produce a book which must become a best-seller.

This novel deals with the trials and triumphs of the three characters whose lives are charted, sometimes dramatically, sometimes humorously, with a great feeling and insight, and it retains, at all times, superb realism.

A former Southport High School girl, who used to work as a 'general dogs-body' at a local hotel, Kathleen Conlon is a true professional.

A Move in the Game is no forgettable romantic novel. It is too realistic, too dramatic and at times too earthy to satisfy a reader who is searching for a happy-ever-after romance.

Nor would I denigrate book or author by recommending it as 'women's reading'. It's a book for everyone, and one which many men would do themselves a favour reading.

A Move in the Game, a Collins hardback, was published on Monday. The lorry drivers' strike will probably cause delays in getting it to our local bookshops.

Keep your eyes open, and find Kathleen Conlon. You may even find yourself.

from The Southport Visiter

EXERCISE 4.24

Have you ever tried to write a book review? If so, you may have found some problems thinking what to say once you'd told the story. Well, the story is important (though if you tell it all you'll spoil it for someone who hasn't read it). But there is more to a book than the story. To help you, try filling in a copy of the questionnaire that follows for a book that you have read recently. This should give you a lot more to write about (and think about).

Book Review (Literature)
(where options are given, delete as applicable)

1) *Title of Book*

   Author   Publisher

   Length   First published in

   Type of book   Price

   Novel/play/collected short stories

2) *Subject Matter*

   History / Crime / War / Mystery / Travel / Romance / Sex / Society / Sport / Politics / Philosophy / Science Fiction / Horror / Other (please state).

3) *Film and TV Links*

   This is/is not a book of a film/TV series.

   A film/TV series has/has not been made of this book.

4) *The Story/Plot (A Summary)*

   (maximum length one paragraph please)

5) *The Beginning*

   It takes time to 'warm up'/It caught my interest right from the start/It never really got going.
   e.g. . . .

6) *The Ending*

   It was what I expected/It was a surprise,
   i.e. . . .

   Everything was sorted out at the end/I was still left wondering
   i.e. . . .

7) *The Characters*

   I learnt about the main characters through:

   what they thought/what they said/what they did/what others thought about them/what others said about them/what others did to them.

   Relationships develop and change/They remain static.

   e.g. . . .

   Characters are complex and do not fit into easy categories/ They are one-dimensional, 'stock' or typical figures.

   e.g. . . .

8) *Themes*

The book dealt with/did not deal with important ideas.

e.g. . . .

These ideas were stated by the writer himself/by a major character/were not explicitly stated but were implied or suggested in some way.

e.g. . . .

9) *Location/Setting/Environment*

Not described/described for its own sake/details described to give a realistic effect of time and place/described to help create an atmosphere/described to show how it affects or is affected by the characters/symbolic.

e.g. . . .

10) Have you read any other books *by the same author/on a similar topic?*

If so, please state them:

Was this book better/worse/about the same as the others?

11) *Style*

(Your answers to the previous six questions will have given you quite a few examples of the writer's style – for example,

what he or she chooses to include and to leave out;

what he or she chooses to describe (or not to describe) about people, places and ideas;

how he or she starts, finishes and otherwise organises the book;

how obtrusive the writer is (does he or she keep making comments, or let the story get on with itself?).

If any characteristics of the writer's style stand out say so and give examples . . .

12) *What kind of readers* (age/sex/interests) would you recommend this book to?

13) *What You Liked about this Book*

I found this book very entertaining/interesting/amusing/exciting/thrilling/sad/tragic/enjoyable/absorbing/other (please state). especially when/for instance when . . .

14) *What You Disliked about this Book*

I found it rather boring/shallow/unimaginative/superficial/predictable/old-fashioned/hard to follow/repulsive/other (please state).

I had difficulty finishing it/couldn't finish it.

What put me off was the language/the subject matter/the story line/the characters/the ideas.

e.g. . . .

15) *Final Assessment*

One of the best books I've ever read.

One of the best books of its kind.

A good book.

Average: readable, but nothing special.

Below average: not especially readable.

One of the worst books of its kind.

One of the worst books I've ever read.

EXERCISE 4.25

That was a questionnaire for a fictional book (novel, short story, etc.). Try making your own questionnaire for a non-fiction book (e.g. on travel, sport, fashion, vehicle maintenance, etc.).

Play reviews ═══

EXERCISE 4.26

Watching a good play performed on stage, in a good production, is quite a different thing from reading through it in class. I've often found my students are surprised at just how much of a difference there can be. Should you be able to go and see a play, here is a short questionnaire to take with you, together with some notes. They should help you notice more about what is going on.

If possible, fill this in while you are watching the play – if you become too interested in the story to do this fill in some sections during the interval. In any case add comments as soon as possible afterwards, – for example, on the coach or train going back if you have travelled far to see a play. The quicker you do the report the more you will remember!

A The Play

Title of play
Writer
Group producing the play
Theatre (or other location)

Was there a good story?
What was the story?
(A very brief summary)

Best part of play
(Why?)

Worst part of play
(Why?)

Were the characters realistic?
(Why/Why not?)

Did the play have something to say?
(Did it have a *point* or a *message?)*
If so – *what?*

Or was it just entertainment?)

What was the language of the play?
modern/old-fashioned? which century?
upper-class/middle-class/working-class?
BBC English/regional English? which region?
natural speech/blank verse/verse?

(Delete above as applicable.)

B The Acting

Audibility (could you hear all the actors?)
(who couldn't you hear – and why?)

Vocal range (speed, intonation, sound, moods displayed by voice etc.)

(Which actor used his or her voice to the best advantage? And which actor used his or her voice to the least advantage? What was the overall standard?)

Best actor (Who – and why?)
Worst actor (Who – and why?)

Consider: (i) movement and use of gesture; (ii) use of the stage; (iii) interaction between actors (were they just making speeches or were they responding to each other?); (iv) credibility (were they believable in the part they were playing?); (v) interest (did they hold your interest and attention?); (vi) pace (did they rush through their speech and movements too quickly – or drag them out too long – or go at just the right speed?)

Overall standard of acting (considering the points above)
Grouping (How did the actors arrange themselves on stage?)

C The Production

Sketch: (i) pictures of the stage; (ii) costumes; (iii) how the actors were positioned in some scenes; (iv) what areas the lights covered, etc.

Type, number etc.	Reason for use	What was added to or lost from performance as a result?
Stage		
Lighting		
Costume		
Make-up		
Scenery		

The questions on pages 113–15 may also be helpful here.

Audience response Was the audience response the same as yours? If not, why not?

What did you learn from this production?

How did it compare with other productions seen?

Was the play a good choice (considering the resources available)?

Play reviews: further suggestions ██████████████████████████

Reviews of plays seen should operate via *evaluation and analysis* – that is, by asking *why and with what effect?* – rather than just description and narrative. Consider the following:

A *Lighting* Was it used to: indicate the time of day or night; replace curtains (e.g. ending scenes by blackout), create atmosphere (romantic, menacing, etc.); focus the audience's attention on certain characters; provide surprise effects/change or reflect mood? Did it combine with effects listed below to give an integrated production (e.g. had make-up and lighting been co-ordinated)?

B *Sound effects* Were they used: to give an impression of what could not easily be presented on stage (e.g. a battle, traffic etc.); to complement what was being shown on stage; to provide/reflect/ change mood and atmosphere (e.g. 'creepy' music)? Were they used in conjunction with lighting? Were they realistic?

C *Costume* Was it used: to indicate social class/occupation/status/ character; to build up an impression of realism (e.g. authentic 'period' costume)? Was the costume accurate in every detail – or were selected but significant details chosen (e.g. Shakespearian stage, a turban for a Turk)? How well did costume work overall (e.g. *all* of the same period/carefully contrasted styles to reflect differences of class, occupation, character etc.)?

D *Staging* Did this: enable the production to flow smoothly; focus attention on, or distract from, the actors; make maximum use of the space available; enable the audience to see or hear particularly well; involve the audience; create atmosphere?

E *Acting*
   (i) *Voice* Was this used to: express feelings (e.g. harsh/tender); indicate social class or regional location (accent and dialect); express character (e.g. a deep manly voice or a high effeminate one)? Was there a significant change of voice (as in *My Fair Lady*)?
   (ii) *Body language* Was this used to: express status (height/ unmoving = dominance?); express feelings (turning back on someone, moving away or vice versa); emphasise what was being said (e.g. a gesture such as banging on the table); contradict what was being said (e.g. a wink or inappropriate facial expression)?

F *Set design* Was this used to: give an impression of detailed realism (exact details); indicate time and place via a few selected items (audience's imagination to do the rest)? Was it dispensed with altogether to focus attention on characters?

G *Make-up* Did it: complement or alter the actor's face (e.g. to change age or sex); integrate with lighting and costume; provide contrast between characters to indicate differences?

Film reviews/previews

EXERCISE 4.27

The extracts that follow describe the same film. In what ways are they the same as, and in what ways are they different from, (i) each other, and (ii) other reviews you have read?

TEETH 'N' SMILES

If you thought that when you'd seen one Alien you'd seen them all think again. In 'Aliens', the sequel, writer/director James Cameron of 'The Terminator' fame, has whole armies of the monsters with the nastiest gnashers in movie history (and legs like Cyd Charisse). It's helter-skelter horror and only Sigourney Weaver between you and a severe case of indigestion.

'ALIENS' PROVIDES yet more evidence of just how elastic the 'science-fiction' hold-all can be. Indeed, along with its predecessor 'Alien', it can raise discussion of just what is definable as 'science-fiction' to interminable degrees. There may have been spaceships in the original but aside from its obvious setting, is 'Alien' not just an efficient fear machine? From an era when most fantasy movies were in fact flights of innocence, romantic wonder and wish fulfilment ('Star Wars', 'Superman', 'Close Encounters') 'Alien' stood out like a sore thumb in its wilful return to the old school of '50s monster movies like 'Creature From The Black Lagoon' or 'Them' [...]

WHILE 'ALIENS' is certainly an even more efficient fear machine than its predecessor, the ground rules have changed a little. Ripley (Sigourney Weaver), last seen shot into the awful solitude of deep space, has survived her 57 years in an escape pod, and landed on a mining colony somewhere. The mining company decide to go back to the original Alien planet to see what has happened to a colony they placed there a little while previously (as if we can't guess). Ripley is persuaded to lead a Marine Combat Patrol on what begins as a reconnaissance mission but which will inevitably turn into

search and destroy. Much of the movie then is taken up with Marine tactics and the stresses and excitements of the classic 'patrol' movie. It is further confirmation that the science-fiction genre can accommodate virtually any material, indeed can make the raw material from another genre its whole substance. The days when it was possible to make a simple 'Steve McQueen storming the pillbox' movie are over. This is probably all that John Milius wanted to do when he made 'Red Dawn', and it certainly governs the initial thrust to 'Aliens', but nowadays it has to be cloaked as science-fiction.

Cameron says, 'Hill wanted me to do a re-run of the "Dirty Dozen" formula for the Marines, which is certainly attractive. In fact, I was more anxious to point up the blue-collar nature of the patrols – how dirty a job it is, and pretty rough. Of course there are lessons learnt from Vietnam here, but that wasn't a primary concern.' It is a route Hill and Giles have travelled before, with their training patrol mission movie 'Southern Comfort' which definitely echoed to the distant trumpets of 'Nam. 'Aliens' however is mostly fear. [...]

In the Alien-infested colony, the only surviving human is a little girl, who has been living in a hiding hole for some months alone, before the Marines come to the rescue. Ripley develops a maternal, protective instinct towards the girl. As the movie is drawing to its climax, the space shuttle is about to leave the planet and the atomic reactor there is about to melt down taking the remaining Aliens with it, alas the Aliens have captured the girl for their own incubating plans. Ripley drops everything and goes after the girl. The movie then enters real time as an extended chase and final battle take place in the disintegrating power station. It's a brave plot move, to hold everything up for such a length of time. Indeed it's a move which puts the whole movie in jeopardy; it could kill it stone dead.

As a bravura move in the just-how-far-can-we-stretch-it game, it also points up just how clever the whole structure of the film is. It may feel like 90 minutes of nerve-crusher but, at just three minutes short of two hours, the movie's plotting is a marvel of carefully constructed manipulation. For the first three-quarters of an hour virtually nothing happens. After that every-thing happens, continuously, like 40 miles of bad road, and all of it utter, raving, hideous, fucking terror. 'It may sound a little simplistic, but in fact it's structured exactly like a roller-coaster ride. You start out in the little car just meandering along enjoying the ride. Maybe there's a little jerk in the ride, to get them going, but not much. Then there's the long slow climb up the first slope. Then it almost comes to a stop at the top of the first hill, teeters on the edge, then topples over. From then on it never stops, just getting faster and faster and more frighten-ing.

THE 'LITTLE JERK' that is given to the audience early on is a sequence in which the famous stomach-burst-ing scene from 'Alien' is re-enacted – just to, uh, whet your appetite. It is worked into the preamble by the clever device of making it Ripley's dream while recovering in hospital. There is a little cheating however in that some vital 'realistic' information is included from other characters which, it transpires, can only have occurred in the dream sequence. 'It's true. We didn't cheat much, but we cheated right,' says Cameron. 'It's just further proof that you can get away with almost anything, provid-ing you do it right.'

The ending is a post-feminist slug-ging match between Ripley and the monster for the maternal custody of the child. Naturally enough Ripley has a little muscular help in the shape of a 'power loader', which is an exo-skeleton rather like a fork-lift truck except that it fits closely around the body of the operator and gives her a decent straight right, and a killer left hook.

from Time Out

ALIENS

Here is a film for which you can safely bask in the role of fan – it is that rare thing, a futuristic adven-ture film with a tough heroine – and not a hero in sight [...]

The storyline continues from where the first film left off (but you don't need to have seen it). Ripley (Weaver), having arrived home to tell of the terrifying Alien which destroyed the rest of the crew, is wearily coerced into returning with a party of troops to find out what's happened since. Has the Alien returned?

Yes, of course, and a high-tension drama ensues.

I'm usually under my seat at the first sign of suspense or gore in movies, but I didn't find **ALIENS** too terrifying – it is action-packed rather than scary.

Is it a touch militaristic? OK, there's a lot of explosion and weaponry (thermal) around.

But the conventional backdrop props are overturned by the completely unconventional dynamics in the narrative. This is not simply sci-fi with women substituting for men. For the principle drama is between two females, between two maternal strengths, Ripley and the egg-laying Alien, deep in dripping, secretory, womb-like caverns.

It is a young *girl*, Newt, who has been the only survivor on the planet. The attachment between her and Ripley is fierce, mutually protective, and becomes the focus of the drama. In giving us such an unusual scenario, the film maintains a precise control, never spilling into the sentimentalism or over-indulgence we usually get from Hollywood. Instead, Weaver as Ripley, while totally physically competent, making all the right decisions and generating all the life-saving acts, remains emotionally weary and strained – real in a way heroes never are.

Wonderfully unreal too, of course: completely gorgeous to watch, whether sweating buckets in a leather jacket, looking worried in her vest, or simply suspicious and exasperated with the men she finds herself amongst.

ALIENS even has an anti-capitalist thread, which seals its position as different from run-of-the-mill macho adventure stories. When I saw it, the audience burst into spontaneous applause twice – at Ripley's daring. This is a perfect Saturday night movie. Go with a bunch of girls and enjoy yourselves.

from Spare Rib

EXERCISE 4.28

1 *Most local papers do a brief weekly review of films on in the area. Collect a few of these to read and discuss. (If you go to see any of them, try comparing what you thought of them with what the newspapers said about them.)*

2 *There are specialist magazines about films (you may find some in your local library). Try to get hold of these and read what they have to say about films. Also try finding some film catalogues (your own library may have some for reference). These often describe and illustrate hundreds of films made over the years.*

3 *Try producing your own film review questionnaire to help you decide what to look for when watching a film. Next time you go to see a film, try it out.*

4 *Choose a type of film you particularly enjoy watching, such as thrillers, romance, science fiction, horror, comedy or musicals. Write a review of the next example of this type of film you see, comparing it with other examples you have seen and enjoyed.*

READING AND RESPONSE

EXERCISE 4.29

1   *Read the passage carefully and answer the questions at the end.*

The sky was dark blue through the dark green mango leaves, and I thought, 'This is my place and this is where I belong and this is where I wish to stay.' Then I thought, 'What a beautiful tree, but it is too high up here for mangoes and it may never bear fruit,' and I thought of lying alone in my bed with the soft silk cotton mattress and fine sheets, listening. At last I said, 'Christophine, he does not love me, I think he hates me. He always sleeps in his dressing-room now and the servants know. If I get angry he is scornful and silent, sometimes he does not speak to me for hours and I cannot endure it any more, I cannot. What shall I do? He was not like that at first,' I said.

Pink and red hibiscus grew in front of her door, she lit her pipe and did not answer.

'Answer me,' I said. She puffed out a cloud of smoke.

'You ask me a hard thing, I tell you a hard thing, pack up and go.'

'Go, go where? To some strange place where I shall never see him? No, I will not, then everyone, not only the servants, will laugh at me.'

'It's not you they laugh at if you go, they laugh at him.'

'I will not do that.'

'Why you ask me, if when I answer you say no? Why you come up here if when I tell you the truth, you say no?'

'But there must be something else I can do.'

She looked gloomy. 'When man don't love you, more you try, more he hate you, man like that. If you love them they treat you bad, if you don't love them they after you night and day bothering your soul case out. I hear about you and your husband,' she said.

'But I cannot go. He is my husband after all.'

She spat over her shoulder. 'All women, all colours, nothing but fools. Three children I have. One living in this world, each one a different father, but no husband. I thank my God. I keep my money. I don't give it to no worthless man.'

'When must I go, where must I go?'

'But look me trouble, a rich white girl like you and more foolish than the rest. A man don't treat you good, pick up your skirt and walk out. Do it and he come after you.'

'He will not come after me. And you must understand I am not rich now. I have no money of my own at all, everything I had belongs to him.'

'What you tell me there?' she said sharply.

'That is English law.'

'Law! The Mason boy fix it, that boy worse than Satan and he burn in Hell one of these fine nights. Listen to me now and I advise you what to do. Tell your husband you feeling sick, you want to visit your cousin in Martinique. Ask him pretty for some of your own money, the man not bad-hearted, he give it. When you get away, stay away. Ask more. He give again and well satisfy. In the end he come to find out what you do, how you get on without him, and if he see you fat and happy he want you back. Men like that. Better not stay in that old house. Go from that house, I tell you.'

'You think I must leave him?'

'You ask me so I answer.'

from The Wide Sargasso Sea *by Jean Rhys*

1   What can you deduce from the passage about the sex, race, status and approximate age of the two people talking?

2   What is the narrator's problem?

3   In no more than 25 words, summarise Christophine's advice to the narrator.

4   How does the writer maintain your interest throughout the passage?

5   Write 400–500 words in response to one of the following:

   (i)   The sky was dark blue through the dark green mango leaves . . .

   (ii) A friend's advice

   (iii) The alternatives open to someone whose marriage is going through a difficult phase

   (iv) 'This is my place and this is where I belong and this is where I wish to stay . . .'

6   You work for the Agony Column of a modern magazine and receive a letter from someone in the narrator's position. Write her a letter offering her your advice.

7   **For discussion**

   Who do you feel are the best people to turn to for advice if you have personal problems – your family, your friends or a specialist agency?

EXERCISE 4.30

Read the passage carefully and answer the questions at the end.

It was several weeks before she stumbled on the case of Varsha Nahri. Sumitra was tidying up the filing cabinet and came upon the Missing Persons section. The name leapt out at her, startling amongst the Jennings and Hutchinsons and Browns. At lunchtime, instead of window-shopping in Oxford Street or meeting a friend for coffee, she opened her file and sat down to read.

The correspondence inside the file related to a young Indian girl who had left home. Her parents had contacted the Agency in the hope of finding their daughter. Mr Farley had agreed to handle the case on one condition; that he would not divulge the girl's address if he managed to trace her. He would find out if she was safe, ask her to contact her parents, but that was all.

At the back of the file were some clips sent in by a Cuttings Service detailing a few suicide cases. All the names were of Asian girls who had killed themselves. One of the Coroner's reports said, 'I dread making out even one more report on a pathetic little girl found floating in a river.'

Sumitra read through the case history of this unknown stranger who suddenly seemed to represent her own dilemma. Varsha, twenty-one years old, had been found living in Ealing in a bedsitter. Mr Farley had spoken to her; Varsha said that she had to leave home – her parents were insisting that she marry an accountant of their acquaintance while she had no desire to do so. She was studying at London University and wanted to complete her studies and have a career before even thinking about getting married.

She agreed to write to her parents regularly, to phone them occasionally, but not to see them, explaining that they would try to pressurize her into returning home, where once again she would be subject to family demands to conform to a way of life she did not want to lead. They had, she said, beaten her, locked her in her room, and threatened to send her to India if she continued to act as she was doing.

Sumitra lit a cigarette. Her hand was shaking. She had heard of Indian girls leaving home, but had never met anyone who had actually done so. Those girls who had run away were talked about in tones of envy by those of her own age, and in hushed voices of disgust and shame by her parents' generation. But as far as she knew no one had ever come into contact with anyone who had left home without their parents' consent.

All her Indian friends discussed leaving home, it was like her parents' wish to own a shop, or the neighbours' longing for a cottage by the sea. It was a myth, a legend to cling to, an empty dream that would never come true, but which was comforting and consoling. One of her friends, Sulima, had often spoken of going away, of finding a flat, and had even got as far as looking in the Accommodation Vacant columns in the papers. But both Sulima and Sumitra knew that she would not leave. It was as if expressing the wish was enough, it defined hopes and needs, but putting the wish into effect would break her mother's heart, disgrace her family, mar her brothers' and sisters' chances of marrying well, bring the family name into disrepute with the rest of the Indian community. Sumitra listened to her, expressed the same desire, and hung back for the same reasons.

She read through the file again and frowned. If she did leave home – and her heart missed a beat at the thought – *if* she left home, how would the family react? Mai and Bap would be devastated. They both relied on her so much, they would never manage without her. But then again, if she married soon, as they wanted her to, they would have to cope without her anyway. This was not really the issue.

She thought about the burden it would throw on Sandya. Sandya would have to manage alone. She seemed so thin and vulnerable, yet in so many ways she had turned out to be stronger, more determined than Sumitra.

Sandya would manage, that was not the real stumbling-block either.

The crucial point was Sumitra, whether she herself possessed enough courage to leave home. She wasn't sure that she did. It was true that other boys and girls of her own age, even younger, set up homes every day on their own, but it was one thing to be independent with the approval and encouragement of a family, and another to do something that meant cutting herself off for ever from the whole way of life and the people she loved.

from Sumitra's Story *by Rukshana Smith*

1   *What do you think Sumitra's job is and why?*

2   *Why was Sumitra so interested in the case of Varsha Nahri?*

3   *What is the 'empty dream' (para. 7) which Sumitra's friends have – and why do they find it so difficult to achieve?*

4   *In no more than 30 words, summarise Sumitra's feelings about her future.*

5   *Consider what your advice would be if Sumitra were your friend and asked for your advice about leaving home. Write a letter to her giving your advice.*

6   *Write 400 words in response to one of the following:*

   (i) *Leaving Home – a one-act play*

   (ii) *An empty dream*

   (iii) *Parental influence*

   (iv) *Sumitra lit a cigarette. Her hand was shaking . . .*

7 For discussion

Given the divorce rate in the Western world, marriage arranged by parents may be worth serious consideration. How far do you agree and why?

EXERCISE 4.31

Read the passage carefully and answer the questions at the end.

Percy Toplis was ambushed by three policemen near a country church on a hot summer's evening in June 1920. Worshippers coming out from evensong scattered for cover among the gravestones to avoid being caught in the exchange of gunfire. The local chief constable's son, armed with an automatic pistol, roared up to join in. Toplis's killing, at the age of 23, was brutal, and its manner unprecedented, but it also came as a great relief to the highest authorities in the War Office and the Secret Service. For with him were buried, for sixty years at least, some of the darker secrets of the First World War.

At the time the case aroused a small amount of adverse comment in the *Manchester Guardian*, slight praise in the *Yorkshire Post*, total approval in local newspapers, and some muted protest at Westminster. It took a jury just three minutes to record a verdict of justifiable homicide. The chief constable who, it was claimed, had authorized the operation was awarded the CBE and then, within weeks, mysteriously resigned. Even in death, Percy Toplis continued to blight the lives of the establishment.

Toplis had been handsome, debonair, a natural actor, a fair pianist, a renowned philanderer. He had a wild sense of humour. Even when on the run for his life, he ostentatiously affected a gold-rimmed monocle. But unknown to the newspaper readers who devoured the scandalous details of his post-war career, he was also the most extravagant anti-hero of the First World War. At a time when he ought to have been dead, executed by firing squad in accordance with rough-and-ready wartime justice, he was rejoining the British Forces with arrogant ease, confident he would not be touched.

It was a very grateful authority that made quiet heroes of the men who finally gunned him down, and who then swiftly swept him under the sod into a pauper's grave overlooking the hills and lakes of Ullswater. The cemetery register simply states: 'Shot dead by police at Plumpton.'

But there are those alive today who still remember Percy Toplis with affection, respect and admiration. They include his closest childhood friend, Earnest Leah of Bilsthorpe, Mansfield. Leah looked so like his friend that he was once actually arrested by police in a case of mistaken identity when the country-wide manhunt was on for Toplis. As Leah recalls:

'He was my best friend. A lovely lad. Today he would have been regarded as one of those intellectual socialists. Then, he had no chance at all. Mind you, he was a bit of a tearaway, was Percy.'

Ernest Leah's brother Raymond, a local councillor in Alfreton, Derbyshire, still keeps Toplis's army belt as a treasured memento.

This, then, is the story of the monocled tearaway. Private alias Lieutenant/Captain/Colonel Percy Toplis, who made the biggest single-handed contribution to the almost unknown mutiny of the British Army in France in the First World War.

In June 1920, less than three years after that rebellion, the authorities no doubt excused themselves for the manner of his death with the thought that Toplis had been too dangerous to bring to trial. The country was not yet ready for regrets and recriminations. Or for a first-hand, eye-witness account of a mutiny which had officially never happened.

Even today, the Ministry of Defence shies away from the word 'mutiny'. It prefers the word 'disturbances', which was the description used in a secret army record on the time. But mutiny it was, and it lasted six desperate days, involved thousands of troops and finished with the authorities surrendering and a brigadier-general being relieved of his command. Toplis's control of another British army – an army of deserters behind the front line – was so complete that when the mutiny brought about a clean sweep of military police personnel, the first and most important task of the new commander, a secret service agent, Edwin Woodhall, was to track Toplis down. But Toplis, as he was to do so many times again, turned Houdini and escaped to thumb his nose at the military and the police through another three years of immaculate effrontery.

But then he had been doing that to authorities of every kind since he was 11 years old.

from The Monocled Mutineer *by William Allison and John Fairley*

1 *What was unusual about the death of Percy Toplis?*

2 *What evidence is there that many people at the time felt his death to have been justified?*

3 *Write a character sketch of Percy Toplis, showing clearly the kind of person he was.*

4 *Why were the authorities relieved that Toplis had been killed?*

5 *Percy Toplis was a private, the lowest rank in the British Army – and yet he seems to have been an important figure. Why and in what way was he important?*

6 *What do you think the writer's feelings are about Toplis and what evidence is there for this?*

7 *Assume yourself to be a local newspaper reporter, sent to report the death of Percy Toplis in 1920. Write a newspaper article based on the event and provide a suitable headline.*

8 *Write 400–500 words in response to* one *of the following:*

    (i) Mutiny – *a play for radio*

    (ii) '. . The cemetery register simply states: "Shot dead by police at Plumpton."'

    (iii) The last week of Percy Toplis – a diary

    (iv) 'He was my best friend'

9 For discussion

    Can there ever be such a thing as justifiable homicide? Why and under what circumstances – or why not?

5 Personal Expression

– 'OPEN' WRITING

Use of words

Read the following passage by the South African writer Alex la Guma.

> Michael Adonis turned into the entrance of a tall narrow tenement where he lived. The floor of the entrance was flagged with white and black slabs in the pattern of a draught-board, but the tramp of untold feet and the accumulation of dust and grease and ash had blurred the squares so that now it had taken on the appearance of a kind of loathsome skin disease. A row of dustbins lined one side of the entrance and exhaled the smell of rotten fruit, stale food, stagnant water and general decay. A cat, the colour of dishwater, was trying to paw the remains of a fish-head from one of the bins.
>
> She came down and stood on the first step, smiling at him and showing the gap in the top row of her teeth. She had a heavy mouth, smeared blood-red with greasy lipstick, so that it looked stark as a wound in her dark face. Her coarse wiry hair was tied at the back with a scrap of soiled ribbon in the parody of a ponytail, and under the blouse and skirt her body was insignificant. She was wearing new yellow leather flat-heeled pumps that gave the impression of something expensive abandoned on a junk heap.
>
> *from* A Walk in the Night

EXERCISE 5.1

Would you like to live in the place he describes? Would you be flattered if you were described as the girl is described? If not:

1   *List the words which you feel give an unfavourable impression. Is there any connection between these words?*

2   *Now rewrite the passage to give the opposite picture – of a charming and attractive location and person.*

Do this by changing the words you have listed. Where possible change the details as little as possible, just the impressions. For example, most qualities can be seen in two ways. A person may seem generous to his or her friends but spendthrift *to those who like him or her less: the same quality viewed two ways. So, in the passage, the girl's 'insignificant' body could be described, more attractively, as 'slim' (without altering her actual appearance we have altered the words to give a different impression).*

This may not always be possible, of course. We may have, for example, to replace 'dustbins' by 'flowers', but alter as little as possible otherwise.

Pen portraits

Here is a pen portrait of one of the main characters in Timothy Mo's novel, *Sour Sweet*.

The first thing that might have struck any casual observer about Ma Lurk Hing would have been his extreme shortness, that and the scars of child-hood smallpox which had endowed his pitted face with the colour and consistency of an amply aereated but half-cooked batter pudding. Had the casual observer spoken Cantonese he would have discerned in Ma's rasping voice – a voice so hoarse, so brutalised that surely the surface mutilations must point to some deeper penetration of the disease into the throat – the twang of a man used to another dialect. He sounded like a Swatownese; an emigrant from a poorer quarter of that teeming dock-town.

Ma had come on since those days. One glance at his clothes told you that. Winter or spring, the details of his under-suiting would be concealed by a long overcoat. This was an expensive garment: a navy blue which became black under street illumination, say on a corner. It was a soft cloth (pure cashmere by its sheen) that seemed poured around the contours of the stocky body which filled it. Brown alligator moccasins, another seasonal perennial, gleamed beneath the unfashionable cuffs of Ma's trousers. His hands were hidden in his over-long coat sleeves but when he consulted his watch (Patek Philippe, the strap again of alligator) it could be seen that the index and adjoining fingers of his right hand had been cleanly amputated from below the line of the second joint. Some industrial accident perhaps? A supposition to be encouraged by Ma's bow-legged longshoreman's stance and trick of carrying his hands curled into pudgy fists, the wrists cocked, facing outwards, as if he might be levering up a hatch by its bar in some atavistic reflex of labour. Giving the lie to this, the flesh of Ma's palms was soft and white, had long been so. But the first two knuckles of each hand were enlarged, protuberant as golf balls, functionally connected (it seemed) by a crinkled web of yellow callus. When Ma balled his fists, his hands, the mutilated and the whole, were indistinguishable; they looked like clubs.

As a Swatow man, Ma was somewhat unusual in the Street, coming neither from Hong Kong, the New Territories, nor even Canton, though the nosiest of his fellow provincials baulked at snooping here. Ma was clearly not a man to trifle with; at the same time there was also something slightly ludicrous about him – connected, perhaps, with a lack of proportion between personal appearance and social consequence. Ma acted on his own estimation of himself and others accepted it but there was nothing inherently prepossessing about the man. It was as if he derived authority from some source external to himself: great wealth, maybe, or the expectation of it . . . but not wealth. But what?

He had no obvious means of support. No business, restaurant, teahouse, car-hire firm, supermarket or travel agency. Judging by the frequency with which he visited the Street's basement gambling houses he might have been a professional gambler, except he was never seen to wager; only to watch impassively with hands in his overcoat pockets. Family? None. Not even the hint of a mistress of whatever race. The groups of young men he was occasionally seen with might point to a proclivity of another kind. In someone else this could have provoked mirth and sarcasm, inspired hilarious witticisms, and the outrageous punning so dear to southern hearts, but not in Ma's case. No one stared at him or at his companions when they took tea at the back tables of restaurants or when Ma passed, in a black German saloon, chauffeured by a single youth, or sometimes accompanied by another young man in the back. Tough-looking boys, these, with an inclination towards pale corduroy or darker leather jackets, their long hair brushing the collar in soft black spikes. They had a fashion for wearing four heavy signet rings, two on each of the fingers that were missing on Ma's right hand, in what might have been construed as a tribute to the older man.

Now ask yourself these questions:

1 How full is the physical description of Ma Lurk Hing? Is every aspect of his manner and appearance described? If not, what kind of details are selected?

2 Are these details given for their own sake? Or are they given to suggest to us aspects of Ma's character and occupation? Does this selection of details excite – leaving your imagination to do the rest?

3 The writer could simply have said that Ma was a Chinese gangster. Would he have produced the same effect? Would he have convinced us of the uniqueness of this man? Would we be as interested to read on and find out what becomes of him?

EXERCISE 5.2

Using the technique of selected *detail, write three pen portraits:*

(i) *one of a friend,*

(ii) *one of a schoolteacher or college lecturer, and*

(iii) *one of a person with an unusual occupation (suggesting but not stating what the occupation is).*

Some general points ▬▬▬▬▬▬▬▬▬▬▬▬▬▬▬▬▬▬▬▬▬▬▬▬▬▬▬▬▬▬▬▬▬▬▬▬

Read the passages which follow. For each of them, ask these questions, so as to decide what ingredients make a good piece of descriptive writing:

1 Does it appeal to the eye, by writing in such a vivid way that we immediately 'see' what is being described? Which phrases made you 'see' most vividly the things described?

2 Does it appeal to the other senses – of hearing, taste, touch and smell? Which phrases helped you 'feel' most strongly what was being described?

3 Are specialised words and terms used, in order to convey a more authentic feeling or atmosphere? (Check the meaning of any words that you do not understand.)

4 Is there a keen and accurate observation of detail? Are the individual details built up, like the bricks used to build a house, to create a description that works as a whole?

5 Is the language used carefully, with every word, phrase and sentence chosen for the maximum effectiveness?

6 Is your interest aroused and your attention held – and if so, by what means?

a) It was about eleven o'clock in the morning, mid-October, with the sun not shining and a look of hard wet rain in the clearness of the foothills. I was wearing my powder-blue suit, with dark blue shirt, tie and display handkerchief, black brogues, black wool socks with dark blue clocks on them. I was neat, clean, shaved and sober, and I didn't care who knew it. I was everything the well-dressed private detective ought to be. I was calling on four million dollars.

The main hallway of the Sternwood place was two storeys high. Over the entrance doors, which would have let in a troop of Indian elephants, there was a broad stained-glass panel showing a knight in dark armour rescuing a lady who was tied to a tree and didn't have any clothes on but some very long and convenient hair. The knight had pushed the vizor of his helmet back to be sociable, and he was fiddling with the knots on the ropes that tied the lady to the tree and not getting anywhere. I stood there and thought that if I lived in the house, I would sooner or later have to climb up there and help him. He didn't seem to be really trying.

from The Big Sleep *by Raymond Chandler*

b) 'The Balinese is a startling and startled figure. Every part of his body is taut. His tense face, with wide-open eyes staring intently at an apparition visible only to himself, is like an erratic thunder-cloud cut by lightning. After an outburst of a few sudden swaggering steps forward the figure stops as abruptly as it had started.

'The forceful Javanese dancer projects no such hypnotic and startling intensity. It is the very expansiveness and stately, regular rhythm of his gestures that make him an unrelenting force, impersonal, impassive. Compared with the sudden outbursts of the hypertense Balinese dancer, the controlled poise of his Javanese counterpart seems an epitome of relentless steadiness.

'The feminine dancers of the Javanese [serimpi] and Balinese [legong] offer even stronger contrasts. The dance of the serimpi, embellished by the unfolding, falling and fluttering of their dance scarves, is stately and restrained. The glance of the dancer is constantly lowered, lending her performance a concentrated inwardness. At her fastest, a serimpi glides tiptoe over the floor in tiny, even steps, with one of her extended scarf-ends fluttering at her side.

'In contrast, the lithe bodies of the Balinese legong are propelled in rapid staccato rhythms. Instead of the delicate tip-toeing of the serimpi, the legong moves in a dust-raising lateral shuffle which sends her scooting in one direction and then in another.'

from Art in Indonesia *by Claire Holt*

c) In the period of which we speak, there reigned in the cities a stench barely conceivable to us modern men and women. The streets stank of manure, the courtyards of urine, the stairwells stank of mouldering wood and rat droppings, the kitchens of spoiled cabbage and mutton fat; the unaired parlours stank of stale dust, the bedrooms of greasy sheets, damp featherbeds, and the pungently sweet aroma of chamber-pots. The stench of sulphur rose from the chimneys, the stench of caustic lyes from the tanneries, and from the slaughterhouses came the stench of con-gealed blood. People stank of sweat and unwashed clothes; from their mouths came the stench of rotting teeth, from their bellies that of onions, and from their bodies, if they were no longer very young, came the stench of rancid cheese and sour milk and tumorous disease. The rivers stank, the marketplaces stank, the churches stank, it stank beneath the bridges and in the palaces. The peasant stank as did the priest, the apprentice as did his master's wife, the whole of the aristocracy stank, even the king himself stank, stank like a rank lion, and the queen like an old goat, summer and winter. For in the eighteenth century there was nothing to hinder bacteria busy at decomposition, and so there was no human activity, either constructive or destructive, no manifestation of germinat-ing or decaying life, that was not accompanied by stench.

And of course the stench was foulest in Paris, for Paris was the largest city of France. And in turn there was a spot in Paris under the sway of particularly fiendish stench: between the rue aux Fers and the rue de la Ferronnerie, the Cimetière des Innocents to be exact.

from Perfume *by Patrick Süskind*

d) The blossom opens slowly, slowly on the apple tree. One day, the boughs are grey, though with the swellings of the leaves to come visible if you look closely. The next day and the next, here and there, a speck of white, and then a sprinkling, as though someone has thrown a handful of confetti up into the air and let it fall, anyhow, over the branches.

The weather is grey, it is cold still. The blossom looks like snow against the sky. And then, one morning, there *is* snow, snow at the very end of April, five or six inches of it, after a terrible stormy night, and rising from it, and set against the snow-filled sky, the little tree is puffed out with its blossom, a crazy sight, like some surrealist painting, and all around us, in every other garden, there is the white apple and the pink cherry blossom, thick as cream, in a winter landscape.

And another day, just before the blossom withers and shrinks back into the fast opening leaves, there is the softest of spring mornings, at last it is touched by the early sun, and the apple tree looks as it should look, if the world went aright, in springtime.

from The Magic Apple Tree *by Susan Hill*

e) There were three dynamos with their engines at Camberwell. The two that have been there since the beginning are small machines; the larger one was new. The smaller machines made a reasonable noise; their straps hummed over the drums, every now and then the brushes buzzed and fizzled, and the air churned steadily, whoo! whoo! whoo! between their poles. One was loose in its foundations and kept the shed vibrating. But the big dynamo drowned these little noises altogether with the sustained drone of its iron core, which somehow set part of the ironwork humming. The place made the visitor's head reel with the throb, throb, throb of the engines, the rotation of the big wheels, the spinning ball-valves, the occasional spittings of the steam, and over all the deep, unceasing, surging note of the big dynamo. This last noise was from an engineering point of view a defect, but Azuma-zi accounted it unto the monster for mightiness and pride.

If it were possible we would have the noises of that shed always about the reader as he reads, we would tell all our story to such an accompaniment. It was a steady stream of din, from which the ear picked out first one thread and then another; there was the intermittent snorting, panting, and seething of the steam-engines, the suck and thud of their pistons, the dull beat on the air as the spokes of the great driving wheels came round, a note the leather straps made as they ran tighter and looser, and a fretful tumult from the dynamos; and, over all, sometimes inaudible, as the ear tired of it, and then creeping back upon the senses again, was this trombone note of the big machine. The floor never felt steady and quiet beneath one's feet, but quivered and jarred. It was a confusing, unsteady place, and enough to send anyone's thoughts jerking into odd zigzags.

from The Lord of the Dynamos *by H. G. Wells*

f) They woke up at dawn the next morning and rode out on three sad horses into the Dead Hills. Their name was perfect. They looked as if an undertaker had designed them from leftover funeral scraps. It was a three-hour ride to Miss Hawkline's house. The road was very bleak, wandering like the handwriting of a dying person over the hills.

There were no houses, no barns, no fences, no signs that human life had ever made its way this far except for the road which was barely legible. The only comforting thing was the early morning sweet smell of juniper brush.

Cameron had the trunk full of guns strapped onto the back of his horse. He thought it remarkable that the animal could still move. He had to think back a ways to remember a horse that had been in such bad shape.

'Sure is stark,' Greer said.

from The Hawkline Monster by Richard Brautigan

EXERCISE 5.3

With these passages in mind, aim to produce your own piece of descriptive writing. Start by focusing on a busy location, as this will provide plenty of potential for description.

Try to convey the bustle, the action and the atmosphere. You can include descriptions of the place itself, the people there, the kind of activity, and specialised acts or movements involved and changes which occur through the day. It is important to choose a place you are familiar with.

Here are a few suggestions of bustling places which might serve as subjects for your description:

A department store at sales time

A college on enrolment day

A seaside resort on a bank holiday

A show at an exhibition centre – such as a motor show or agricultural show

A busy day at an amusement park like Disneyland or Alton Towers

EXERCISE 5.4

Write a short passage of about 500 words on one of the following topics.

(i) A portrait in words.

(ii) The coldest day of the year.

(iii) Street life.

(iv) A view from a high place.

(v) The storm.

(vi) Sunset.

(vii) Your journey to school or college on a delightful summer's day compared with the same on a cold unpleasant winter's day.

(viii) The work involved in a part-time or holiday job you have.

(ix) The odd couple.

(x) A popular holiday spot early in the morning, before the crowds have arrived, and later in the day, when it is full of people.

(xi) A work of art or piece of machinery that intrigued you.

(xii) The rubbish tip.

(xiii) The land that time forgot.

(xiv) In response to a particularly evocative photograph or piece of music.

NARRATIVE WRITING

The report on yesterday's controversial football match in the sports pages of the newspaper; your account of what really happened at the party in a letter to a friend; Samuel Pepys' *Diary* (or anyone else's diary for that matter); many folk song and pop song lyrics; most myths, legends, fairy stories and nursery rhymes; novels and short stories – these may all seem very different in content, but they are all examples of narrative writing. They all relate a series of events (and they don't even need to be factual to count as narrative writing – telling a story is narrative just the same).

Narrative is therefore an extremely common form of writing. As it usually follows the order of events ('First . . . Then . . . Next . . . Finally . . .'), it is easy to remember and easy to follow. Indeed, people will often slip into narrative even when it *isn't* wanted, because it comes so easily. For instance, it is a common complaint of examiners that many literature students end up telling the story (narrative writing) rather than answering the questions set (analytical writing).

In one sense, then, narrative is the one type of writing you as a student should need least help with, as it is the kind that seems to come most naturally. However, it is still worth considering these four rules. Normally the events described should be:

● *interesting in themselves* – if they are not, why are you writing about them?

- *told without irrelevant sidetracking* – a stock comic character is the one who starts off telling a story but never quite gets to the end, as each event sparks off some extra thought or memory which is then pursued at length.

- *told in an interesting and varied manner* – an interesting start always helps, and some sort of message or moral at the end may give the account added weight.

- *told in such a way as to involve and sustain your interest* – common techniques here are the use of mystery, strange or unusual events, crises, suspense or characters you can sympathise with.

EXERCISE 5.5

Now read the passages that follow. Do they follow the four rules of narrative writing? Is there more to narrative than the four rules suggest – and if so, what?

a) 1. Joe is skeletal. His legs are piteous sticks. His red bathing-suit is the baggy boxer type. His voluptuous girl-friend is with him. Her thighs are thicker than his. The calm sea beyond contrasts with Joe's ordeal. A man with a grand physique is humiliating him. We cannot see the torturer's face, but the girl informs Joe that the man is a well-known local nuisance.

2. A tiny sail has appeared on the horizon. We see the bully's face. We appreciate his beery chest. The girl-friend has drawn up her knees and is wondering why she ever dated this no-assed weakling. Joe has been pulled to his feet by the bully and now must sustain a further insult.

3. The sail is gone. Some miniscule figures play ball at the edge of the sea. Seagulls appear. An anguished Joe stands beside the girl he is losing.

Joe: The big bully! I'll get even some day.

Her: Oh, don't let it *bother* you, little boy!

4. Joe's room, or the remains of it. A cracked picture hangs askew on the green wall. A broken lamp is in motion. He is kicking a chair over. He wears a blue blazer, tie, white ducks. He clenches his fist, a clawlike articulation from a wrist thin as a bird leg. The girl-friend lies in some panel of the imagination snuggling in the bully's armpit, winking out a thousand shameful anecdotes about Joe's body.

Joe: Darn it! I'm sick and tired of being a scarecrow! Charles Axis says he can give me a REAL body. All right! I'll gamble a stamp and get his FREE book.

5. LATER. Could this be Joe? He flexes a whole map of jigsaw muscles before his dresser mirror.

Joe: Boy! It didn't take Axis long to do this for me! What MUSCLES! That bully won't shove me around again!

Is this the same red bathing-suit?

6.   The beach. The girl has come back. She is having a good time. Her body is relaxed and hips have appeared. Her left hand is raised in a gesture of surprised delight as her vision of Joe undergoes a radical transformation. Joe has just thrown a punch which lands in an electrical blaze on the bully's chin, knocking him off balance, knitting his eyebrows with amazed pain. Beyond we have the same white strand, the same calm sea.

Joe: What! You here again? Here's something I owe you!

Her: Oh, Joe! You ARE a real man after all!

An attractive girl sitting on the sand nearby: GOSH! What a build!

The envious man beside her: He's already famous for it!

Joe stands there in silence, thumbs hooked in the front of his bathing-suit, looking at his girl, who leans lasciviously against him. Four thick black words appear in the sky and they radiate spears of light. None of the characters in the panel seems aware of the celestial manifestation exploding in terrific silence above the old marine landscape. HERO OF THE BEACH is the sky's announcement.

from Beautiful Losers *by Leonard Cohen*

b)   When we had finished eating I took the plates back to the kitchen. I was determined not to start washing up, but the masculine squalor of the sink and its surroundings compelled me. Nothing had been touched since the morning before: the sink-hole was stopped with a mound of tea leaves, and there was a pile of dirty cups and saucers all over the draining board. I looked anxiously for a glass or two but there were none: my suspicions were right, he must be a secret abstainer.

When I tore myself away from it we went and sat down on the settee, and kissed in some discomfort. After a while he said that perhaps we might go up and lie on the bed, and I said that perhaps we might, so we went up to the bedroom. But it was useless. I couldn't bring myself to think about it at all.

'What's the matter?' he said, after a while. 'What's the matter with me? What have I done? Don't you want me to make love to you, Emma?'

'Not particularly,' I said, turning over and lying on my back to stare at the ceiling. 'Not particularly, to tell you the truth.'

'Why not?'

'Oh, I don't know,' I said. 'All that washing-up, and I can see that there's a button off your shirt, and I know that any minute now you're going to ask me to sew it on for you, aren't you? Be honest, tell me, you were, weren't you?'

'Well, it had crossed my mind. But not immediately, of course, not now.'

'No. After.'

'Yes, I suppose so. After.'

I started to laugh. 'Oh well,' I said. 'At least you admitted it. If you hadn't admitted it, that would have been that. Tell me, Wyndham, what makes you think that I'm better at sewing on buttons than you are?'

'Well, you're a woman. More practice.'

'You could start practising now. Then you wouldn't have to take a woman to bed with you in order to get your buttons sewn on. I'll give you a lesson.'

from The Garrick Year *by Margaret Drabble*

c)   Opportunity

Opportunity
Came to my door
When I was down
On my luck
In the shape
Of an old friend
With a plan
Guaranteed

Showed me the papers
As he walked me to the car
His shoes
Finest leather
He said
You could wear this style
If you follow my advice

He owned a gun
The calibre escaped me
But I noticed
Straight away
It made me itch
Carried an address
With numbers on the back
And an L-shaped
Bar of iron

What's that for
I asked my man
With eyes
Wide opened

And the knowledge in my head
And he said
Opportunity
World wide adventure
Money in the bank

We did the job
The work was so well done
No one saw us coming
Much less leave
But what I dropped
Carried my credentials
And a black and white
Shot of you and me

What's that for
I asked the cop
With eyes of innocence
And the knowledge in my head

And he said
Opportunity
World wide adventure
Let me have your hand.

from Show Some Emotion *by Joan Armatrading*

d)   They crouched with their rifles in the pineapple field, watching a man teach his son how to ride a horse. It was the summer of 1902 in Hawaii.

They hadn't said anything for a long time. They just crouched there watching the man and the boy and the horse. What they saw did not make them happy.

'I can't do it,' Greer said.

'It's a bastard all right,' Cameron said.

'I can't shoot a man when he's teaching his kid how to ride a horse,' Greer said. 'I'm not made that way.'

Greer and Cameron were not at home in the pineapple field. They looked out of place in Hawaii. They were both dressed in cowboy clothes, clothes that belonged to Eastern Oregon.

Greer had his favourite gun: a 30:40 Krag, and Cameron had a 25:35 Winchester. Greer liked to kid Cameron about his gun. Greer always used to say, 'Why do you keep that rabbit rifle around when you can get a real gun like this Krag here?'

They stared intently at the riding lesson.

'Well, there goes a thousand dollars apiece,' Cameron said. 'And that God-damn trip on that God-damn boat was for nothing. I thought I was going to puke forever and now I'm going to have to do it all over again with only the change in my pockets.'

Greer nodded.

The voyage from San Francisco to Hawaii had been the most terrifying experience Greer and Cameron had ever gone through, even more terrible than the time they shot a deputy sheriff in Idaho ten times and he wouldn't die and Greer finally had to say to the deputy sheriff, 'Please die because we don't want to shoot you again.' And the deputy sheriff had said, 'OK, I'll die, but don't shoot me again.'

'We won't shoot you again,' Cameron had said.

'OK, I'm dead,' and he was.

The man and the boy and the horse were in the front yard of a big white house shaded by coconut trees. It was like a shining island in the pineapple fields. There was piano music coming from the house. It drifted lazily across the warm afternoon.

Then a woman came out onto the front porch. She carried herself like a wife and a mother. She was wearing a long white dress with a high starched collar. 'Dinner's ready!' she yelled. 'Come and get it, you cowboys!'

'God-damn!' Cameron said. 'It's sure as hell gone now. One thousand dollars. By all rights, he should be dead and halfway through being laid out in the front parlour, but there he goes into the house to have some lunch.'

'Let's get off this God-damn Hawaii,' Greer said.

from The Hawkline Monster by Richard Brautigan

e)   **Vergissmeinnicht***

Three weeks gone and the combatants gone,
returning over the nightmare ground
we found the place again, and found
the soldier sprawling in the sun.

The frowning barrel of his gun
overshadowing. As we came on
that day, he hit my tank with one
like the entry of a demon.

Look. Here in the gunpit spoil
the dishonoured picture of his girl
who has put: "Steffi. Vergissmeinnicht"
in a copybook gothic script.

We see him almost with content
abased, and seeming to have paid
and mocked at by his own equipment
that's hard and good when he's decayed.

But she would weep to see to-day
how on his skin the swart flies move;
the dust upon the paper eye
and the burst stomach like a cave.

For here the lover and killer are mingled
who had one body and one heart.
And death who had the soldier singled
has done the lover mortal hurt.

Homs, Tropolitania, 1943
by Keith Douglas

*Forget-me-not

f)   Gupis, 9 June

If anyone ever asks you to drive three donkeys and a foal for twenty-four miles through the Karakoram Mountains, be *very* firm and refuse to do so – it really *is* more than flesh and blood was ever meant to endure. The position, as explained to me this morning, was that the four were being exchanged for a pony mare and foal from Gupis, but the latter was too young to travel for another fortnight whereas the donkeys were urgently required in Gupis, and a donkey foal, although looking so much frailer, is presumed tougher – therefore, would I please take the donkeys with me and save a villager the journey to Gupis? Green as I am I foresaw some of the complications and said, 'Couldn't a villager come with me, riding half the way on Rob, and when the pony foal was able to make it, couldn't a Gupis villager bring them up?' But no – it was in the bargain that the donkey village was responsible for herding both lots. So off I went at 5.45 a.m., armed with a long switch which would, in theory, enable me to steer my charges without difficulty. Well, maybe a local on horseback could do it, but those donkeys knew they were onto a soft thing. Everyone remained happy while there was, on one side, a sheer drop of hundreds of feet into the river and, on the other side, an equally sheer wall of rock – then the brutes had no alternative but to go in a straight line. The fun started when the mountains receded in places, or the track dropped to river level and there came level stretches between river and track. Then the quartet merrily gambolled off at about ten times the rate they'd go on the road, in divers directions, through deep, yielding sand and thorny bushes, and between boulders and over streams and behind trees and around cliffs. (It's all right for you to sit back and laugh, but if *you* were galloping under a blazing sun trying to reassemble *in one place* a herd of apparently demented donkeys, you mightn't think it so amusing.) Rob was again wonderful – this is obviously a frequently recurring crisis in her life. She went after them like a sheep-dog and on the track kept reinforcing my rather half-hearted use of the switch by pushing the last donkey's rump with her nose; twenty-four miles at the pace of ambling donkeys is decidedly wearing. I passed a lovely pool, but did not dare to swim because the caravan would have been half-way to Peking by the time I came out. After twelve miles I saw that the foal couldn't possibly be driven any further without positive cruelty: from his point of view the whole idea was cruel anyway. (He was the smallest foal I've ever seen, with a mother hardly bigger than an Irish donkey foal.) So then I did what they do in Afghanistan with tiny foals and calves – tied his forefeet and hind-feet and put him across Rob in front of the saddle. I had to climb onto a rock to get him in place – he seemed amazingly heavy despite his dwarfishness – and he took a very dim view of the performance, as did his mother. (Rob was the only one to accept the situation philosophically.) By the time this was accomplished the two donkeys not involved had vanished and as I didn't feel like going into the unknown with the foal *in situ* I pursued them on foot, leaving Rob tied to a bush, the foal tied to Rob and the mother psychologically tied to the foal. A twenty-minute chase followed over burning sand and loose rocks (my biggest fear was that one of the wretches would break a leg) and then we were off again. We arrived here at 7.45 p.m., having had several pauses to dismantle the foal for feeding.

from Full Tilt *by Dervla Murphy*

EXERCISE 5.6

Three narrative extracts follow. Each describes an execution. Consider:

(i) the point of view each is seen from.

(ii) which aspects are concentrated on in each case.

(iii) what each passage seems to be telling you, about the people involved, and about life and death.

Finally, draw up a list of useful narrative techniques, that is, methods you can use when writing narrative accounts to make them more effective and interesting.

a)   A small man came out of a side door: he was held up by two policemen, but you could tell that he was doing his best – it was only that his legs were not fully under his control. They paddled him across to the opposite wall; an officer tied a handkerchief round his eyes. Mr. Tench thought: But I know him. Good God, one ought to do something. This was like seeing a neighbour shot.

Of course there was nothing to do. Everything went very quickly like a routine. The officer stepped aside, the rifles went up, and the little man suddenly made jerky movements with his arms. He was trying to say something: what was the phrase they were always supposed to use? That was routine too, but perhaps his mouth was too dry, because nothing came out except a word that sounded like 'Excuse'. The crash of the rifles shook Mr. Tench: they seemed to vibrate inside his own guts: he felt sick and shut his eyes. Then there was a single shot, and opening them again he saw the officer stuffing his gun back into his holster, and the little man was a routine heap beside the wall – something unimportant which had to be cleared away. Two knock-kneed men approached quickly. This was an arena, and the bull was dead, and there was nothing more to wait for any more.

from The Power and the Glory *by Graham Greene*

b)   The gallows stood in a small yard, separate from the main grounds of the prison, and overgrown with tall prickly weeds. The hangman, a grey-haired convict in the white uniform of the prison, was waiting beside his machine. He greeted us with a servile crouch as we entered. At a word from Francis the two warders, gripping the prisoner more closely than ever, half led, half pushed him to the gallows and helped him clumsily up the ladder. Then the hangman climbed up and fixed the rope round the prisoner's neck.

We stood waiting, five yards away. The warders had formed in a rough circle round the gallows. And then, when the noose was fixed, the prisoner began crying out to his god. It was a high, reiterated cry of 'Ram! Ram! Ram!' not urgent and fearful like a prayer or cry for help, but steady, rhythmical, almost like the tolling of a bell. The hangman, still standing on the gallows, produced a small cotton bag like a flour sack and drew it down over the prisoner's face. But the sound, muffled by the cloth, still persisted, over and over again: 'Ram! Ram! Ram! Ram! Ram!'

The hangman climbed down and stood ready, holding the lever. Minutes seemed to pass. The steady, muffled crying from the prisoner went on and on, 'Ram! Ram! Ram!' never faltering for an instant. The super-intendent, his head on his chest, was slowly poking the ground with his stick; perhaps he was counting the cries, allowing the prisoner a fixed number – fifty, perhaps, or a hundred. Everyone had changed colour. The Indians had gone grey like bad coffee, and one or two of the bayonets were wavering. We looked at the lashed, hooded man on the drop, and listened to his cries – each cry another second of life; the same thought was in all our minds: Oh, kill him quickly, get it over, stop that abominable noise!

Suddenly the superintendent made up his mind. Throwing up his head he made a swift motion with his stick. 'Chalo!' he shouted almost fiercely.

There was a clanking noise, and then dead silence. The prisoner had vanished, and the rope was twisting on itself. We went round the gallows to inspect the prisoner's body. He was dangling with his toes pointed straight downwards, very slowly revolving, as dead as a stone.

The superintendent reached out with his stick and poked the bare brown body; it oscillated slightly. '*He's* all right', said the superintendent. He backed out from under the gallows, and blew out a deep breath. The moody look had gone out of his face quite suddenly. He glanced at his wrist-watch. 'Eight minutes past eight. Well, that's all for this morning, thank God.'

from A Hanging *by George Orwell*

c) It seemed to him that they had been walking along this corridor for several minutes already. Still nothing happened. Probably he would hear when the man in uniform took the revolver out of its case. So until then there was time, he was still in safety ...

A dull blow struck the back of his head. He had long expected it and yet it took him unawares. He felt, wondering, his knees give way and his body whirl round in a half-turn. How theatrical, he thought as he fell, and yet I feel nothing. He lay crumpled up on the ground, with his cheek on the cool flagstones. It got dark, the sea carried him rocking on its nocturnal surface. Memories passed through him, like streaks of mist over the water.

Outside, someone was knocking on the front door, he dreamed that they were coming to arrest him; but in what country was he? ...

A shapeless figure bent over him, he smelt the fresh leather of the revolver belt; but what insignia did the figure wear on the sleeves and shoulder straps of its uniform – and in whose name did it raise the dark pistol barrel?

A second, smashing blow hit him on the ear. Then all became quiet. There was the sea again with its sounds. A wave slowly lifted him up. It came from afar and travelled sedately on, a shrug of eternity.

from Darkness at Noon *by Arthur Koestler*

EXERCISE 5.7

Write a short passage of about 500 words based on one of the following:

The great escape

Angel of mercy

Once upon a time . . .

A short story in one of the following styles:
science fiction/horror/whodunnit/romantic

. . . so the moral is . . .

After midnight

The first time

I'll never forget . . .

DIARIES, JOURNALS AND AUTOBIOGRAPHIES – PERSONAL NARRATIVE

Writing about our own lives and experiences ought to be a good starting point for writing generally. We are writing about something we know intimately and can record easily. However, there is a danger. Is what we are writing likely to be of interest to anyone but ourselves? Why should anyone else want to read about us?

The danger is illustrated by this extract from *The Diary of a Nobody* by George and Weedon Grossmith:

November 20. Have seen nothing of Lupin the whole day. Bought a cheap address-book. I spent the evening copying in the names and addresses of my friends and acquaintances. Left out the Mutlars of course.

EXERCISE 5.8

Compare this with the diary extracts which follow and ask yourself these questions:

1   *Does it matter who has written the diary and whether he or she is famous or has led a particularly interesting or eventful life?*

2   *Alternatively, is the diary written in a way which makes you want to keep on reading – by amusing you, or creating suspense, or involving your feelings and emotions?*

3   *Is there an ideal period of time a diary should cover?*

4   *Should the diary include everything that happens, or be selective? If it should select, in what way?*

5   *Should the emphasis be on thoughts or events, or is this less important than the way the diary is written?*

6   *Diaries are intended to contain factual narrative rather than fiction. Does this mean they are written in a different tone or register from a work of fiction? If so, what are the differences?*

7   *Diaries are not necessarily written to be read by other people. Does this more personal approach affect the way they are written and how readable they may be?*

a)   DD,

Judy slept over, and you know what? – we called Jeffrey! We didn't say who we were or anything. Judy did most of it. Well, first I dialed but his father answered so I hung up fast. I couldn't believe it – his father! Then Judy said she'd do it. She made this really sexy voice by holding her nose and said, "Hello, Jeffrey, this is Marilyn, remember me?" and then she started laughing so hard she couldn't talk so I grabbed the phone and slammed it down. Then she called again!!!!!!!!!!!!!! This time she said, "Is this Jeffrey Dobkin speaking?" and when he said yes, we both shouted, "Jeffrey, we want your body." We had total and complete hysterics. We couldn't stop laughing. After that she called back one more time but his father answered and said to stop calling. I wondered if he was going to trace the call and find out it was us!!!!!!!!!!!

I'm so glad Judy is my best friend.

from Teenage Romance *by Delia Ephron*

b)   *Tuesday, January 16* – Camp 68. Height 9760. T. $-23.5°$. The worst has happened, or nearly the worst. We marched well in the morning and covered $7\frac{1}{2}$ miles. Noon sight showed us in Lat. 89° 42′ S., and we started off in high spirits in the afternoon, feeling that to-morrow would see us at our destination. About the second hour of the march Bowers' sharp eyes detected what he thought was a cairn; he was uneasy about it, but argued that it must be a sastrugus. Half an hour later he detected a black speck ahead. Soon we knew that this could not be a natural snow feature. We marched on, found that it was a black flag tied to a sledge bearer; near by the remains of a camp; sledge tracks and ski tracks going and coming and the clear trace of dogs' paws – many dogs. This told us the whole story. The Norwegians have forestalled us and are first at the Pole. It is a terrible disappointment, and I am very sorry for my loyal companions. Many thoughts come and much discussion have we had. To-morrow we must march on to the Pole and then hasten home with all the speed we can compass. All the day-dreams must go; it will be a wearisome return.

from Scott's Last Expedition – The Personal Journals of Captain R. F. Scott, C.V.O., R.N.

c)   AUGUST 1940

Sunday, August 18th

I said, half seriously, that my motive for coming to stay was to see one of these great air battles. I got my wish: after several warnings in the morning, we eventually had a grandstand view of a fight from the terrace of the house. It was after lunch and we were sitting on the terrace looking towards Thorney Island with the Portsmouth balloons just visible over the trees to our right. Suddenly we heard the sound of A.A. fire and saw puffs of white smoke as the shells burst over Portsmouth. Then to our left, from the direction of Chichester and Tangmere, came the roar of engines and the noise of machine-gun fire. "There they are," exclaimed Moyra, and shading our eyes to escape the glare of this August day we saw not far in front of us about twenty machines engaged in a fight. Soon a German bomber came hurtling down with smoke pouring from its tail and we lost sight of it behind the trees. A parachute opened and sank gracefully down through the whirling fighters and bombers. Out of the mêlée came a dive-bomber, hovered like a bird of prey and then sped steeply down on Thorney Island. There were vast explosions as another and then another followed, and my attention was diverted from the fight as clouds of smoke rose from the burning hangars of Thorney aerodrome. In all, the battle only lasted about two minutes and then moved away seawards, with at least two German aircraft left smouldering on the ground.

from The Fringes of Power – Downing Street Diaries *by John Colville*

EXERCISE 5.9

Keep a diary for the next week. Aim to write in a way which will make the diary interesting for someone else to read as well as yourself.

EXERCISE 5.10

Now take the questions on page 146 and apply them to these extracts from autobiographies.

a) Bert was in charge of all the drivers and was responsible to the foreman. For some reason he liked me and one day when a driver was fired, he shouted across from the T23 in which he sat, 'Come here, Dublin! Can you drive?' I couldn't. 'Well, you might as well learn by starting on one of these. Hop up and I'll show you.' On a road gang this was like an initiation into manhood. The machines were gargantuan. Driving one was like sitting on top of the world. On the move between sites you felt you were part of a convoy of tanks. They did about forty-five miles per hour when they got their speed up and even unloaded they must have weighed around forty ton. They were unstoppable and quite frightening. Doing the edging work on steep sliproads, they would sometimes topple over. It was because of the brute power of the T23s that ordinary cars were barred from the motorway while it was under construction. I found out why one day as I came slowly around a corner and there in the middle of the main haul road was a little Renault 4 with a local corporation site inspector sitting in the front seat. I slammed on the brakes, but there wasn't sufficient air in them. Normally on a haul road that wouldn't have mattered, you would simply have let the machine drift to a halt. I waved madly at the driver to get out of the way. In slow motion I saw the front of the little car disappear between my gigantic wheels. I heard the crunch beneath me. I was screaming at the man to get out. I was sure I had killed him. The T23 ground to a halt. The front wheel had crushed his engine flat. The car had gone under the T23 itself. I backed off and jumped down. There inside the car sat the man, trapped in his driving seat, his face the colour of cold ash. It was him that got the sack, not me. He shouldn't have been there, and the report on my vehicle showed that it was the brakes which were faulty, not my driving. The other drivers thought the whole incident hilarious. After the accident, they would constantly get on their radios and broadcast mock warnings that all traffic should beware because Dublin was within a two-mile radius.

from Is That It? *by Bob Geldof*

b) A clean-up operation of a quite different kind brought considerable changes in my daily walk to school: the crackdown on the cigarette smugglers who stood at street corners or in doorways whispering offers of "Dutch merchandise." The cheapest legally acquired cigarette cost at least two and a half pfennigs, a feeble object, half as firmly packed as a Juno or an Eckstein, which cost three and a third pfennigs each. The Dutch product was pale gold, firm, a third plumper than an Eckstein, and was offered at one to one and a half pfennigs each. Naturally that was very enticing at a time when Brüning's penny-pinching policies were still having their effect, so my brother Alois would sometimes give me money to buy him illegal Dutch cigarettes. Between Rosen-Strasse and Perlen-Graben, the focal point being somewhere around Landsberg-Strasse, with scattered outposts extending as far as the Eulen-Garten (the smugglers' headquarters that were located close to our school on Heinrich-Strasse), I had to be both wary and alert, had to appear both confidence-inspiring and eager to buy. Apparently I succeeded, and that early training or schooling (which, as I say, cannot be acquired in school but only on the way to school), that education, if you prefer, turned out to be very useful to me in later years in many of the black markets of Europe. (I have dealt elsewhere with the fact that a dedicated feeling for legality does not form part of the Cologne attitude to life.)

So the Dutch merchandise would reach home safe and sound, and I would receive my cut in the form of fragrant cigarettes. On one occasion, I must admit, I was diddled: the neat little package with its Dutch revenue stamp contained, instead of twenty-five cigarettes, approximately twenty-five grams of ... potato peelings! To this day I fail to understand *why* potato peelings, and not, say, sawdust or woodshavings. They had been carefully weighed, evenly distributed, packed in foil. (Contempt for wax seals, lead seals, bailiff's seals, revenue stamps – also a kind of seal – ingrained in me by my mother, turned out, after the war, to be my undoing when I broke the seal of an electricity meter and tampered with it – unfortunately in a detectable manner. Bailiff's seals were promptly removed as a matter of course.) I was enjoined by my brother in future to check the goods and was still puzzling over *how*, since everything had to be done so quickly, when suddenly the entire smuggling operation was smashed. Certain streets were virtually under siege, and I recall at least one armoured vehicle. Police and customs agents – in the end without shooting – cleared out the whole smugglers' nest: there were rumours of millions of confiscated cigarettes and numerous arrests.

from What's to Become of the Boy? *by Heinrich Böll*

EXERCISE 5.11

 Look back over your life so far and write a short chapter which could form part of your autobiography.

SHORT STORIES

A check list

As you read a short story ask yourself these questions – they may help you to decide how good the short story is, and *why*:

1 How short is the story actually? Would it have been better longer – or even shorter?

2 Are there any characters in the story who are unnecessary – who would have been better left out because they distract your attention from the central figure?

3 Are there any actions or events in the story which are unnecessary – which would have been better left out because they distract your attention from the main actions or events?

4 Look again at the beginning. How far advanced is the situation before the story opens? Is there too much background information given? Could it have been left out/condensed/introduced incidentally as the story progressed?

5 Does the story line (plot) follow a common formula? Such a formula might be:

  (i) the eternal triangle (two men both in love with the same woman, or two women both in love with the same man).

  (ii) a mistaken identity, or a mistake about someone's status (e.g. the poor beggar boy turning out to be a rich prince).

  (iii) a love story (e.g. boy meets girl, boy loses girl, boy gets girl back).

  (iv) a mystery (e.g. a whodunnit).

6 Look again at the ending. Is there a 'twist' in it? If so, does it seem artificial or natural?
Does a short story need a 'twist' at the end?

7 Does the story follow Edgar Allen Poe's prescription for a short story: i.e., it should work out a single idea; make a single point; close with a single 'punch'; convey a single effect; the opening paragraph (and even sentence) should strike the keynote – and no diversion should be allowed?

8 Did you enjoy the story – and if so was it because of, or despite, the points considered above?

The short story that follows is set in South Africa.

The waste land

The moment that the bus moved on he knew he was in danger, for by the lights of it he saw the figures of the young men waiting under the tree. That was the thing feared by all, to be waited for by the young men. It was a thing he had talked about, now he was to see it for himself.

It was too late to run after the bus; it went down the dark street like an island of safety in a sea of perils. Though he had known of his danger for only a second, his mouth was already dry, his heart was pounding in his breast, something inside him was crying out in protest against the coming event.

His wages were in his purse, he could feel them weighing heavily against his thigh. This was what they wanted from him. Nothing counted against that. His wife could be made a widow, his children made fatherless, nothing counted against that. Mercy was the unknown word.

While he stood there irresolute he heard the young men walking towards him, not only from the side where he had seen them, but from the other also. They did not speak, their intention was unspeakable. The sound of their feet came on the wind to him. The place was well chosen, for behind him was the high wall of the convent, and the barred door that would not open before the man was dead. On the other side of the road was the waste land, full of wire and iron and the bodies of old cars. It was his only hope and he moved towards it; as he did so he knew from the whistle that the young men were there also.

His fear was great and instant, and the smell of it went from his body to his nostrils. At that moment one of them spoke giving directions. So trapped was he that he was filled suddenly with strength and anger, and he ran towards the waste land swinging his heavy stick. In the darkness a form loomed up at him, and he swung the stick at it and heard it give a cry of pain. Then he plunged blindly into the wilderness of wire and iron and the bodies of old cars.

Something caught him by the leg, and he brought his stick crashing down on it, but it was no man, only some knife-edged piece of iron. He was sobbing and out of breath, but he pushed on into the waste, while behind him they pushed on also, knocking against the old iron bodies and kicking against tins and buckets. He fell into some grotesque shape of wire; it was barbed and tore at his clothes and flesh. Then it held him, so that it seemed to him that death must be near, and having no other hope he cried out, 'Help me, help me!' in what should have been a great voice but was gasping and voiceless. He tore at the wire, and it tore at him too, ripping his face and his hands.

Then suddenly he was free. He saw the bus returning and cried out in the great voiceless voice, 'Help me, help me!' Against the light of it he could plainly see the form of one of the young men. Death was near him, and for the moment he was filled with a sense of the injustice of life, that could end thus for one who had always been hardworking and law-abiding. He lifted his heavy stick and brought it down on the head of his pursuer, so that the man crumpled to the ground, moaning and groaning as though the world had been unjust to him also.

Then he turned and started to run again, but ran first into the side of an old lorry that sent him reeling. He lay there for a moment expecting the blow that would end him, but even then his wits came back to him, and he turned over twice and was under the lorry. His very entrails seemed to be coming into his mouth, and his lips could taste sweat and blood. His heart was like a wild thing in his breast, and seemed to lift his whole body each time that it beat. He tried to calm it down, thinking it might be heard, and tried to control the noise of his gasping breath, but he could not do either of these things.

Then suddenly against the dark sky he saw two of the young men. He thought they must hear him; but they themselves were gasping like drowned men, and their speech came in fits and starts . . .

Then some more of the young men came up, gasping and cursing the man who had got away.

'Freddy,' said one, 'your father's got away.'

But there was no reply.

'Where's Freddy?' one asked.

One said, 'Quiet!' Then he called in a loud voice, 'Freddy'.

But still there was no reply.

'Let's go,' he said.

They moved off slowly and carefully, then one of them stopped.

'We are saved,' he said. 'Here is the man.'

He knelt down on the ground and then fell to cursing.

'There's no money here,' he said.

One of them lit a match, and in the small light of it the man under the lorry saw him fall back.

'It's Freddy,' one said, 'He's dead.'

Then the one who had said 'Quiet' spoke again.

'Lift him up,' he said. 'Put him under the lorry.'

The man under the lorry heard them struggling with the body of the dead young man, and he turned once, twice, deeper into his hiding place. The young men lifted the body and swung it under the lorry so that it touched him. Then he heard them moving away, not speaking, slowly and quietly, making an occasional sound against some obstruction in the waste land.

A short story by Alan Paton

EXERCISE 5.12

1 *Now look back at 'Short stories: a check list' (page 149) and discuss the effectiveness of this particular example.*

2 *Complete any two of the following:*

(i) *A record was still playing softly somewhere in another room. Her arm hung over the side of the bed.*

(ii) *Once upon a time and in a land very different from our own . . .*

(iii) *'Is this the first time?' I asked.*

(iv) *As aliens go this one was almost human in appearance – apart from the transparent green skin, of course.*

(v) *I have a confession to make.*

(vi) *'I shouldn't worry if I were you,' she said reassuringly.*

(vii) *The beach was empty that morning. Even the wind was somewhere else.*

(viii) *She turned slowly towards me. That was when I saw her eyes.*

(ix) We would have got there in the end I suppose, we really would.

(x) You may find this hard to believe . . .

DRAMA AND DIALOGUE

Read the three examples of dialogue which follow. The first is from a phone-in programme on the radio, the second is dialogue from a play, and the third is dialogue from a novel.

a) The place: LBC radio studio where Tony Foale is the guest expert in an hour-long motorcycle problem/diagnosis phone-in.

DJ – And next on LBC, Thomas from Bethnal Green. Hallo Thomas.

Thomas – Oh hello. Er good afternoon. I'm phoning er. Can I speak to the man please?

DJ and Tony Foale – Yes.

Thomas – I'm phoning on behalf of my brother yer know. He asked me to give you a ring because he's not on the phone himself. He's got a bike – a 650 Norton 1952 and he's had it a long time and he does a lot of mileage on it. It's a lovely bike, a powerful bike like, you know. And he lent it to this guy some weeks back, about seven or eight weeks ago and when he got it back, the back wheel spins the wrong way round.

DJ and Tony Foale – Pardon!

Tony Foale – Sorry, could you repeat that. The back wheel . . .?

Thomas – The back wheel spins the wrong way around. It goes backwards instead of ordinary-like, you know, instead of frontwards like, y'know.

Tony Foale – You mean when you get on it and start it up . . .

Thomas – When he gets on it and selects first gear to take it off, to go with it, it spins round backwards.

Tony Foale – And the bike actually goes backwards?

Thomas – Yes. And he took it to the shop and everything and they put new bearings and everything into it for him and it still wouldn't do nothing. So he got a new wheel and the same thing happened.

Tony Foale (with certainty) –Yes, I'm not surprised at that.

Thomas – See. I don't know what's happened to it like, y'know except it's the gears maybe but er . . .

Tony Foale – They haven't put the handlebars on the wrong end have they?

Thomas – No . . . no the bloke says the gears are perfect and everything and he can't find nothing wrong with the bike. Cos it's a powerful bike, it's a lovely bike, y'know. He wouldn't give it away for the world like. He wouldn't do away with it, y'know.

DJ – It sounds like a very special bike Tom.

Thomas – It is a special bike yes.

Tony Foale – Other than putting the seat and the handlebars on the wrong end . . .

Thomas – Yes.

Tony Foale – All I can suggest is um, er . . . (*long pause*). No I can't suggest anything really . . . (*Much studio laughter between Foale and DJ*) No, it's not unheard of for two-strokes to run backwards and then everything from there on in goes backwards as well but it's fairly unusual for a four-stroke . . .

Thomas – It is unusual yes. He tried everything. He took it to a shop in Stratford y'see – a bicycle shop in Stratford. And they done it for him and it's still going the wrong way round, y'know what I mean?

DJ – Well, I'd hang onto it Tom.

Tony Foale – Yes, I think that's going to increase in value quite a bit.

Thomas – Oh he will hold onto it. Cos it's like new. He used to keep it lovely y'know what I mean and he didn't disregard it or anything y'know. It's like his bed like, y'know. He looked after it really well y'see but he's really upset over it. . . .

(*The sound of a police car siren can be heard in the background.*)

DJ – Thomas?

Thomas – Yes.

DJ – I think they've arrived for you.

Thomas – Pardon?

(Much laughter in the studio as they neatly cut Thomas off and get on with the next caller.)

from Superbike

b)   [*The street door is broken open and heavy steps are heard in the hall, punctuated with shouts of "Old the light 'ere, 'Put 'em up', etc. An Auxiliary opens the door of the room and enters, revolver in one hand and electric torch in the other. His uniform is black, and he wears a black beret.*]

The Auxiliary	'Oo's 'ere?
Seumas	[*as if he didn't know*] Who – who's that?
The Auxiliary	[*peremptorily*] 'Oo's 'ere?
Seumas	Only two men, mister; me an' me mate in t'other bed.
The Auxiliary	Why didn't you open the door?
Seumas	We didn't hear you knockin', sir.
The Auxiliary	You must be a little awd of 'earing, ay?
Seumas	I had rheumatic fever a few years ago, an' ever since I do be a – I do be a little deaf sometimes.
The Auxiliary	[*to Davoren*] 'Ow is it you're not in bed?
Davoren	I was in bed; when I heard the knockin' I got up to open the door.
The Auxiliary	*You're* a koind blowke, you are. Deloighted, like, to have a visit from us, ay? Ah? [*Threatening to strike him*] Why down't you answer?
Davoren	Yes, sir.

The Auxiliary	What's your name?
Davoren	Davoren, Dan Davoren, sir.
The Auxiliary	You're not an Irishman, are you?
Davoren	I-I-I was born in Ireland.
The Auxiliary	Ow, you were, were you; Irish han' proud of it, ay? [*To Seumas*] What's *your* name?
Seumas	Seuma . . . Oh no; Jimmie Shields, sir.
The Auxiliary	Ow, you're a selt [*he means a Celt*], one of the seltic race that speaks a lingo of its ahn, and that's going to overthrow the British Empire – I don't think! 'Ere, where's your gun?
Seumas	I never had a gun in me hand in me life.
The Auxiliary	Now; you wouldn't know what a gun is if you sawr one, I suppowse. [*Displaying his revolver in a careless way*] 'Ere, what's that?
Seumas	Oh, be careful, please, be careful.
The Auxiliary	Why, what 'ave I got to be careful abaht?
Seumas	The gun: it-it-it might go off.
The Auxiliary	An' what prawse if it did; it can easily be relowded. Any ammunition 'ere? What's in that press?

> *from* The Shadow of a Gunman *by Sean O'Casey*

c) 'Miss Storey,' said Sister, 'you are behaving most foolishly, and I must ask you to leave at once.'

'I won't leave,' I said. 'You'd much better take me straight there, I don't want to be compelled to wander round upsetting the whole of your hospital until I find my baby.'

'Now then, now then,' said Sister, 'this is neither the time nor the place for hysterical talk like that. We must all be grateful that your child is . . .'

'Grateful,' I said. 'I am grateful, I admire your hospital, I admire your work, I am devoted to the National Health Service. Now I want to see my baby.'

> *from* The Millstone *by Margaret Drabble*

Some points to consider ▬▬▬▬▬▬▬▬▬▬▬▬▬▬

A *Variety* can help. For instance, don't just write '". . ." he *said*'. Consider the appropriate alternatives, such as *asked/replied/called/shouted/ whispered/muttered.*

B *Examples* can help to liven up a dialogue; for example, when a character says 'I remember ...' and goes on to give an interesting anecdote or memory.

C *Conflict* is perhaps even more effective in this respect. In plays some of the most interesting moments come when there is conflict between characters (physical or verbal) – or sometimes even within a person's mind ('Should I, shouldn't I?', as in Hamlet's famous line, 'To be or not to be?').

D Dialogue can be used to *indicate*:
- *country of origin* – in passage **b)** which countries are the characters from and how do you know?
- *occupation* – a soldier might use military terms, a doctor medical terms, etc.
- *social class* – in passage **c)** the indications are, from the way Miss Storey speaks, that she is middle class: there is no dialect and she speaks in long but coherent articulate sentences.

E *Dialect: a warning.* This can be difficult to keep up. Remember that dialect may have a different grammar (e.g. *I be* for 'I am') as well as a different vocabulary (e.g. *thee* for 'you'). If you write in dialect some examiners may wonder whether you can actually write 'correct' English. Sometimes dialect is more effective if used as a *contrast* to standard English.

F Dialogue should be *appropriate* to the *type* of character and the *situation* he or she is in. One lorry driver is not likely to say to another, 'I say, look here, old chap!'

G Dialogue can help make each character a *distinct individual*; for instance, when a character is given a particular way of talking or a characteristic catch phrase.

H The way people *actually* talk (see passage **(a)** and also Chapter 1, 'The English Language – What's Yours Called?') is not always a good guide – in particular the way they 'um' and 'er' and 'well' and repeat themselves. Don't bore your reader to death. Keep the language appropriate – but keep it moving!

I Unless you are writing a play, remember the *punctuation rules* for dialogue – that is, new speaker, new line.

EXERCISE 5.13

Write on one of the following:

(i) *A conversation between two different kinds of people*

(ii) *'What are you doing here? . . .'*

(iii) *A difficult conversation I have taken part in*

To help you consider how drama works, whether on stage or television, consider the following points. Then use them to analyse the play extracts which come later.

A A play must catch the audience's attention. It must be built around a situation which is interesting in itself and with the potential to develop further.

B A play must maintain the audience's interest. It helps if there is some tension between what the audience can see happening on stage and what they sense is likely to happen later.

C There should be a character, or characters, the audience can identify with – in other words a hero or heroine, or an anti-hero or anti-heroine.

D Conflict is essential, whether between people or between ideas and values.

E Plays, because they are intended to be presented before an audience rather than read privately, tend to present bold, emphatic, simplified characters and ideas. They often deal in extremes, with larger than life events and characters.

F Drama is able to utilise both sound and visual effects, such as songs, noises off stage, costume and scenery. While this can sometimes be simply decorative a good play will mingle verbal, visual and sound effects to produce a cumulative dramatic effect.

The opening lines of Brecht's play, *Mother Courage*

Spring, 1624. In Dalarna, the Swedish commander Oxenstierna is recruiting for the campaign in Poland. The canteen woman Anna Fierling, commonly known as Mother Courage, loses a son.

Highway outside a Town

A sergeant and a recruiting officer stand shivering.

The Recruiting Officer   How the hell can you line up a company in a place like this? You know what I keep thinking about, Sergeant? Suicide. I'm supposed to knock four platoons together by the twelfth – four platoons the Chief's asking for! And they're so friendly round here, I'm scared to go to sleep at night. Suppose I do get my hands on some character and squint at him so I don't notice he's pigeon-chested and has varicose veins. I get him drunk and relaxed, he signs on the dotted line. I pay for the drinks, he steps outside for a minute, I have a hunch I should follow him to the door, and am I right? Away he's gone like a louse from a scratch. You can't take a man's word any more, Sergeant. There's no loyalty left in the world, no trust, no faith, no sense of honour. I'm losing my confidence in mankind, Sergeant.

The Sergeant   What they could do with round here is a good war. What else can you expect with peace running wild all over the place? You know what the trouble with peace is? No organization. And when do you get organization? In a war. Peace is one big waste of equipment. Anything goes, no one gives a damn. See the way they eat? Cheese on pumpernickel, bacon on the cheese? Disgusting! How many horses have they got in this town? How many young men? Nobody knows! They haven't bothered to count 'em! That's peace for you! I've been in places where they haven't had a war for seventy years and you know what? The people haven't even been given names! They don't know who they are! It takes a war to fix that. In a war, everyone registers, everyone's name's on a list. Their shoes are stacked, their corn's in the bag, you count it all up – cattle, men, *et cetera* – and you take it away! That's the story: no organization, no war!

A scene midway through David Cregon's play, *Transcending*

Mother, *dressed in ordinary clothes, is putting breakfast on the table.* **Father** *marches in buttoning up his jacket, having obviously just got dressed.*

Father	[*as he enters*] The dirty old man wants my daughter to sleep with him.
Mother	No!
Father	Why not?
Mother	[*horrified*] Why not?
Father	He's got good taste. You want to sleep with my daughter? Certainly. Fifty pounds.
Mother	[*horrified*] What?
Father	A hundred pounds.
Mother	How dare you!
Father	Money doesn't enter into it, Mr. Lemster. You should respect the finer feelings of sex and take it for free.
Mother	He shouldn't take it at all!
Father	Ah! Caught you in an attitude! Now stick to it and we might get somewhere. Where's breakfast?

The closing lines of Brendan Behan's play, *The Hostage*

Rio Rita *covers the body with one of the nun's cloaks.* **Teresa** *kneels by the body. The others bare their heads.*

Teresa	Leslie, my love. A thousand blessings go with you.
Pat	Don't cry. Teresa. It's no one's fault. Nobody meant to kill him.
Teresa	But he's dead.
Pat	So is the boy in Belfast Jail.

Teresa It wasn't the Belfast Jail or the Six Counties that was troubling you, but your lost youth and your crippled leg. He died in a strange land, and at home he had no one. I'll never forget you, Leslie, till the end of time.

She rises and everyone turns away from the body. A ghostly green light glows on the body as **Leslie Williams** *slowly gets up and sings:*

The bells of hell,
Go ting-a-ling-a-ling,
For you but not for me,
Oh death, where is thy sting-a-ling-a-ling?
Or grave thy victory?
If you meet the undertaker,
Or the young man from the Pru,
Get a pint with what's left over,
Now I'll say good-bye to you.

The stage brightens, and everyone turns and comes down towards the audience, singing:

The bells of hell,
Go ting-a-ling-a-ling,
For you but not for him,
Oh death, where is thy sting-a-ling-a-ling?
Or grave thy victory.

Curtain

EXERCISE 5.14

 Working in groups of four or five, discuss and agree an idea for a play, the main characters and the basic storyline. Then, individually, draft your own version of the opening two scenes of the play, with the dramatic situation unfolding and characters appearing and developing.

 If you have time, rejoin your original group. Then choose the draft which seems most effective as the starting point. Develop it for presentation to the rest of the class, taking ideas from the group as a whole. Keeping a tape or cassette record of progress may help this process.

PERSONAL LETTERS

Despite advertisements extolling the cheapness of telephone calls, letter writing remains a particularly cost-effective way of keeping in touch with friends who live some distance away. To help you consider what makes an interesting and effective letter, read the questions and the letters which follow and discuss what you can learn from them.

1   How far are the personal feelings and emotions of the writer conveyed?

2   Is the language lively and vivid – appealing to your imagination?

3   Is the tone personal and informal, speaking directly to you as if in conversation?

4   Do the letters focus on everyday life or on new or unusual experiences?

5   What atmosphere, if any, does each convey?

6   Is there a diary-like quality to any of the letters?

7   How is each letter organised? Does it deal with events in the order they happened, move rapidly from one impression or experience to another, develop and express a feeling or emotion, keep returning to an underlying question or theme, make a series of comparisons, or adopt some other approach?

8   How fluent and readable is each letter and what causes this?

9   Is the emphasis on people, places, ideas or the writer?

10   From each letter, what can you deduce about the relationship with the person written to, how long it is since they have seen each other, and the reason for writing?

"I know that it is hopeless (Caroline wrote), but I don't mind. If that sounds pathetic, I don't mean it to be. What I've had and have (?) with you has been like a windfall. I've always told myself that – even when it seemed that it could go on forever. I've always held onto that thread which takes me back to what I was.

Except that you've changed me a lot, I think. In some ways I'm unhappier: I know this can't work out, I know how much I want it to. [. . .]

I've re-written this letter scores of times in my head and it's always been more fluent and less mournful than this. I just don't have the energy to do this as well as I would like to. You see, my love, I have to leave you.

I can't believe I'm really saying this. After meeting Marion I know that she is your fundamental commitment whatever else you might say or do. I suppose I can't bear the realisation that I will never be that. I didn't feel jealous of her, though; just tired. Suddenly tired, as if I'd been hit by vertigo. I wish you were here. Isn't it funny how it all comes down to clichés? "I wish you were here," "I'll never stop loving you," "I can't go on like this." The English teacher at school used to chastise us if we used clichés.

Good luck darling: God bless, and thank you.

Love,

Caroline"

from Love and Glory *by Melvyn Bragg*

December 14th

Dear Daddy-Long-Legs,

I dreamed the funniest dream last night. I thought I went into a book store and the clerk brought me a new book named *The Life and Letters of Judy Abbott*. I could see it perfectly plainly – red cloth binding with a picture of the John Grier Home on the cover, and my portrait for a frontispiece with, 'Very truly yours, Judy Abbott', written below. But just as I was turning to the end to read the inscription on my tombstone, I woke up. It was very annoying! I almost found out whom I'm going to marry and when I'm going to die.

Don't you think it would be interesting if you really could read the story of your life – written perfectly truthfully by an omniscient author? And suppose you could only read it on this condition: that you would never forget it, but would have to go through life knowing ahead of time exactly how everything you did would turn out, and foreseeing to the exact hour the time when you would die. How many people do you suppose would have the courage to read it then? Or how many could suppress their curiosity sufficiently to escape from reading it, even at the price of having to live without hope and without surprises?

Life is monotonous enough at best; you have to eat and sleep about so often. But imagine how deadly monotonous it would be if nothing unexpected could happen between meals. Mercy! Daddy, there's a blot, but I'm on the third page and I can't begin a new sheet.

I'm going on with biology again this year – very interesting subject; we're studying the alimentary system at present. You should see how sweet a cross-section of the duodenum of a cat is under the microscope.

Also we've arrived at philosophy – interesting but evanescent. I prefer biology where you can pin the subject under discussion to a board. There's another! And another! This pen is weeping copiously. Please excuse its tears.

Do you believe in free will? I do – unreservedly. I don't agree at all with the philosophers who think that every action is the absolutely inevitable and automatic resultant of an aggregation of remote causes. That's the most immoral doctrine I ever heard – nobody would be to blame for anything. If a man believed in fatalism, he would naturally just sit down and say, 'The Lord's will be done', and continue to sit until he fell over dead.

I believe absolutely in my own free will and my own power to accomplish – and that is the belief that moves mountains. You watch me become a great author! I have four chapters of my new book finished and five more drafted.

This is a very abstruse letter – does your head ache, Daddy? I think we'll stop now and make some fudge. I'm sorry I can't send you a piece; it will be unusually good, for we're going to make it with real cream and three butter balls.

Yours affectionately,
Judy

from Daddy-Long-Legs by Jean Webster

14 East 95th St
New York City

September 18, 1952

Frankie, guess who came while you were away on vacation? SAM PEPYS! Please thank whoever mailed him for me, he came a week ago, stepped out of four pages of some tabloid, three honest navy-blue volumes of him: I read the tabloid over lunch and started Sam after dinner.

He says to tell you he's overJOYED to be here, he was previously owned by a slob who never even bothered to cut the pages. I'm wrecking them, it's the thinnest India paper I ever saw. We call it 'onion skin' over here and it's a good name for it. But heavier paper would have taken up six or seven volumes so I'm grateful for the India. I only have three book-shelves and very few books left to throw out.

I houseclean my books every spring and throw out those I'm never going to read again like I throw out clothes I'm never going to wear again. It shocks everybody. My friends are peculiar about books. They read all the best sellers, they get through them as fast as possible, I think they skip a lot. And they NEVER read anything a second time so they don't remember a word of it a year later. But they are profoundly shocked to see me drop a book in the wastebasket or give it away. The way they look at it, you buy a book, you read it, you put it on the shelf, you never open it again for the rest of your life but YOU DON'T THROW IT OUT! NOT IF IT HAS A HARD COVER ON IT! Why not? I personally can't think of anything less sacrosanct than a bad book or even a mediocre book.

Trust you and Nora had a fine holiday. Mine was spent in Central Park, I had a month's vacation from joey, my dear little dentist, he went on his honeymoon. I financed the honeymoon. Did I tell you he told me last spring I had to have all my teeth capped or all my teeth out? I decided to have them capped as I have got used to having teeth. But the cost is simply astronomical. So Elizabeth will have to ascend the throne without me, teeth are all I'm going to see crowned for the next couple of years.

I do NOT intend to stop buying books, however, you have to have SOME-thing. Will you see if you can find me Shaw's dramatic criticism please? and also his music criticism? I think there are several volumes, just send whatever you can find, now listen, Frankie, it's going to be a long cold winter and I baby-sit in the evenings AND I NEED READING MATTER, NOW DON'T START SITTING AROUND, GO FIND ME SOME BOOKS.

hh

from 84 Charing Cross Road by Helene Hanff

How far would you say each of these letters was written to a particular individual and how far was each written for a wider audience? What clues are there about this?

N.B. The kind of personal letters you may be asked to write as part of your course work or in your examination may differ in two ways from the letters you are used to writing. Sometimes you may be asked to write taking on a new role or personality, which requires a degree of imagination and sympathy so as to put yourself in someone else's position. Usually, you will also be expected to write in a reasonably organised way and perhaps a shade more formally than your normal letter writing style. It is worth trying to balance the best of your own personal style with what you have learnt about effective writing on the course so far.

EXERCISE 5.15

1   *One of your friends has left the area and is now living with relatives in Canada. Write a letter bringing him or her up to date with what has been going on since he or she left.*

2   *In the film* Letter to Brezhnev, *a girl meets and falls in love with a Russian sailor visiting Liverpool. However, he has to return to Russia with his ship. Afraid that she will never see him again she writes to the Soviet President asking his help. Put yourself in her situation and write the letter.*

3   *Write a letter to a foreign penfriend describing a particularly memorable experience you have had recently.*

4   *After a particularly heated argument you leave home vowing never to return again. Three weeks later and two hundred miles away you have been unable to find a full-time job or to afford a place of your own to stay – and you have flu. While you value your independence, you are beginning to feel that it might have been a mistake to leave quite so dramatically. Write a letter home.*

EXERCISE 5.16

Letters to the Editor

Letters to the editor of a newspaper are a special kind of personal letter. Collect a selection of such letters, from a range of local and national newspapers. Working as part of a group of from five to seven students, try to decide what makes an effective letter and draw up a checklist of key characteristics. (Look at the sections on 'Persuasive Writing' beginning on pages 103 and this page. These might provide a useful starting point.)

Then working individually, find a letter with which you disagree particularly strongly. Using the techniques you have identified, write an effective reply. Compare the different letters produced within your group and decide which you would publish if you were a newspaper editor. Where there are letters that you wouldn't publish, discuss how you could amend them to make them more effective and thus worth publishing.

It might be interesting to send the letter you consider most effective to the relevant newspaper and see if the editor does publish it.

N.B. *To check how to set out a formal handwritten letter, see the example on page 186.*

PERSUASIVE WRITING: ARGUING A CASE

'Well look this isn't an argument!'
'Yes it is!'
'No it isn't, it's just contradiction!'
'No it isn't!'
'It is!'
'It is not!'
'Look you just contradicted me!'
'I did not!'
'Oh you did!'
'No, no, no!'
'You did just then!'
'Nonsense!'
'Oh look, this is futile!'
'No it isn't!'
'I came here for a good argument!'
'No you didn't, you came here for an argument.'
'Well an argument isn't just contradiction.'
'It can be!'
'No it can't. An argument is a connected series of statements intended to establish a proposition.'
'No it isn't!'
'Yes it is! It's not just contradiction!'
'Look, if I argue with you I must take up a contrary position.'
'Yes, but that's not just saying. "No it isn't".'
'Yes it is!'
'No it isn't! Argument is an intellectual process. Contradiction is just the automatic gainsaying of any statement the other person makes.'

'No it isn't.'
'Yes it is!"   -
'Not at all.'
'Now, look!'

from Monty Python's Previous Record

This passage shows one of the problems of argumentative writing. In everyday life an argument can be simply two people shouting at one another. When presenting an argument in writing, however, more is needed. For instance:

A   A collection of *facts* which, taken together, support your case is obviously useful. So, do some appropriate background research first. (It helps to indicate where the 'facts' came from, to indicate how reliable, up to date they are etc.)

B   *Opinions* can also prove useful – but the opinions should be those of relevant *experts*. For example, if it is a medical question the views of doctors, and particularly of specialists, would be most appropriate. The views of famous figures (film stars, singers, politicians, etc.) may have a certain glamour, but are no more reliable on areas they are not expert in than the views of anyone else.

C   *Anticipating* opposing views, by listing them and explaining their weaknesses, may sometimes seem difficult. If you can do it, however, it makes your case much stronger. In a sense it suggests that *you* are an expert, familiar with *all* the arguments.

D   *Variety of wording* helps avoid monotony. Suppose you were writing about marriage. One of the facts your research came up with was that last year in England and Wales there were 356,000 marriages and 146,415 divorces. This indicates to you that many people are now dissatisfied with marriage (though to 'prove' this you would also need to know how many of those who divorced, later married again, i.e. were they dissatisfied with marriage or just their current husband or wife?) and that it is no longer stable (more figures, showing how long marriages last, and how this compared with the past, would also be needed to 'prove' anything).

You could word this point in a variety of ways – for example:

- The fact that marriage is no longer the stable institution it once was is now clear from official figures – 146,415 divorces last year alone!

- Official figures on divorce (146,415 last year) suggest that marriage is no longer a permanent institution.

- The fact that marriage is no longer seen as permanent is indicated by official figures: there were 146,415 divorces last year alone.

Complex figures can also be simplified. Our figures above could be restated as: for every two marriages in England and Wales there is now one divorce.

You may still find it difficult to put this advice into practice, so let us look at a few examples.

a) It can be said to its credit that advertising has cultivated appreciation of better living. It has encouraged the desire for a varied and sensible diet. It has introduced appliances and tools which make home and office and factory work less tedious and tiring. It has stimulated our ambition by awakening desires which we can only satisfy by increasing our earning power.

This extract lists points in favour of advertising – but offers no proof. For example, we have to take the writer's word for it that advertising has encouraged sensible diets – he gives no facts or figures to support his claim. This, then, is a *weak* argument.

(Can you think of any examples to support the points made about advertising, and thus help to produce a stronger argument?)

b) Now most people take in most of their information from pictures. The washing instructions on your shirt or skirt and the markings on the knobs and levers in your car are symbols not words. And you don't have to read any more to find the right 'loo': an outline figure tells you which door.

This is a *stronger* argument because the main point, that most people take most of their information from pictures, is supported by *three* separate examples. Even so, is the argument conclusive? If pictures are so important why doesn't the writer use some himself?

c) TV – renting or buying

The advantages of renting a television set are that the cost for the first year is less than the outlay would be for buying, and you do not have to pay for repairs or service calls. However, the set never becomes yours, so you cannot sell it, and you have to go on paying rent for as long as you keep the set.

All in all, if you have the money, it is cheaper to buy. Even if you buy on credit, by the end of the third year you will have paid for the set and for the next few years the set will have a resale value, too. Your only expenses would be on repairs.

from Which?

Here we see a more *balanced* argument. The writer gives some of the advantages of renting, and then some of the advantages of buying, before reaching the conclusion ('it is cheaper to buy'). This weighing up of the arguments gives us more confidence, because the writer seems to be giving an unbiased and objective account, based on the facts. However, even here, some specific figures, showing the costs of renting as against buying a typical TV, would have helped.

As *Which?* magazine does regular tests on consumer goods, like TVs, we can also count their advice as *expert* opinion. So, even though they don't give specific figures, we can take it that they know what they are talking about.

d)   The 'essay' as traditionally conceived has many disadvantages, especially in the form in which it usually appears in an examination paper. It is very unfair to expect candidates in their predicament as silent prisoners, without access to information sources, notes, dictionaries etc., and with only an hour in which to write, to produce lively, relevant, and intelligently robust comment on generalised topics such as 'The Right to Strike', 'Living in Suburbs', '"A House is a Machine for Living in" (*Le Corbusier*)'.

from Notes on the Setting and Marking of Examinations in English
for National Certificates and Diplomas in Business Studies

e)   Girls are still encouraged to think that their only aim in life is to get married, have children, and then vaguely live happily ever after. There are two things wrong with this life: first, it has become a sentence of solitary confinement with hard labour, leaving the prisoner with no role to play on release; second, society has such a low opinion of it that it doesn't seem worth doing at all.

from His and Hers *by Joy Groombridge*

These two passages are interesting because the two writers, although concerned with quite different topics, have both used the same technique. They have both used the same *emotive* word to appeal to the reader's emotions. Passage **d)** describes candidates as 'prisoners'; passage **e)** describes housewives as 'prisoners'. The idea, in both cases, is to produce sympathy for the people described by poetic exaggeration of their plight.

This is permissible in persuasive writing, and is a very powerful technique. But it should be used *as well as, and not instead of*, hard evidence (facts, figures, etc.).

f)   'Well, we have ideas too,' the lieutenant was saying. 'No more money for saying prayers, no more money for building places to say prayers in. We'll give people food instead, teach them to read, give them books. We'll see they don't suffer.'

'But if they want to suffer . . .?'

'A man may want to rape a woman. Are we to allow it because he wants to? Suffering is wrong.'

from The Power and the Glory *by Graham Greene*

Sometimes it is worth taking an argument to its logical conclusions to see if it is still sound. In this passage, the argument of the second speaker is that people should be allowed to do what they want (even if what they want is to suffer). This may seem fair enough. However, this argument can be taken too far, as the first speaker's reply shows. Some things a person may want to do cannot be allowed, such as rape. So, allowing something *just* because a person wants to do it, may not be a good argument.

When considering an argument, therefore, it is sometimes worth asking *what if?*, and taking the argument one stage further.

EXERCISE 5.17

Several extracts follow. For each one, consider the following:

1 *What is the main point the writer is making?*

2 *Does the writer make it at the beginning or end of the writing?*

3 *What evidence does the writer give? (How many examples and illustrations, what facts or figures? How much is fact and how much opinion?)*

4 *Does the writer take different points of view into account? (If so, which?)*

5 *Does the writer use emotive words to argue his or her case? (If so, which?)*

6 *How varied is the writing? Is it interesting to read?*

7 *What kind of reader do you think it is aimed at? Give reasons for your choice.*

8 *Finally – do you think the writer has made out a good case?*

a)
ALCOHOL
Public Enemy No. 1?

For young people in the 18–24 age group, here are two stark facts:

1. Of all chemical substances, alcohol presents the major threat.

2. Alcohol-related injury in accidents is the commonest cause of death.

It has not always been so. During the 1940s, a survey in England showed that over half the population did not drink alcohol at all, or drank less than once a week. And, amazingly in view of later developments, the authors of the survey observed: 'as might be expected, the largest percentage of men who never take alcohol is found in the youngest age group (16–24)'.

Now, the 18–24s are the heaviest drinkers in the entire population.

Starting early

Especially during the past twenty years, the number of young people drinking alcohol has sharply increased. They begin drinking at a younger age, their drinking is more frequent, and the amount they drink has increased.

There was a time when most people drank on special occasions only. Gradually, new styles of drinking have crept in. Wine is drunk with meals, and the habit of weekend drinking has now extended into the week. Drinking is no longer excluded, as it used to be, from home, work and places of leisure. It is now a part of everyday life.

Problems

Alcohol brings with it two main kinds of problem:

1. Acute problems that are the result of a single drinking episode, such as drunkenness and accidents.

2. Chronic problems that are the result of long-term heavy drinking, such as cirrhosis of the liver.

Drunkenness offences in boys under 18 rose by 296% between 1964 and 1980, and by 265% in boys under 21. The rise among young girls is even more dramatic: 583% in girls under 18 and 633% in the under 21 group.

These huge increases have, of course, coincided with the rise of hooliganism and violence on the football terraces, culminating in the dreadful events in the Heyssel Stadium in Belgium in 1985.

All the evidence shows that, for many young people, the first step into trouble is drinking. Of 200 consecutive admissions to a Scottish Young Offenders Institution, 63% admitted being drunk when they committed their offence. A probation service reports that, of the last 416 reports prepared, 210 (50.5%) involved cases where drink was related to the defendant's offence.

Accidental death

An analysis of road accidents has shown that for young drivers a sharp acceleration in accident proneness occurs at much lower blood alcohol levels than with other drivers. With young drivers, accident proneness begins to accelerate when the blood level is 15 milligrams. At 50 mg it trebles, and it quintuples at 80 mg.

The risks for girls are worse than for boys, because their blood alcohol level builds up more quickly. They become accident prone that much sooner, and the rate of acceleration is greater.

Alcohol contributes to the death of over 1,000 16–24 year olds each year. This takes into account accidents caused by young people with raised blood alcohol levels, including road accidents, home accidents, fire fatalities and drownings, plus sober young people who are killed by drunken drivers. The total figure is the equivalent of three Jumbo air crashes.

Apart from accidents, the other bad news is that the earlier you start drinking, the more likely you are to become a heavy drinker as the years go by. That carries with it the possibility of alcohol-related disease . . . and, of course, the risk of becoming an alcoholic.

High and dry

The real danger of alcohol is that it is a socially acceptable drug, and in some circles it is considered almost antisocial not to drink. Young people might well ask, 'Why don't older people set us a better example?'

Many young people who do not wish to drink find themselves isolated by the pressures of social habit. For them, though, there is new hope in the movement towards the formation of High and Dry Societies, promoted by the National Union of Students. A number of these societies already exist on college campuses, and there is the prospect that they may also be extended to fifth and sixth form activities in schools.

The formation of these societies is one result of the 'Stay Dry' campaign, which was launched about a year ago by Martin Shaw, the actor. At the launching he set the tone of the campaign by saying, 'It's such a natural thing to be alcohol free.'

from Over 16

b)   The Hidden Curriculum

As the children grow older, their ideas of sex roles begin to be influenced by factors beyond the home, the most significant of these influences being the school, the peer group and the media. Since the only factor controlled by teachers is the school, every effort should be made to present a non-discriminatory environment. Many small but significant procedures can affect the development of a non-discriminatory environment and teachers need to give consideration to the following points:

— Do boys and girls line up separately to move about the school?

— Are boys more often given the unattractive, heavy, messy jobs requiring little or no sensitivity?

— Are girls more often given the unexciting, monotonous tasks requiring more patience and concentration?

— Do boys always carry the milk crates?

— Are girls ever encouraged to operate the school's audio-visual or other mechanical aids?

— In thematic work, do girls always investigate clothes, food, home life, etc., while the boys research into weapons, building techniques, space travel, engines, etc.?

— Are boys and girls segregated in classroom and assembly seating arrangements?

— Do you invite workpeople in non-traditional jobs to talk to pupils (e.g. female bus driver, male nurse, etc.)?

— Are girls and boys treated the same? Care should be taken not to react like the teacher who told a boy who could not knock a nail in to "get on with it", but responded to a girl in the same situation by taking the wood, nail and hammer and doing it for her!

— Do the boys usually cover areas of work such as traffic surveys while the girls always do the work connected with plants, trees and pets?

— Are out-of-school activities organised so that the football club and the recorder club meet at the same time, thus becoming mutually exclusive?

This list can be extended, and the staff of every school needs to co-operatively consider its policies in these areas and assess the influence they are having upon pupils in perpetuating sex stereotypes.

Positive action

Primary school teachers need to take positive action to eradicate sex stereotyping in their schools, not only by altering certain structural features in the schools and by giving greater consideration to the impact of the "hidden curriculum", but also by introducing positive de-stereotyping elements into their teaching. This can be done in a number of ways, including:

— Using non-sexist reading books and materials.

— Incorporating reversals of traditional sex roles into drama activities.

— Writing mathematics work-cards which have men going shopping, etc., and women using bank accounts, driving cars, etc.

— Making girls and women the central characters in writing adventure stories.

— Focusing on the achievements of women in projects (e.g. women astronauts, sailors, mountaineers, explorers, scientists).

— Including non-traditional roles and types of employment in projects or thematic work. Many themes cover topics such as "People at Work", "People Who Help Us", "At Home", "The Family", "Our Town", and they provide a wide range of opportunities for developing the children's awareness of the opportunities for moving outside the barriers of traditional sex roles.

Interviewing people in non-traditional roles, or inviting them into a school to talk to the children.

from Do You Provide Equal Education Opportunities?
by the Equal Opportunities Commission

c) Do not go gentle into that good night

Do not go gentle into that good night,
Old age should burn and rave at close of day;
Rage, rage against the dying of the light.

Though wise men at their end know dark is right,
Because their words had forked no lightning they
Do not go gentle into that good night.

Good men, the last wave by, crying how bright
Their frail deeds might have danced in a green bay,
Rage, rage against the dying of the light.

Wild men who caught and sang the sun in flight,
And learn, too late, they grieved it on its way,
Do not go gentle into that good night.

Grave men, near death, who see with blinding sight
Blind eyes could blaze like meteors and be gay,
Rage, rage against the dying of the light.

And you, my father, there on the sad height,
Curse, bless, me now with your fierce tears, I pray.
Do not go gentle into that good night.
Rage, rage against the dying of the light.

Dylan Thomas

d) The Case for Nuclear Power in Britain

FOUR FALLACIES bedevil Britain's energy strategy and, with it, our chances of economic improvement in the long-term. The French, who are not making our mistakes, must be amazed at our ill-preparedness, as they get ready to sell us electricity in future at prices they will command.

The first fallacy stems from a fool's paradise: because oil and gas are plentiful today, they will always continue to be readily available. But the peak in North Sea production which we are enjoying today is a narrow one. Output will be well down at the end of the century and Britain will be forced to import energy on a large scale from world markets in which oil, gas and coal prices will be shooting up rapidly.

The second fallacy comes from an oversight: from the assumption that the only problem is the depletion of North Sea supplies and that this can be overcome by improved methods of extraction. But even if Britain aims at only a modest rate of economic growth, e.g. 2 per cent a year – in order to create more jobs and better social services – then by the year 2020 our economic turnover will be twice as large as today's. To support such a growth, our energy consumption will have practically to double by then. Even with an exceptional increase in energy conservation measures, some 50 per cent more energy will still be required.

Third is the fallacy of the quick fix: that, by a last-minute improvisation we could always overcome an energy crisis, as and when it arrives, and so do not need a long-range policy. Unfortunately, some decades are needed to build a great new energy industry of a size to match our future needs. The French have a clear appreciation of the long time-scales involved for this and are building now for the future, while we are not.

Finally, the fallacy of redundancy: that the development of other energy sources can make nuclear power unnecessary. To satisfy a 50 per cent increase in energy demand by 2020, in the face of the North Sea decline, we will need to double our total supplies from sources other than the North Sea. Even this assumes a spectacularly successful energy conservation policy; otherwise, even more energy will be needed. There is no practical possibility of output from our coal, hydroelectric and renewable energy resources being able to expand to anything like the level necessary to meet this requirement.

Crippling prices

The only way, then, to avoid major economic decline will be to meet most of the short-fall with nuclear power, which could necessitate a four-fold expansion over the next 30 years. The alternatives to this are either to suffer an almost zero rate of economic growth and the social consequences of stagnation, or to attempt to import large amounts of energy, bought on world markets at crippling prices, using mainly borrowed money so long as our credit holds out. Each nuclear power reactor that we might build could, over a 30-year life, save the importation of about 100 million tons of coal or, equivalently, about 500 million barrels of oil. Careful estimates have forecast that, even by the year 2000, the world price will be about $50 a barrel (in 1980 dollars).

As well as economic self-interest, there is another reason why Britain should develop more nuclear power. The Third-World countries will continue to seek fuel and power to build up their economies and support their growing populations. It will surely be right for advanced industrial countries, such as Britain, to limit their demands for the world's remaining fossil fuel resources in order to leave as much as possible for the Third World. The advanced countries ought thus to turn almost exclusively to nuclear power (and, to the limited extent that is practicable, also to renewable energy sources) for expanding their own future electrical supplies.

The radiation hazard associated with nuclear power is, of course, a matter of great public concern at the present time. In considering this, the effects of the normal operations of the nuclear power industry (including inevitable minor incidents, such as those at Sellafield) have to be distinguished from those of big accidents such as that at Chernobyl.

Normal operations and minor incidents undoubtedly expose the general public to radiation, but the amounts involved are too small to produce detectable medical effects. This is because they are much smaller than the natural radiations to which we are all exposed from the soil, the air, building materials, even from naturally radioactive atoms belonging to our own bodies, radiations to which mankind has always been exposed, but which have never been shown to have any medical effects.

Tragic casualties

The accident at Chernobyl is of course a very different matter, with its real and tragic casualties. Although the number of its victims is not large, by comparison with those killed in other kinds of energy disaster (e.g. 15,000 at the Gujarat Dam in India in 1979; 4,000 in the London smog of 1952; 500 in a Mexican gas explosion in 1984; 180 due to an accident to a fuel-tanker vehicle in Spain in 1978; 144, mostly children, at the Aberfan coal tip in 1966; 123 on an overturned North Sea rig in 1980), nevertheless there must clearly not be another Chernobyl.

Can this be guaranteed? In a very specific sense, yes, at least in countries outside the USSR, for only the USSR has the particular kind of reactor that went wrong at Chernobyl and only this kind of power reactor contains the combination of both water and graphite that was responsible for the nuclear instability which turned the operators' mistakes into a major accident. Britain rejected the water-graphite type of reactor system, on safety grounds because of this instability, in 1947.

More generally, a strong assurance if not an absolute guarantee should be possible, because the Chernobyl accident began with a most extraordinary sequence of wrong actions by the operators, which included running the reactor for several hours leading up to the accident with the emergency cooling system switched off. In general, power reactors are protected against such actions by various safety circuits and operational controls. The USSR intends to alter its Chernobyl type of reactors to prevent such operators' mistakes and there is every reason to think that an extremely high standard of safety will now be reached.

The confidence in this is shown by the fact that, despite Chernobyl, the USSR intends to continue giving priority to its nuclear power programme. In the words of the head of the USSR delegation to the recent Vienna Conference on Chernobyl, without nuclear energy the USSR would be unable to master the next stage in the development of its society; a view which could be applied equally to Britain and to many other countries, in the face of the coming gap between energy demand and fossil fuel supplies.

Without sufficient energy the world will become a cold, hungry, economically depressed place, with countries competing ruthlessly for dwindling supplies of fossil fuel. These risks are surely worse than those of well-controlled nuclear power.

Sir Alan Cottrell, FRS, is Master of Jesus College, Cambridge, and a member of the UK Atomic Energy Authority.

from The Observer

EXERCISE 5.18

Fact and opinion

These words are often used when describing argumentative or persuasive writing. What do they all mean, and can you give an example of each?

fact	rationalise	reasoned
opinion	substantiate	radical
evidence	satirise	reactionary
conjecture	ironic	exaggerated
interpretation	emotive	objective
generalisation	biased	evaluate

EXERCISE 5.19

Here are some sample topics for research, persuasive writing, group discussion or formal debate.

'Fashion is a form of ugliness so intolerable that we have to alter it every six months.' (Oscar Wilde)

Is marriage an outdated institution?

The conservation policy Britain needs in the 1990s.

The education I should want for my child.

The role of the police in modern Britain.

The case for voluntary euthanasia.

'Government of the rich by the rich for the rich.' Do you think this is an apt description of Britain today?

Love is . . .

Can hijacking and terrorism ever be justified?

Making cities better places to live in.

How far is our health in our own hands?

An action plan to combat football hooliganism.

What's wrong with sport in Britain today?

Youth unemployment.

Is man the weaker sex?

6 *Writing to Order*

– 'CLOSED' WRITING

Is this the train to Birmingham?

Where can I find out more about holiday jobs?

How old is her brother?

When will you be getting some more in stock?

What happens if there's a power failure?

Who should I ask for when I get there?

Unless you're a vegetable there'll be times in your life when you want to find things out – even if it's just the time of the next bus or train. A lot of things you can just ask. You can ask a complete stranger what the time is and have a good chance of an accurate reply. But some things even your friends or family might not know. Look at the questions above. How would you find the answers?

Now look at the passage below. Does it help you answer the second question?

> **WHERE TO START   First of all decide where you want to work: near home; elsewhere in the UK or abroad; if you want to make money (be paid); or simply earn your keep (voluntary). Then consider *what* it is you want to do – though it's not always a matter of choice these days.**
>
> **WORKING AT HOME**
>
> **For a paid job near home:** Look in your local newspaper and on the boards of newsagents. Go to your local Jobcentre. Be brave and fearless, knock on doors, go round local shops and restaurants, ring or write to companies located nearby. Use contacts. Seasonal work at the Post Office, etc., should be applied for early, there'll be a queue. If you live in the country try 'picking' jobs.
>
> **For a paid job in the UK:** Look in national newspapers like *The Times, The Sunday Times, The Observer* and *The Guardian*, the 'Personal' column and 'Situations Vacant'. Look in specialist magazines if you have a specialist interest. As a last resort try commercial agencies. Don't forget holiday camps: Butlins, Pontins and others.

176

An excellent all-round directory to buy is:
SUMMER JOBS, BRITAIN (£4.95),
Vacation Work Publications, 9 Park End Street,
Oxford OX1 1HJ (Telephone 0865 241978).

For a voluntary job in the UK: If you want to stay close to home ring
your local Council Offices and ask whether any help is required with play
schemes, the disabled, Senior Citizens etc. They should be able to direct
you to relevant voluntary agencies.

Interesting organisations are:
CONSERVATION VOLUNTEERS,
36 St. Marys Street, Wallingford, Oxfordshire
(Telephone 0491 39766).
If 16 + (18 if from abroad) you can help keep the countryside in good shape.
COUNCIL FOR BRITISH ARCHAEOLOGY
112 Kennington Road, London SE1 6RE
(Telephone 01-582 0494).
Use voluntary help on sites.

WORKING ABROAD

For paid work abroad: See the world and tuck a second language
under your belt! But there are pitfalls: visas, jabs, work permits etc., vary
from country to country. If you get into trouble always make the British
Consul your first point of call. If you have a full British Passport it's
normally easy to work in the EEC, but check for all relevant information
from the relevant Embassy before you go.

Good basic guides to jobs are:
WORKING HOLIDAYS (£4.00)
Central Bureau for Educational Visits and Exchanges
Seymour Mews House, Seymour Mews, London W1H 9PE
(Telephone 01-486 5101).
*Offices in Edinburgh and Belfast too. Hotel work, grape picking etc. Govern-
ment publication.*

WORKING ABROAD – THE DAILY TELEGRAPH GUIDE (£6.95)
*Published by Kogan Page: aimed at those wanting permanent work but full
of ideas.*

SUMMER JOBS ABROAD (£4.95)
Practical with endless listing. Work in 14 European countries.

SUMMER EMPLOYMENT DIRECTORY OF THE UNITED STATES (£6.95)
*Full of ideas plus info on applying and entry regulations. (These two publi-
cations also from Vacation Work Publications, above.)*

Organisations to contact are:
AU PAIRS UNIVERSAL
The Dell, 180 Toms Lane, King's Langley, Herts WD4 8NX
(Telephone 09277 66524).
Looking after children 'en famille'; light domestic duties.

CONCORDIA
8 Brunswick Place, Hove, East Sussex BN3 1ET
(Telephone 0273 772086)
Agricultural work. Also volunteer service. Send S.A.E. Registration Fee.

CANVAS HOLIDAYS LTD
Courier Dept. A, Bull Plain, Hertford,
Herts SG14 1DY (Telephone 0992 59933).
Looking after camping sites and customers in Europe.

from Cheque In, *published by the Midland Bank*

As the question was a fairly specialised one it needed fairly specialised information to answer it. For anything else a little bit out of the ordinary you'll probably need to check with a specialist book, guide or instruction manual. Asking people probably won't be enough.

However, specialised information can be a problem. In particular, it can be difficult to follow – especially if it uses specialist terms. How much sense does the following piece of information make, for instance (for you, anyway)?

The behaviour of 'absorption currents' in polyethylene was observed to be similar to that of polypropylene (Das Gupta and Joyner 1976) except that the onset of a quasi-steadystate conduction current in the charging transients occurred at earlier times and lower temperature and field in the present case. As in the case of polypropylene, the 'absorption current' in polyethylene also showed a marked increase with temperature above 273 K in comparison with its behaviour below it. The observed magnitude of n in the low-temperature range of 113–273 K and the absence of any thickness dependence and any significant electrode material effect will rule out tunnelling (Wintle 1973), electrode polarisation (Macdonald 1971) and charge-injection-forming trapped space charge (Walden 1972, Wintle 1974) as possible mechanisms for 'absorption currents'.

from Journal of Physics D: *Applied Physics*

EXERCISE 6.1

Now, have a look at the passages that follow. How well do they put over their information? To help you here are a few questions to consider:

1 *Is there one big block of information, or is it broken up into separate points? (And which is easier to follow?)*

2 *Is the language easy to follow (e.g. not too many technical terms, or complicated sentences)?*

3   *Is there any variety of presentation, to attract and keep your interest (e.g. pictures, different sizes and types of print, numbered points etc.)?*

4   *Are some points more memorable because of the way they're expressed? (Which, and why?)*

5   *Does the passage seem to be written to you? How personal is the approach?*

6   *How relevant is the information to you? Could you go out and use it – now/next week/next year/ever?*

7   *So far as you can judge, how accurate is the information?*

8   *After reading each piece do you feel like following the advice? (If so, why? If not, why not?)*

9   *Does it help to be told why you should do something – or do you just prefer to be told what to do?*

10   *Does the amount of information you're given affect your response?*

11   *If things need to be done in a definite order, is the order clearly stated and easy to follow?*

12   *If some points are more important than others, is it clear what the order of importance is?*

a)   **Car in deep water** If your car plunges into a lake or river it will probably take up to eight minutes to sink, provided that all the windows are tightly closed and it has no structural damage. If you are trapped inside use these eight minutes to effect an escape. Try to wind down the nearest window and climb out through it. If you can't do this, climb into the section of the car farthest away from the engine because this will be the last bit to go under water, and try to break the nearest window by hitting it with a sharp pointed object like a pen or penknife.

Even if you are in the car when it reaches the bottom you still have time to get out because even though it fills with water there is practically always a little pocket of air left inside to enable you to breathe. Wait until the water has stopped pouring in, and the pressure inside the car is the same as that outside, then you will be able to open a door or window. Take a deep breath from the pocket of air and either swim or float to

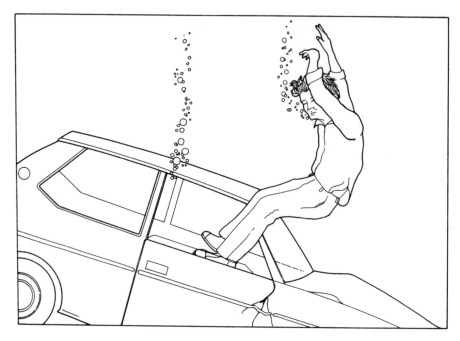

To escape from a car under water, wait until the water pressure equalises. It will then be possible to open a door or window and float out.

the surface. It is important *not* to panic or struggle, but to conserve as much energy, oxygen and common sense as you possibly can in order to survive.

from Help *by Jennifer Curry*

b) The Debt Trap
. . . Living away from home
CHRIS BURGESS

Dramatic increases in the numbers of young people falling into debt now place 18–25 year olds as the largest group of problem debtors in the UK in the eighties. Easy credit, high unemployment and the pressures of advertising are some of the reasons why the debt trap is so easy to fall into – especially when you're living away from home.

The Real Cost of Living

Living at home with a supportive family shields young people from any real knowledge of the cost of accommodation and all that goes with it; gas, electricity, and perhaps general rates, water rates, and even maintenance and decorating.

These costs, plus food and clothing, are basic to living. They must be the first items on your budget, so that you are left with a clear view of what remains for other spending, including leisure.

Indeed, these basic costs should be thoroughly investigated when leaving home to start a new course or a job. It is far better to find out what you cannot afford than blindly falling into the debt trap. But if you do get into debt, don't panic.

The Professionals

Professional help is available, and the sooner young debtors get it, the better. The longer you wait, the more difficult it becomes to sort out the mess.

Worry about debt is a very private thing, and it can become almost impossible to talk about it to friends and relatives – so talk to the professionals. The professionals are Debt Counsellors and a 'phone call to your local Citizens Advice Bureau is all that is needed to make an appointment to talk to one of them.

People who take their troubles to a Debt Counsellor experience an immediate and immense relief from the mere fact that the worry is shared with someone who is totally impartial, and who will deal with their case in absolute confidence. There are many ways of dealing with debt, and the Counsellor will know which way is most appropriate for each individual case. Furthermore, the people and companies who are owed the money welcome the intervention of the Debt Counsellor, because they know that they are likely to receive far more of what they are owed, with far less bother than if they have to pressurize the debtor without the benefit of a 'go-between'.

The Debt Counsellor's job is to help both sides. Sensible arrangements can be made to pay the debts gradually over a long period. The Counsellor can help the debtor with the budgeting of living expenses – and the relief from worry often helps the debtor to improve his or her ability to cope with life.

Start Right

The very worst start you can make when you're trying to stand on your own two feet away from home is by getting into debt. Remember that a debt is not just the money you borrow, but also the interest. Debts grow, even when you don't borrow any more.

If you do borrow for some good reason, make sure that the repayments – including the interest – are within your means. If at all possible, shop around for the lowest interest rates.

Warning! Do not borrow to cover a temporary shortfall in income due to illness or for some other reason. Cut back temporarily on your outgoings, until your income comes back to normal.

Do not become responsible for other people's debts. This can happen if you sign as a guarantor for money being borrowed by someone you know. If they cannot keep up the agreed payments then the responsibility for the debt will become yours. Your own debts are bad enough, but someone else's are even worse.

But if, despite all this advice, you do get into a position where you cannot see a way of clearing debts, then go to a Debt Counsellor.

Your nearest Citizens Advice Bureau is listed in the 'phone book.

from Over 16

c) Use the following checklist. Keep it by you and tick off the energy-saving action points as you go around the home.

YOUR ENERGY-SAVING CHECKLIST

Some of the tips may require you to spend a little time, effort or money, but you will benefit immediately. The savings on your fuel bills can cancel out any initial outlay in a remarkably short time. But you don't have to **spend** a lot of money to save energy. You'll be surprised how much you can **save** by following these tips.

COOKING

plan your menu well in advance to make full use of the oven for a whole meal

use a portable toaster if you have one; it is far more economical than the electric cooker grill

do not drown the vegetables – it wastes energy and ruins the flavour; a little water in the pan is all that is usually necessary

cut vegetables small; they cook more quickly and evenly that way

cover pans with lids to cut down cooking time

simmer pans on smallest cooker rings where you have a choice

use correct size pan for the ring you are using; pans should completely cover the heat

adjust the size of flame or use a dual ring to fit the pan you are using

limit the number of burners or rings in use

use a steamer or metal colander over a saucepan and cook one lot of vegetables over another

use segmented or divided pans to cook more than one vegetable on the same ring

invest in a pressure cooker for complete meals (it can save fuel, time and nutrients)

do not overfill kettles; boil *just* the amount you need – but be sure to cover the element in electric kettles

turn off kettles as soon as they have boiled; don't allow to steam away unattended

let warm food cool before putting it into the fridge

defrost fridges and food freezers regularly; when ice builds up you waste energy

keep your food freezer at least three-quarters full

do not open the fridge or food freezer door unnecessarily

de-scale kettles regularly for quick, efficient boiling time (but follow instructions on thorough rinsing)

keep the cooker clean and have appliances regularly serviced

from Energy Saving in the Home, *published by the Department of Energy*

d)

> FELL WALKERS!
> READ THIS
> and live a little longer . . .
>
> British mountains can be killers if proper care is not taken. The following notes cover the **minimum** precautions if you want to avoid getting hurt or lost, and so inconveniencing or endangering others as well as yourselves.
>
> CLOTHING. This should be colourful, warm, windproof and water-proof. Wear boots with nails or moulded rubber soles, not shoes, plimsolls, or gum-boots. Take a woollen cap and spare jersey; it is always colder on the tops.
>
> FOOD. **In addition** to the usual sandwiches take chocolate, dates, mint cake or similar sweet things which restore energy quickly. If you don't need them yourself, someone else may.
>
> EQUIPMENT. This **must** include map, compass, and at least one reliable watch in the party. A whistle and torch (a series of six blasts or flashes repeated at minute intervals signal an emergency) and, in winter conditions, an ice-axe and survival bag are **essential**.
>
> COMPANY. Don't go alone, and make sure party leaders are experienced. Take special care of the youngest and weakest in dangerous places.

e) **Q.** What and who is **No Body's Perfect?**

A. No Body's Perfect is a safe way to exercise to music, catering for all levels of fitness. Angela and Caroline run and teach these classes to a high professional standard. Both have had thorough training in the fitness, nutrition and beauty field.

Q. What is Bodyworkshop?

A. If you are at a loss where to start exercising try Bodyworkshop, which concentrates on exercising problem areas such as thighs, bottoms and abdominals.

Q. What are Aerobics?

A. Aerobics are one of the few forms of exercise which provides total or 'holistic' fitness – stamina, strength and flexibility. We offer Aerobics at two levels – Low impact for Beginners and Intermediate for those who want to work that bit harder!

Q. But I already play squash/tennis/badminton etc. – why should I come to **No Body's Perfect?**

A. In our classes we aim to work the whole body whereas when playing most other sports, only certain parts of the body are used. Therefore our classes can work all the muscles you have not been using.

Q. Why should I exercise at all?

A. Exercise is now being recognised as therapy for many 20th-century 'ills'.

It helps to reduce tension and stress. It delivers more oxygen to the brain and tissues, which in turn banishes feelings of sluggishness and improves circulation, and generally gives an all-over improvement of body shape. In fact, whatever your lifestyle, a relaxed body and mind helps you to cope with day to day chores and problems more easily.

Q. Why exercise to music?

A. According to the experts, music and exercise go together to form 'selective perception', in other words you get so engrossed in the words and rhythm that you achieve a better workout.

Q. If I have any problem areas, can you help?

A. Yes. Please feel free to ask.

f)

By now you should have a fair idea about what makes a good piece of informative writing. Try these exercises and see:

EXERCISE 6.2

1 *Prepare a clear and interesting guide to:*

   (i) a sport or indoor game which is not well known (as a test, when it is written your friends who do not know the sport or game should be able to play it just by following the guide).

   (ii) a useful skill, hobby or activity.

2 *Prepare a short instruction manual on how to work a machine you are familiar with (a motorbike, sewing machine, lawn mower, washing machine, typewriter, etc.) for someone who knows nothing about one.*

3 *Prepare a short handbook of useful information for someone who is leaving home for the first time to live on his or her own. (Assume he or she will not be leaving the area he or she was living in.)*

4 *Prepare a school or college handbook, introducing the place to new students.*

BUSINESS LETTERS

Confusion is sometimes caused by the fact that there are different rules for typewritten business letters and for handwritten letters. Read the two examples which follow, and see how many differences you can find and list:

a) Handwritten letter

55 Blantyre Crescent,
Derwent Road,
Coventry
CV5 8PT

1st March 1987

The Bookings Manager,
Wyvern Castle,
Wyvern,
Warwickshire
CV34 6HW

Dear Sir,

As part of a college project we have to organise a visit to a place of historical interest. Could you please send me details of the admission fee to the castle, when you are open and possible reductions for a party of twenty students.

We also wondered if you had any special events, shows or entertainments for young people.

If possible we would hope to come on a Wednesday, early in May. Please let me know if this would be possible.

Yours faithfully,

D. Livingstone

D. LIVINGSTONE

b) Typed (business) letter

WYVERN CASTLE
Wyvern   Warwickshire   CV34 6HW
Telephone: 0409 5757

Our Ref:

Your Ref:

5th March 1987

Mr. D. Livingstone
55 Blantyre Crescent
Derwent Road
Coventry
CV5 8PT

Dear Mr. Livingstone

Thank you for your letter of 1st March enquiring about a possible visit
to the Castle by a group of college students early in May. We are open
every day from 10 a.m. to 5 p.m. during the months of March to October
and would be very happy to welcome you.

The admission fee is £3 but our party discount rate allows one free
admission for every ten persons in a group. Thus if you are able to
bring a party of twenty students we can allow two of those students
free admission.

We do have a number of special events planned and I am enclosing
our programme for May and June.

I hope this information will prove useful and look forward to your visit
in May. Please do not hesitate to contact me if you require further
details.

Yours sincerely

Anne McGregor
Bookings Manager
enc.

N.B. The use of 'Yours sincerely' and 'Yours faithfully' does not depend on whether the letter is handwritten or typed. The rule remains, whether for typed or handwritten letters:

Dear Sir/Madam – Yours faithfully

Dear Mr/Ms/Miss/Mrs – Yours sincerely

EXERCISE 6.3

For discussion: business letters

1   *Why do you write the name and address of the person you are writing to on the letter as well as the envelope?*

2   *What is a 'Ref:' and why is one given?*

3   *What advantages have a fully blocked style[1] and open punctuation[2] for typists – and thus for their employers?*

4   *Has the traditional handwritten layout any advantages?*

   [1] *A fully blocked style begins each line at the same distance from the edge of the paper. Whereas a traditional handwritten letter would signal the start of a new paragraph by indenting, a business letter simply leaves a gap and then starts a new line.*

   [2] *Open punctuation means punctuating only the body of the letter (the part between 'Dear _____' and 'Yours _____'), i.e. only the part where punctuation is absolutely necessary to make the meaning clear. No punctuation is used in the address, for instance.*

We are now going to consider two sorts of letter that you might need to write: one for a job application, the other to complain.

Job applications

There are three possible ways in which you might apply for a job:

A   You may send a brief letter requesting an application form and then simply fill in the form and return it (with no further letter needed).

B   Alternatively you may, when returning the application form, be asked to send an accompanying letter giving more information – for instance, stating why you feel you are suited to the job. In that case, work out what qualities the employer is looking for (what qualifications, what experience, what interests), using the original job advertisement and any further information you have been sent.

Then, assuming you have most of the qualities looked for, write a short letter showing this (see 'Making words work harder for you', pages 190–1).

C   If no application form is provided, you will have to include all the relevant information in your letter. It is often easier to write a short covering letter, and then to enclose a separate list of your qualifications and experience. (This list can be photocopied if you are applying for many jobs, leaving you only a different covering letter to write for each new job.) An example follows. (**N.B.** Delete items marked * as appropriate.)

Your Address,
(Telephone Number)
Date (in full)

Name and
Position (of person dealing with applications)
Name and
Address of Firm applied to

Dear Mr*/Mrs*/Miss*/Ms*

   I should like to apply for the post of   , as advertised in the   of   (date).

   This job*/This post*/This kind of work*/Your Company* particularly interests me because   . Also, my qualifications and experience (a summary of which I have enclosed) seem very relevant.

   I hope you will be able to offer me an interview, so that I can provide any further information you may need.

Yours sincerely,
(Signature)
Name printed underneath

A summary to accompany the letter could look like the one that follows. (**N.B.** Headings in *italics* should appear as they are. Fill in the rest with your personal details.)

Full Name: *Qualifications and Experience*

1   *Personal Details:* (i) Full Name, (ii) Age, (iii) Sex, (iv) Marital Status.

2   *Education:* (i) Full-Time – Name and Address of Schools/Colleges + dates attended + subjects studied, (ii) Part-Time – (as above).

3   *Qualifications:* (indicating dates taken, types of exam, and grades),

    (i) GCSEs, GCEs, RSAs, + any other relevant certificates/ qualifications.

    (ii) Exams still to be taken.

4   *Previous Experience:*

    (i) Gained at school/college – where relevant to job.

    (ii) YTS Traineeship (if you have been a trainee).

    (iii) Any jobs done (inc. holidays or Saturdays) – position, employer, duties.

    (iii) Any relevant special interests.

5   *Other Material Relevant to Application:*
e.g. interested in nature of work, willingness to train, do day release, etc.

6   *Referees* (usually two):
Name and position at school/college/firm + address.

(You can also include copies of testimonials where relevant – although employers will usually take more notice of references, as these are given in confidence.)

These days competition for jobs can be tough. Hundreds of people may be applying for one job, with maybe only five or six of these being short-listed and invited for interview. To get an interview your letter of application, or application form, has to stand out from the rest. It needs to be:

● neat and well set out,

● carefully worded, and

● correctly spelt.

To avoid crossings out do a rough draft first, and then a good copy for sending off.

Making words work harder for you

When it's results we're after, we should forget about expressing ourselves, and concentrate on getting through to the other person ... shift the focus from 'What do I want to say?' to *'What results do I want?'*

Read this application that was sent to the personnel manager of a big company:

I am writing in reply to your advertisement for a secretary/ assistant to your Export Manager.

Your advertisement mentions good typing, and although I can type accurately at 60 wpm, I want a position where I do not have to type very much.

You also say that a knowledge of French would be an advantage. I do know some French, and would be very glad if the job you are offering would help me improve it.

I have always wanted to work for a company like yours, because I like all the social contacts you can make in a big organisation. In fact the kind of job I'd really like is a job dealing with people.

I've already booked up my holidays for this year, and the dates are . . .

The letter goes on like that. The personnel manager said wearily, 'The only thing left out is what she'd like for lunch!'

The writer of the letter did not get on the short list, although the job might have been just right for her. She could have asked about holidays and all the other things at an interview, which she would have been offered if she'd written:

I can type accurately at 60 wpm. But I am also good at dealing with people, so could bring other things to the job, as well as typing. I already know some French and would work hard at learning more in order to help your Export Manager.

It is saying the same thing – but in a very different way.

from Getting Through *by Godfrey Howard*

EXERCISE 6.4

Look through the 'Situations Vacant' columns of your local and regional newspapers, or visit your local Jobcentre. (If the week you are looking at doesn't produce anything relevant, try back copies in the local library.) Find two jobs you are interested in and could realistically apply for. For each write a letter of application. The letters should be different in content and emphasis to the extent that the two jobs are different.

Letters of complaint

HELP! offers some tips on letters of complaint: how to write, who to write to, and how to make your complaint more effective.

Some years ago, as complaints clerk at the world's biggest bookshop, I was astonished to find how diffident the British are when it comes to complaining. Americans whose orders had gone astray phoned from their hotels demanding to know what we were going to do about their missing books. British victims, in contrast, tended to write in apologetic vein: 'Last November I ordered some books for Christmas presents, but I am sorry to say that they have not arrived. It may be that they have gone astray in the post, but as it is now July I would appreciate it if you could check to see if they were duly despatched.'

Such a low-key approach is probably as effective as aggressiveness, and illustrates the first of the ten rules for writing letters of complaint.

(1) *Be polite.* Abuse may be satisfying, but is usually counterproductive. Recipients are likely to respond more seriously to a letter which shows the complainant as a reasonable person – and therefore someone who is the more dangerous. People organising a calm campaign of attrition are more formidable than those who operate by temperamental outbursts.

(2) *Be concise.* Strong points in an argument can be lost or swamped in too much detail. One-page letters are the best letters. A story told in chronological order is the best story.

(3) *Produce evidence.* You should always keep invoices or copies of letters sent to you by a firm or other organisation. Then if promises are not fulfilled, you can write enclosing a photocopy of the document. Keep copies of your own letters too.

(4) *Get the name right.* If you are phoning an organisation and are transferred from one office to another, always ask who you are speaking to. If you are writing, phone beforehand to establish who you should address the letter to. If you simply write to 'The Manager' you may find it impossible, later, to track down the person on whose desk it eventually arrived.

(5) *Take advice.* Epistles along the lines of: 'I want my money back straight away or I'll sue' do not impress professional troubleshooters. It is better to consult with an advice agency in order to establish what your rights are and the best procedure to pursue. The advice centre may help you draft your letter – or might even take up the case themselves.

(6) *Send copies.* An effective and economical way of adding weight to your complaint is to send a copy of your letter to other interested parties. So that if, for example, you are writing to a local shop manager, send a carbon or photocopy to the head office as well. Or, in the case of public utilities, despatch a duplicate to your MP.

(7) *Publicise.* Even more effective, if you are getting nowhere, is to send a copy to your local newspaper, or perhaps one of the consumer columns of a national paper. Or Esther Rantzen? In extreme cases – if the roof of your council flat has fallen in and no one has come round to repair it – write to the paper direct and suggest it might make a news story. Other sorts of direct action – such as setting fire to a defective car outside the garage you bought it from – are tempting but costly.

(8) *Persist.* Many bureaucracies operate on the principle that the machine has more stamina than the individual. Prove they are wrong. If they seem to be procrastinating, badger them to such an extent that it is easier for them to negotiate with you than ignore you.

(9) *Give up.* On the other hand there comes a point when a grievance becomes obsessive, and then it is probably better to forget the whole business. As Christopher Ward sensibly writes in his book *How to Complain*, 'Just walk away from petty disputes and get on with something more useful, more enjoyable.'

(10) *Where credit is due* ... Similarly, when you receive exceptionally good service or value for money, it is only fair you should recognize this by penning the occasional letter of appreciation.

from Radio Times

EXERCISE 6.5

1   *Test on business English and letters*

     (i)   *How many addresses would you put on a personal letter – and whereabouts on the page?*

     (ii)   *How many addresses would you put on a formal/business letter?*

     (iii)   *If you were handwriting a formal/business letter would you indent the addresses? i.e.*   _____

                                             _____

                                             _____

                                             _____

     (iv)   *Should you write the date in full on formal letters?*

     (v)   *If you start a letter 'Dear Sir' how should you finish it?*

     (vi)   *If you start a letter 'Dear Mrs', how should you finish it?*

     (vii)   *When writing a letter of application for a job what information would you include about yourself?*

                                                        (1 mark for each point)

     (viii)   *You have written off for a clock radio as a Christmas present. When the clock radio arrives it is the wrong colour and the figures do not light up. What points would you include in a letter of complaint?*

                                                        (1 mark for each point)

2   *Write a letter in answer to the following advertisement: 'Found in Baker Street, Newtown, on July 15, a leather purse/wallet* containing a sum of money. Will be returned on satisfactory identification. Write: Smith, 24 Butcher Street, Newtown.'*

                                                        (*delete as applicable)

3   *Write a letter to the local travel agent, explaining that you and your friend will have to cancel your booking for a week's holiday, and asking for the deposit to be returned.*

4   *Write a letter to a former headteacher/teacher/tutor asking if he or she will agree to act as a referee for you. Tell him or her about the post you have in mind.*

5   *Write a second letter of complaint to a mail order firm. The firm sent you a garment which was not only torn but also the wrong size. Because you liked the style and the colour you wrote to ask for a replacement rather than a refund. However, it is now four weeks later and you have still received no reply.*

6 *You are a student who has been asked to leave college by the Principal halfway through the academic year. Write a letter to the Principal appealing against the decision and giving reasons why you should be allowed to continue your course. Supply all the necessary details.*

(If you are at school assume you have been asked to leave by the head-teacher. Again, write an appropriate letter to him or her, appealing against the decision.)

BUSINESS REPORTS

If you want to see change in an organisation, whether a school or college or a major company, it may not be enough simply to express your feelings or organise a petition. You may, instead, be asked to make a case more formally. This should help your idea to be considered more seriously. A report is one common approach in this situation.

In addition, many people in business have to fill in *routine reports*, especially:

(i) a standard form to be completed – as in the case of accidents or equipment or stock control reports.

(ii) a summary, letter or memo, as for instance with end-of-week sales or progress reports.

A *special report*, which is usually longer, requires investigation or research and is a 'one-off'. The layout may look like this:

> To:
> From:
> Date:
> Report on..
> ....
> INTRODUCTION
> a) Terms of reference (who asked for the report, why, and on what area?)
> b) Procedure (how you found out the information)
> INFORMATION/FINDINGS (The facts – set out via headings, subheadings, numbered points, etc. Like the whole report this should be easy to 'skim' through – disregarding points which don't interest. Make this part, although the longest part, easy for the reader.)
> CONCLUSIONS (A summary of the main points)
> RECOMMENDATIONS (If asked for: what should be done, now the facts are known.)
> APPENDIX (Information, illustrations etc., too bulky to fit in earlier but to which the report refers)
>
> Signature

Organisation of reports

A   Remember the 'Terms of Reference'. Leave out anything not strictly relevant – that is, anything not specifically asked for!

B   When you are clear:

    (i)   what the facts are,

    (ii)   what they indicate, taken as a whole, and

    (iii)   what will need to be quoted to make the point,

then arrange them in order – *most important points first*; less important points later.

C   Traditionally reports were written in a formal/impersonal register – for example:

    It was found that . . .

rather than

    We found that . . .

However, this sometimes resulted in ambiguity and misunderstanding. Current advice would be: keep your style simple and help others to understand. Don't write 'officialese'.

Read the report which follows and check how far it follows the advice given:

To: The Principal   Date: 20th November 1987

From: Pete Jolley,
        Head of Student Services

REPORT ON THE SUBSEQUENT PROGRESS OF STUDENTS WHO COMPLETED THE POST-16 COURSE IN JUNE 1987

Terms of Reference

To report on destination of students who left the Post-16 course in June and recommend means of improving student success – as requested by the Principal on 13th October 1987.

Method

The sixty students who were on the course in 1986–7 were contacted. The names of those who had continued at college were taken from the college computer and they were invited to a short meeting. The others were contacted by letter and asked to telephone or write into college.

Findings

(a) Students progressing to more advanced courses at college

   (i) Fifteen students had continued their studies at 'A' level or BTEC National Diploma level. Of these:

   (ii) ten had wanted to enrol on the courses originally but needed to improve their grades;

   (iii) five had applied for jobs but didn't succeed so came back to college.

(b) Students continuing their studies at other colleges

   (i) Twelve students had enrolled at other colleges. Of these:

   (ii) two had moved to another district;

   (ii) nine wanted to follow courses that are not offered at this college;

   (iv) one wanted a change of atmosphere.

(c) Students finding employment

   (i) Twenty students had found employment. Of these:

   (ii) four had joined their parents' businesses after failing to find suitable employment elsewhere;

   (iii) three were working successfully in banks and coming to college on day release;

   (iv) six were working in various aspects of the retail trade and enjoying their work;

   (v) one was working in a warehouse but hoped to find something better;

   (vi) six had part-time or casual work.

(d) Students currently unemployed

   (i) Thirteen students were unemployed. Of these:

   (ii) ten had been to job interviews but had not been offered employment;

   (iii) three were considering YTS schemes.

Conclusions

   (i) The course had successfully prepared students for more advanced or specialist courses. Nearly half had progressed to such courses.

(ii) Of those in employment only a small group seemed likely to remain in their present jobs on a long-term basis.

(iii) Students are failing to gain employment at the interview stage rather than because they lack the necessary qualifications.

Recommendations

The employment situation in this area is better than average but in order to improve student chances:

(a) More attention should be paid to interview skills, incorporating more practice into this year's tutorials and using a range of college staff and local employers.

(b) There should be closer liaison with the Careers Service.

(c) Students should be encouraged to make early applications, whether for employment or places on college courses.

Pete Jolley

EXERCISE 6.6

In each of the following, first discuss or work out what would be realistic terms of reference – for example, who might want to know and why. (See the notes on 'Questionnaires', pages 28–32, for the best ways of finding out and analysing information.)

Prepare reports on the following:

Leisure facilities for the young people in your area

Study facilities in your college or school

Public transport facilities to and from your college or school

Fashions worn at your college or school

Services provided by a college students' union

Employment opportunities for students in your group:
 (i) in your immediate area
 (ii) in the region as a whole
 (iii) nationally

Opportunities for part-time or holiday work locally

How the average student spends his or her week

Tobacco/alcohol consumption by the average school or college student

The value of your current school or college course

NEWSPAPER AND MAGAZINE ARTICLES

Your local newsagent will usually carry a selection of national daily newspapers, Sunday newspapers, local and regional newspapers and magazines on a range of subjects from fashion to cars and from pop music to computers. For many of us, they provide a more immediate source that can be read more quickly than novels or poetry. Writing an article for a newspaper or magazine is a particular skill – but again, quicker and more immediate than writing, say, a novel.

Think about what makes a good newspaper or magazine article. The following questions should help you.

1 *What is news?*

   (i) Is there an element of novelty, newness or unusualness, as in the classic 'man bites dog'?

  (ii) Is there a degree of scandal or a secret revealed?

      The founder of the *Daily Mail* and *Daily Mirror*, Lord Northcliffe, once said, 'News is what someone somewhere wants to suppress: all the rest is advertising', and some popular newspapers now rely heavily on this approach.

 (iii) Is there 'human interest' and do the people need to be known to you (either because they are famous or because they live locally)? For instance, if you were going to visit China, it could well be considered worth reporting by your local newspaper, whereas a national newspaper would be more interested in reporting a visit by the Queen, Prime Minister or other well-known figure.

 (iv) Is there an element of drama, suspense or conflict, as with the outcome of a military, political or sporting encounter?

  (v) Are there likely to be important consequences for the community, such as major job losses or a threat to health?

2 *Who are the readers?*

   (i) Is there a local, regional, national or international readership?

  (ii) Is the appeal to young or old, men or women?

 (iii) Is there a definite social, political, religious or ethnic audience in mind?

 (iv) Is the appeal to people with particular interests, such as fashion, music, films, motor bikes, computing, photography or sport?

3 *Why do people read the articles?*

Is it:

(i) to gain up-to-date information on current affairs?

(ii) to find out more about a specialist topic?

(iii) because they identify with the people involved?

(iv) to find a solution to a problem or gain some benefit for them-selves?

(v) to have something to talk about with their friends?

(vi) for general interest and entertainment?

(vii) to satisfy their curiosity?

EXERCISE 6.7

Now ask these questions about the articles which follow and note down your findings:

a) The day the jets hit Sidon

When the first sortie of Israeli jets swept over the coast of Lebanon and homed in on Palestinian positions near the port of Sidon, Newsweek's *Sanaa Issa was on the scene:*

Minutes before the Israeli raid, I was in Sidon haggling with a taxi driver over the fare to a Palestinian camp just southeast of the city. Suddenly, there was a tremendous sonic boom as a wave of Israeli jets thundered overhead. I leaped out of the car and, perhaps foolishly, rushed to the roof of a nearby building. All was chaos. Drivers honked their horns. Children screamed and pedestrians rushed to take cover. Four planes wheeled high in the sky, diving again and again to drop their bombs. A huge column of black smoke rose from the camp, as machine-gun and antiaircraft fire erupted all around. Ambulances with sirens wailing careered through the crowded streets.

One wave of jets followed another, raid after raid. That has happened before, but this occasion was different. For the first time since 1982, an Israeli jet was shot down. On the fifth sweep, one of the planes exploded in a gigantic ball of red-yellowish flame. Two parachutes plumed open and I could see the pilots dangling in the sky. For the townspeople, it was a moment of joy. They clapped their hands, danced and sang. At the Ain al Hilweh camp, where I arrived a short while later, jubilant men kissed and embraced. The shrill and ululating women's chant, the zulghota, echoed everywhere.

Soon, Israeli helicopters began combing the area where the pilots had ejected. Palestinian gunmen kept up their barrage to prevent then from landing. To find out whether either Israeli had been captured, I walked to the office of the Popular Front for the Liberation of Palestine. There I was told that a radio operator had intercepted a message on a frequency often used by the rival Amal militia. 'The pigs were able to rescue one cockroach,' it read. 'The other cockroach has been taken to Beirut.'

As it turned out, a 19-year-old militiaman, Rafiq Ibrahim, found one pilot hiding in some bushes. Reportedly, Ibrahim ordered the pilot to raise his arms, then wrestled him to the ground when he raised only one arm. Ibrahim assumed the pilot was concealing a pistol; in fact, he was wounded. Shortly afterward, Amal soldiers took the pilot away.

from Newsweek

b) Joanne Catherall and Susan Sulley are surprisingly glamorous. They are both very slim, very tall (although this is helped by the wickedly high heels they are wearing) and they look as though they model themselves on Sue-Ellen from *Dallas*. It transpires that they do. The only thing that dispels the image is their voices – instead of having a drawl they speak with unmistakable Yorkshire accents.

We meet in the photographer's studio. Joanne is lolling in a chair and flicking through a fashion magazine, Susan is hiding behind a pair of dark glasses. The first thing I notice is that she has the most evil-looking blood-red nails I've ever seen. They both look rather fed-up, but greet me politely and explain apologetically that they've had 'one of those days'. They have a reputation for being awkward, and moody, so it's astonishing to find that they are completely the opposite.

As they are having their make-up done they thaw out a little, start gossiping, chattering and discussing, amongst other things, Holly from Frankie goes to Hollywood. Joanne thinks he's quite nice looking and Susan chimes in, 'Well, I won't tell you what I think he looks like.' But we all agree that he looks like Neil Tennant of the Pet Shop Boys because, says Joanne, 'They've both got the same shaped head.'

Meanwhile Susan scrutinises herself in a full-length mirror and laments the fact that her bum is getting smaller, so her trousers are now too baggy.

When their make-up is done they don't look any different from when they walked in the door – they are both wearing the same clothes and their faces are exactly the same. Their make-up artist tells me how much of a hard time she has trying to get them to experiment with their make-up. They always know exactly what they want, and getting Joanne to wear green eye shadow in the video was something of a breakthrough. 'But I'm working on you, aren't I?' she says.

The way they look, give or take a bit of thick eye-liner, is remarkably similar to the way it was when they joined the Human League in 1981. 'We like the glamorous look – the *Dallas* look,' says Joanne, and it's pretty obvious they do.

'We like make-up,' says Susan, 'we never go *au naturel*. It's not a pretty sight,' she laughs.

Now that their photo-session is over, we are sitting in a quiet corner of the studio and they seem quite relaxed. It's hard to believe that they have the reputation for being ogres. They are both very animated in conversation, giggle a lot, and know each other so well that frequently one of them will start a sentence and the other will finish it.

'The way we look,' explains Susan, anxious to continue where she left off, 'is not contrived. You saw us when we came in. That's what we look like.'

'Maybe it didn't start off like that,' she admits, 'Phillip with the funny hair-cut and me and Joanne looked quite . . . outrageous, or whatever you'd like to call it.'

'We've grown up now,' says Joanne. 'We feel "Ooooh, we can't wear daft make-up because we're too old for that now", even though we're not old.' (They are 23.)

'But you start to worry a bit when your mum finds you acceptable,' says Susan, and describes the raptures her mother went into after she'd seen them on Wogan. 'Our image within the group has always been classical,' says Joanne. 'Phillip always said that one of the main reasons he asked us to join the group was that in a club full of outrageous people we stood out as two girls who could fit into any type, who didn't have pink spikey hair or whatever . . .'

When I ask if they buy more expensive clothes now than they did then, they both shake their heads and say no in unison. They buy their clothes from anywhere: 'And I mean anywhere,' says Joanne, who has to stop and think whether they possess a designer outfit.

'We've not made that much money out of the group,' Joanne explains. 'We can't afford really expensive clothes. I know that people think that all people in groups are really rich, but we're just averagely well-off, and we both get overdrawn at the bank. We only get a wage. And it's not a very big wage. And when it comes down to it,' she continues (whilst Susan is nodding in agreement), 'we've not had a record out for two years and we're not making any money.'

When I ask exactly what they have been doing for the last two years, they tell me that they've been recording their new album, *Crash*. Two years to record one album?

'Well, we've done the album twice so that's just about taken up the last two years,' says Joanne. 'We wanted a dance album, and it didn't work out the way we wanted it.' So they did it again. They had four months off in Sheffield whilst they waited for the right producers to finish with their other commitments. Then it was four months in Minneapolis recording the album again, which they hated. 'Minneapolis is the coldest place on earth – it was horrendous,' says Joanne.

'If anything goes wrong with a group, then it's our group it goes wrong with,' says Susan, by way of explanation. 'So everything takes three years longer. What can I say? We're a bit . . . slow.' The band haven't toured since 1981, and although they both say they enjoy it, it's just another thing they haven't got round to doing. They plan to tour at the end of this year. 'Although we did a one-off concert two years ago in Sheffield with Alvin Stardust,' remembers Susan. 'But he was top of the bill!'

Now that they're back in the swing of things with the new single, I enquire whether they enjoy the lifestyle that goes with being in a group. The parties, the nightclubs.

'We just don't go to parties like that,' says Susan, and Joanne continues, 'It always seems so pompous that if you're in a pop group, you should only mix with other pop groups. Though we did have a party once. At The Venue in London.' She starts giggling. 'They wouldn't let us in! They wouldn't believe we were the group! This hefty bouncer had Ian (the keyboard player) up against the wall, threatening to beat him up because he had said, "We're the group, you've got to let us in." We were saying, "Look! We really are the group!" They finally let us in because someone from the record company rescued us.'

from Just Seventeen

c) Fur protest pair caught red-handed by police patrol

As two animal rights protesters ran away from a fur shop where they had daubed graffiti, they were literally caught red-handed by patrolling police officers, a court heard on Wednesday.

Sarah Louise Chesworth, aged 17, pleaded guilty to two charges of criminal damage at Brian's Furs in Regent Street, when she appeared before magistrates in Leamington along with a 15-year-old youth.

The youth, whose identity was withheld by order of the bench, also admitted the charges.

Mr Kenneth Caley, prosecuting, told the court that the proprietor of the shop, Mr Brian McCracken, had locked up at the end of the trading on Saturday, May 10.

But he was called back to the shop the following day and spent most of Sunday along with his wife, trying to remove red-paint graffiti from the shop window and walls.

The words 'Fur trade out' had been painted on the pavement outside the shop in red paint and the initials 'ALF' had been sprayed on the walls.

Mr Caley told the court that it looked as though a pot of paint had also been thrown at the window. The red paint had run down the glass onto the woodwork and onto the pavement.

The damage to the shop window was £212.54 because the glass needed to be replaced. Warwick District Council also had to employ men using a high powered hose to remove the paint solvent stains from the pavement at a cost of £108.74, the court heard.

The defendants had been arrested by officers WPC Helen Stokes and PC Richard Stokes who were on patrol in Kenilworth Street around 1.23 a.m.

The pair ran towards the police officers but suddenly stopped and began to walk when they saw them. WPC Stokes spoke to the couple while her colleague went off to investigate. He saw a pool of fresh paint outside the shop.

The youth was then seen to drop what looked like a tube of glue. Chesworth was also discovered to have a can of spray paint in her possession. Both had red paint on their hands.

They were arrested on charges of criminal damage and taken to Leamington police station where they were interviewed. The couple refused to co-operate and answered all questions by saying 'no comment', Mr Caley said.

The prosecution said that the fur shop had been the victim of a series of such attacks. In fact, the following evening an acid substance was thrown on the window although this was nothing to do with the defendants.

Mr Richard Armitage, defending, said his clients had a 'real and profound' regret for what they had done although they did not apologise for holding the views that they did.

He said that both were committed to continuing their campaign against the fur trade but would now do so within the law.

Both, he said, had become 'frustrated and disillusioned' after their lawful campaign failed, and they had resorted to criminal damage.

Unemployed Chesworth, of Radford Road, Leamington, and the youth were given conditional discharges for 12 months but were ordered to pay the £312 compensation order between them.

In the case of the youth who, the court heard, was still at school, the £160 would have to be paid by his parents.

from Leamington Spa Courier

EXERCISE 6.8

Collect together copies of each of the national newspapers on a particular day. Then, in groups of four or five:

(i) *Compare the stories each newspaper has chosen to feature on its front page and discuss what this tells you about the newspaper and its readers.*

(ii) *Compare the way one particular piece of news has been presented in each of the newspapers – in particular how much importance the story is given, how much detail is reported and what the newspaper's attitude seems to be.*

EXERCISE 6.9

1 Either: *Having won a competition to spend a day with the pop star, film star or sports star of your choice, write a magazine article describing the day.*

or: *Write a magazine article describing an imagined interview with the pop star, film star or sports star of your choice.*

2 Either: *Write an article for a school or college magazine on a topic you feel particularly interested in or concerned about.*

or: *Write a feature article on one of the following for a local newspaper:*

> *Life as a college student*
> *A guide to local leisure facilities for the under-25s*
> *A guide to clothes/fashion shops in the area*
> *The problems young people face today*

3 *Choose a novel or play which both interests you and has particularly dramatic moments. In the role of newspaper reporter, take one of the dramatic scenes and transform it into an article for front page publication.*

EXERCISE 6.10

Research and prepare a report on one of the following:

A career in journalism

Magazines for the 16–19 age range

How a newspaper is produced

Newspaper coverage of sport, pop music or television programmes

Good news and bad news

Any other topic concerning newspapers or magazines which you would like to investigate further

N.B. *If you collect together the best of the work done on these exercises, you should have enough material to form the basis of your own course or class magazine.*

THE END?

Although this is the end of the main part of the book, I hope it won't be the end of your interest in English. A lot of sections in the book are worth following up further – as are many of the extracts. Good luck with your present English course, and in any English examinations you are due to take.

Reference

– GRAMMAR AND PUNCTUATION

Grammar

You will probably have come across these terms before. Check that you know and understand them. They will help you understand the way English grammar works.

Part of Speech	How it is used	Examples
Noun	To refer to someone or something – the name of a person, creature, place, thing, state or quality	Napoleon, nightingale, Norway, nose, nostalgia, neutrality
Pronoun	To replace a noun – thus avoiding unnecessary repetition	He, she, it, they, that, those, who, which
Adjective	To describe a noun or pronoun	attractive, artistic, awful, appalling, red, your, my, few, much
Verb	To represent an action or state of being – a 'doing' word	vanish, vaccinate, vary, exist, be
Adverb	To tell more about, or modify, a verb – can also tell more about an adjective or adverb	attractively, artistically, acutely, actively, soon, very, nearly, quickly, badly

Preposition	To show the relationship between people or things, especially *where* they are in relation to each other	under, over, in, on, between, with, for, to
Conjunction	To connect two words, phrases or sentences	and, but, or, not, since, before, because, although
Interjection	As an exclamation	Oh! Well! Oh dear! Help!

EXERCISE 7.1

1 *Find four more examples of each of the parts of speech.*

2 *Find at least one example of each part of speech in the following:*

Whew! I nearly missed the last bus and had to walk to my brother's.

N.B. While finding examples you may have discovered that some words could be counted in several different ways, depending on how they were being used. Compare these two sentences, for instance. In which is 'love' being used as a noun and in which as a verb?

They all think our love won't last.

To know you is to love you.

SOME MORE POINTS ABOUT GRAMMAR

Your school or college library will usually have books which explain English grammar in more detail. Here is a useful selection of points to remember.

Further useful terms

Subject   Whoever or whatever is doing the action in a sentence, as in the underlined examples below:
He enjoys reading.
Margaret overslept yesterday.
Life goes on.
The car ground to a halt.

Object   What or who is being affected by the verb in a sentence, as in the examples underlined below:

        She likes <u>pizza</u>.
        He plays <u>the guitar</u>.
        Smoke enveloped <u>the hotel</u>.

'I' is the subject – 'Me' is the object

Which of the following are correct?

    John and I are coming later.
    John and me are coming later.
    The lecturer told Anna and me himself.
    The lecturer told Anna and I himself.

- In cases like this follow the grammatical rule that *'I' is the subject* and *'me' the object*. Simply take away the '– and' to see which version is correct in each case.
  Thus 'I am coming later' is correct but, 'me am coming later' is not; 'The lecturer told me himself' is correct but 'The lecturer told I himself' is not. The correct versions are therefore:

      John and I are coming later.
      The lecturer told Anna and me himself.

- After prepositions always use 'me' (the object form), as in this sentence:

      It is a secret between her and me.

EXERCISE 7.2

To illustrate the point to someone who is having difficulty write a short poem or limerick beginning:

    There was a young man from Dundee
    Who often confused 'I' and 'me'
    . . .

Make sure the subject and verb agree in number

Usually this isn't a problem. We write:

            singular   singular
            subject   verb

His new | record | | is | the best yet,

but

        plural   plural
        subject   verb

Those | records | | are | half price.

We can usually make sure the subject and verb agree even if something comes between them:

a) His new record, despite some rather critical reviews, is the best yet.
We know it is the record which is the best so far, even though the phrase 'despite some rather critical reviews' has come between subject and verb.

b) The records in the sale are half price.
We know it is the records which are half price, even though the phrase 'in the sale' has come between subject and verb.

Some words may occasionally cause confusion. Note the following:

• Each of the following pronouns counts as a singular subject and takes a singular verb:

anyone	anybody	anything
everyone	everybody	everything
no one	nobody	nothing

Note that parts of these words give us a clue: 'one', 'body' and 'thing' are all singular.

The following also count as singular subjects and take singular verbs:

kind	sort	type
each	either	neither

Examples would be:
Everyone is happy today – nobody is sad.
That sort of person annoys me.

• Each of the following counts as a plural subject and takes a plural verb:

several	both	few

Examples would be:
Few were surprised by the news.
Both of us were sad to be leaving.

EXERCISE 7.3

Complete the following by adding the correct form of the verb 'to be':

(i) *Everybody in the audience _____ standing and applauding.*

(ii) *The sky at night, although rather darkened by the oncoming clouds, _____ still quite bright.*

(iii) *Nothing said by the villains _____ true.*

(iv) *Anyone who eats so many pizzas _____ sure to be overweight.*

(v) *Either you or he _____ going.*

(vi) *Both _____ possible answers.*

Avoid ambiguity
Make sure it is clear what you are referring to ════════════════

- Pronouns are useful, but be careful when writing a long sentence. Is it clear who 'he' is, 'she' is, 'they' are and so on?

  For instance is it clear *who* blushed in the following sentence?
  As soon as Kathy began to speak to her sister, she blushed.

  We would have to find a way of making the meaning clear. Examples would include:
  As soon as she began to speak to her sister, Kathy blushed.
  Kathy blushed as soon as she began to speak to her sister.
  Her sister blushed as soon as Kathy began to speak to her.

EXERCISE 7.4

Write four sentences, each giving a clear but different meaning for the sentence below:

Warren asked George whether his bicycle would be safe in his shed.

- The sentence which follows illustrates a similar problem:
  Floating down the river, Kirsty saw a boat.

  Is the boat or Kirsty floating down the river? Again we would have to find a way of making the meaning clear. If the boat was floating down the river we could write:
  Kirsty saw a boat floating down the river.

  If you want to impress your friends you can describe the example above as *correct usage of the participial modifier*. In practice you're just making sure that your writing is clear and not likely to be misinterpreted.

EXERCISE 7.5

Go back through work you have done recently and check whether there are any examples of ambiguity.

- Make sure that words like *almost, even, hardly, scarcely* and *only* are correctly positioned. The examples below show how changing the position within a sentence can change the meaning:
  Only we accept bookings during office hours.
  We accept only bookings during office hours.
  We accept bookings during office hours only.

EXERCISE 7.6

Think of, and write down, a sentence where you could place the word almost in different positions so as to give three different meanings.

Avoid double negatives

Just as in maths two minuses make a plus, so

I don't want nothing

actually means

I want something.

Use *one* negative only –

either: I don't want anything
or: I want nothing.

EXERCISE 7.7

1 *What does the following sentence mean?*

She doesn't know neither of them.

2 *Write two sentences, each giving a correctly-worded version of what the example is trying to say.*

Make sure you have the right time

Below you will see:

• the main times we refer to when speaking or writing.

• common occasions when we use them.

• examples of the ways verbs change as the time changes (often known as the 'tenses' of verbs).

Past	Present	Future
Narrative and storytelling	Presenting an argument, stating a fact, and describing a regular action or one happening now	Horoscope, prediction, expectation, or statement of intent
He *stared* out of the window and nervously *tapped* the sill. He *was* still *staring* out of the window when the siren *sounded*.	I *believe* in nuclear disarmament. Water *freezes* at 0°C. I *wait* here every day. I *am waiting* for you.	You *will meet* a tall, dark handsome stranger. We *will be paid* soon. He *is arriving* tomorrow. We *leave* at dawn.

Past in the Past	Past	Future in the past	Present	Future
What happened before the point in the story		What will happen after the point in the story		
He *had been* in the Secret Service before the war.		We thought the worst was over but the worst *was* still *to come*.		

EXERCISE 7.8

1   *Write a paragraph about an event that took place last week. Use the past tense throughout.*

2   *Write a paragraph on the differences between night and day. Use the present tense throughout.*

3   *Write the kind of monthly horoscope you would like to read under your star sign. Use several different ways of referring to future time.*

SUMMARY – SYNCHRONISE YOUR GRAMMAR

Avoid sudden, unnecessary or ambiguous changes which might confuse your reader – especially changes of:

Tense (Past, Present and Future)
Person (I, you, he, she, it, we, you (plural), they)
Number (singular or plural)

Write accurately – be consistent!

Punctuation

SENTENCES

- Each sentence, of course, starts with a capital letter and finishes with a full stop – like this one.

- There are no rules about length, a sentence can be either short or long, depending who you are writing to, what you want to say, and the effect you want to produce.

- Each sentence, however, must make sense standing on its own. Nothing will need to be added for it to make sense.

- As a check, then, each sentence must have a subject (someone who, or something which, is doing something) and a verb (usually what is being done).

    N.B. A verb ending in '-ing' can't be the only one in a sentence. The example following is *not* a sentence:

    Referring to your letter of 17 January.

    It should be:

    I refer to your letter of 17 January.

    (But you could write this:

    Referring to your letter of 17 January, I see that . . .)

- When reading aloud you will usually pause for breath at the end of a sentence, when you see the full stop. The pause should make sense. As a rough guide, then, when you have made one point it is time for a pause (when reading aloud) or a full stop (when writing) before you start another point.

- You will sometimes, though, want to link two points closely together. Then two or more short sentences can be combined by a conjunction (linking word) to make one longer sentence. Common conjunctions are *and, but, although,* and *however.* For example:

    (i) He went to his room. He opened the drawer.
    (two short sentences)
    He went to his room *and* opened the drawer.
    (one longer sentence)

(ii) She is old. She is still very fit.
      (two short sentences)
      Although she is old, she is still very fit.
      (one longer sentence)

- As another check, look at each paragraph you write. If the whole paragraph has only one or two sentences as you have punctuated it, look again. Unless it is a short paragraph, it will probably need breaking up into more sentences.

EXERCISE 7.9

Read the following extract aloud and check how each sentence works.

> Now he noticed that the sky had grown much darker. The rain was heavier every second, pressing down as if the earth had to be flooded before nightfall. The oaks ahead blurred and the ground drummed. He began to run. As he ran he heard a deeper sound running with him. He whirled round. The horse was in the middle of the clearing. It might have been running to get out of the terrific rain except that it was coming for him, scattering clay and stones, with an immensely supple and powerful action. He let out a tearing roar and threw the stone in his right hand. The result was instantaneous. Whether at the roar or at the stone the horse reared as if against a wall and shied to the left.
>
> *from 'The Rain Horse' by Ted Hughes, in* Modern Short Stories *ed. Jim Hunter*

PUNCTUATION MARKS

Full stops (.)

- These are used to: end sentences (see 'Sentences' section above).

- show abbreviations.

  Examples include:

  e.g., i.e., Dr., Mr., B.B.C., U.S.A.

  However, there is a tendency nowadays to omit full stops in abbreviations, particularly between capitals. Your television screen refers to ITN for Independent Television News (not I.T.N.) and computer users write of BASIC (i.e. Beginners' All-purpose Symbolic Instruction Code), not B.A.S.I.C.

Commas (,)

- They are used to show the reader that you want him or her to *pause* in order to make sense of the passage.

- But the pause is *not* as great or important as a full stop.

- Commas sometimes act like brackets: they go on either side of a phrase which could be left out without changing the main sense of the sentence. For example:

  Doreen, before embarking on a career as an air hostess, learnt to speak two foreign languages fluently.

- Commas are sometimes used to *separate* the words in a list. For example:

  Cars, perfume, cheese and many types of fruit are imported from France.

- Commas are also used to *introduce or interrupt* quotations (see 'Quotation Marks', p. 215). For example:

  The young man protested, 'This is not my wife.'
  'This,' the young man protested, 'is not my wife.'

- Commas are sometimes used to separate *different units of time or space* in a sentence. For example:

  She walked for four hours, twenty minutes, and was tired out.

EXERCISE 7.10

Insert the necessary commas in the following:

1   *On a bright sunny afternoon in March 1959 Robert Foster a young scientist nearly killed himself by holding his breath underwater for thirteen minutes forty two and a half seconds a world record which still stands.*

2   *'Some people are taking pictures of war and pollution' she says 'and it's very important for people to do this. But my photographs are not like that. Nature happiness beauty – people need those things too.'*

3   *The Rolls-Royce Camargue the world's most expensive production car has a V8 3528 cc engine automatic transmission a top speed of 120 miles per hour and an urban fuel consumption of 10 miles per gallon.*

Apostrophes (') ▬▬▬▬▬▬▬▬▬▬▬▬▬▬▬▬▬▬▬▬▬

- These often show *possession* or *belonging*. For example:

  the sheik's harem
  the soldier's rifle
  the victim's scream
  the mother's entreaties

- If the objects belong to several people or things (i.e. their *owners* are plural not singular), then the apostrophe comes after the s – . . . s' instead of 's. For example:

  the magazines' editors
  (more than one magazine with more than one editor)

  the girls' opinion
  (more than one girl with the same opinion)
  the bosses' conference
  (more than one boss at the same conference)

- The other major use of the apostrophe is to show where a part of a word has been left out, usually in more casual English. For example:

  could not shortens to *couldn't*
  we are shortens to *we're*
  I will or *I shall* shortens to *I'll*

- To form the plural of single letters or figures, 's is sometimes used to avoid confusion. For example:

  Do you spell your name with two t's?
  There are ten 6's in sixty.

EXERCISE 7.11

Insert apostrophes where necessary in the following:

  (i) *Ill see you at Sarahs next Wednesday.*

 (ii) *Hes going to his friends brothers villa for his holiday.*

(iii) *Well call the doctors if you havent time.*

(iv) *The secretaries typewriters all need cleaning.*

 (v) *Whats the new secretarys name?*

(vi) *Im not sure yet whos going to Peters sisters party.*

Quotation marks (' ' or " ")

"What are you after? Open the door," he said.

"We shan't – not till you've chosen!" said Muriel.

"Chosen what?" he said.

"Chosen the one you're going to marry," she replied.

He hesitated a moment.

"Open the blasted door," he said, "and get back to your senses."

He spoke with official authority.

"You've got to choose," cried the girls.

"Come on!" cried Annie, looking him in the eye. "Come on! Come on!"

from 'Tickets, Please' by D. H. Lawrence, in Modern Short Stories *ed. Jim Hunter*

- Quotation marks go round *all the words actually spoken*, enclosing them thus: ". . ."

- Start *a new line* when another person starts speaking.

- The first word spoken starts with a *capital letter.*

- Only put a full stop at the end of the words spoken if they are also the last words of the sentence (as in line 6 in the passage quoted).

- If the sentence continues after the last words spoken (as in the first four lines of the passage above) only put a comma, or, if necessary, a question mark or exclamation mark, after the last word spoken and before the last pair of quotation marks (").

- Where what is being said is interrupted halfway through a sentence by some such phrase as *she said*, continue the second part of the sentence being quoted with quotation marks (") and give the next word a small first letter, *not* a capital letter, to show it is all part of the original sentence (as in line 6 above).

  Where what is being said after is a new sentence you will, of course, start it with a capital letter (as in line 9 above).

- When using quotation marks you may use either '. . .' or ". . .". It may be necessary to use both if someone speaking is quoting someone else speaking – to show who is saying what:

  'I don't understand,' Alan confessed. 'What *did* Molly mean when she said "Expect a few surprises on Thursday"?'

  What Molly said has been put inside ". . .". The question mark denotes *Alan's* question. It comes inside the '. . .' but *not* inside the ". . .". Think about it!

- Quotation marks may be used to give stress to particular words, names of individual items, or titles of books:

    The word for this sort of action is 'lunacy'.
    Flirtatious Angela was often referred to as a 'tease'.
    I've just started reading 'Watership Down'.

    (Alternatively, in print, we could use italics, without the quotation marks: *lunacy*, *tease* and *Watership Down*.)

Question mark (?)

- This is used at the end of a *direct* question – either to someone else as indicated by quotation marks ("...") or to the reader (without quotation marks). For example:

    'Where are you going for lunch?' she asked.
    Where are you going for lunch?
    (a note on my desk)

- It is *not* used after an *indirect* question, that is, one in indirect speech. For example:

    She asked me where I was going for lunch.

- Nor is it used after a *request*, although the request may be disguised as a question. For example:

    Will you please send me a copy of the new catalogue.

EXERCISE 7.12

Punctuate the following:

> What vengeance can you mean asked my father in increasing amazement I mean to decapitate the monster he answered and his clenched hand was at the same moment raised as if it were grasping the handle of an axe what exclaimed my father more than ever bewildered to strike her head off cut her head off cut her head off aye with a hatchet with a spade or with anything that can cleave through her murderous throat
> *from* Carmilla *by J. Sheridan le Fanu*

(You will have to do more than simply add quotation marks!)

DIRECT SPEECH AND INDIRECT OR REPORTED SPEECH

- Direct speech consists of the words actually spoken and is usually indicated by quotation marks around it ("..."). For example, a conversation between a shop assistant and a customer:

  "Could I have a copy of *Zig Zag* magazine, please."

  "I'm sorry, it hasn't come yet. I'll save you a copy when it does, though."

  Here we have the actual words of the speakers, i.e. *direct speech*.

- If the general idea of what was said (but not the exact words) is related by someone else, then we have indirect or reported speech. There are no quotation marks and the word 'that' usually precedes the reporting. All present tense verbs are changed to the past tense. Thus the conversation above, in indirect speech, would become:

  A customer asked the shop assistant for a copy of *Zig Zag* magazine. The shop assistant replied he was sorry but the magazine hadn't arrived. He would, however, save a copy when one arrived.

EXERCISE 7.13

Which of the following are direct and which indirect speech?

(i) *Dr Johnson said, "The man who is tired of London is tired of life."*

(ii) *The Prime Minister admitted that unemployment had risen again.*

(iii) *The Leader of the Opposition said he did not accept the government's arguments.*

(iv) *She said, "What will be, will be."*

(v) *She said that what would happen would happen.*

EXERCISE 7.14

Put the following into reported speech:

There was a silence.

'*You're* not going to tell me everything I shall do, and everything I shan't,' she broke out at last.

He lifted his head.

'I tell you *this*,' he said, low and intense. 'Have anything to do with Sam Adams, and I'll break your neck.'

from The White Stocking *by D. H. Lawrence*